THE MONSIGNOR

THE MAN, HIS MISTRESSES & THE MISSING MONEY

COLM KEANE & UNA O'HAGAN

CAPEL ISLAND

Copyright Colm Keane & Una O'Hagan 2023

First published in Ireland in 2023

by

CAPEL ISLAND PRESS
Baile na nGall,
Ring, Dungarvan,
County Waterford,
Ireland

ISBN 978-1-9995920-4-2

Typeset by Palimpsest Book Production Limited, Falkirk, Stirlingshire
& Typeform Ltd., East Wall Road, Dublin 3
Printed and bound in Great Britain by Clays Ltd, Elcograf S.p.A.

For Seán

Colm Keane has published 30 books, including nine No.1 bestsellers, among them *Journey's End, Going Home, We'll Meet Again* and *Heading for the Light*. He was a graduate of Trinity College, Dublin, and Georgetown University, Washington DC. As a broadcaster, he won a Jacob's Award and a Glaxo Fellowship for European Science Writers.

Una O'Hagan is a No.1 bestselling author and former newsreader with Radio Telefís Éireann. A journalism graduate, she has presented all the main news programmes on Ireland's national station. This is her fifth book.

CONTENTS

Prologue   1

1. A Star is Born   3
2. Sunny Days at Pau   12
3. The Rise to Fame   21
4. Apostle to the Genteel   31
5. The Educator of Kensington   40
6. Decline and Fall   51
7. The Mary Stourton Scandal   61
8. The Mrs. Bellew Affair   71
9. The Housemaid's Tale   78
10. Commission of Investigation   83
11. Money Matters   93
12. The Ruin of Miss Plues   99
13. The Mayor, the Maid & the Widows   107
14. The Battle for Rome   115
15. Mrs. Rutherford Smith   121
16. Infamy and Disgrace   129
17. Bankruptcy   137
18. The Reckoning   145
19. America   153
20. On the Road   162
21. Farewell New York   171
22. California   177
23. Mrs. Valensin   185
24. Arno   193

Epilogue   202
Acknowledgements   205
Notes   214

Picture a man of the rarest personal gifts, with voice, presence, eloquence, grace, physical beauty, manly strength, learning, persuasiveness, zeal, sympathy, patrician breeding, and that mysterious quality we call magnetism – picture all this and more to the uttermost limits of your imagination and you will still probably fall short of realising what Monsignor Capel was to the England of the middle of the century.

Evening Express, Cardiff, 4 December 1900

PROLOGUE

One evening in autumn 1876, close to midnight, a policeman named Sergeant Robert Ahern was on patrol in the London borough of Kensington. As he turned into Wright's Lane from Abingdon Villas, not far from Kensington High Street, he heard loud, angry voices coming from the doorway of a house. Out of the gloom he recognised that the property belonged to one of the most famous personalities in Britain – Monsignor Thomas John Capel.

The sergeant noted two women standing on the first step of the house, engaged in animated conversation. Facing them, standing at the open front door, was the readily recognisable Monsignor and Prelate of the Pope. It was "an angry altercation," the policeman later reported. So intense were the words being exchanged that no one heeded his arrival.

In an instant, the seasoned policeman deduced what was happening. The women were of ill repute, from nearby Chelsea, and from the remarks being exchanged and the tone of the confrontation he ascertained that they were arguing with the 40-year-old Monsignor over payment for sexual favours.

One woman was young and a prostitute, he later said; the other, who was old, seemed to be the keeper of a brothel. The impression he got was that they were arguing with Capel because "they were dissatisfied with the payment for his intercourse." Alarmed by the tenor of the disturbance, the sergeant "laid his hand upon the younger woman and pulled her off the step and ordered her off."

He then addressed Monsignor Capel, saying, "You had better go in, Sir." The Monsignor replied indignantly: "Mind your own business!" He added: "How dare you interfere!" among other remarks. As the two women fled into the dark Kensington night, the sergeant had "no doubt whatever" that the Monsignor was blind drunk.

1

Sergeant Ahern, who was a Catholic, never pursued the incident primarily "to avoid a scandal to the Catholic religion," as he explained. The Kensington police force also did not want to cause a "scandal and disturbance" over such a famous man. As a result, the details of the event remained buried until a secret investigation of Capel's behaviour was instigated more than two years later by the Cardinal Archbishop of Westminster.

By then, the Monsignor's file was bulging with allegations of his profligate womanising, heavy drinking, and exploitation of vulnerable ladies, old and young, whose savings supported his lavish lifestyle. His career as the most admired sermoniser in Europe, as converter of nobility and gentry to the Catholic faith, and as Rector of a prestigious Catholic University College lay in ruins.

His debts were enormous, and he was bankrupt in all but name. Finance houses, moneylenders, businessmen, and ordinary women and men pressed for monies he owed them. Court cases were looming. Gentlemen's clubs and parlours buzzed with rumours of his licentious behaviour. The Catholic Church, caught in the headlights, feared that his sordid activities would undo their revival in Great Britain.

"He cannot be stopped," a Church investigator of the Monsignor exclaimed in exasperation. He wasn't alone in his frustration. It was, indeed, baffling how such a handsome, eloquent man, with the world at his feet, could have blown it all so decisively in such a short span of time.

A STAR IS BORN

Ardmore

onsignor Thomas John Capel first saw light of day on 28 October 1836 in the fishing village of Ardmore, County Waterford, Ireland. The son of a coastguard boatman, his tiny cottage home was located on the edge of a sandy beach, surrounded by a small sheltered bay. At his doorstep was the water's edge, with its rock pools and pebble-strewn strand. To the left and right were rolling cliffs. The sea shimmered in summer; large waves raged during winter storms. It was a remote yet wonderful place to begin life in.

The Monsignor's father, John, was an Englishman, born in Brompton, Kent, where his early childhood was immersed in stories of the sea, the art of seamanship and other maritime matters. Located near the Thames estuary, Brompton was surrounded by dockyards and naval establishments. Lord Nelson's HMS *Victory* had been built nearby. Sir Francis Drake had learned how to sail in the area. If ever it could be said that a person had salt water in his blood, that person was John Capel.

Unsurprisingly, John Capel enlisted in the Royal Navy, joining at the age of 13, which was common at the time. Entering as a boy sailor, he served on naval ships during an era when Britain ruled the waves. His postings included HMS *Aboukir*, HMS *Glory*, HMS *Unicorn*, HMS *Ranger* and HMS *Prince Regent*. He saw action with the 52-gun frigate

HMS *Southampton* during a tense and dangerous blockade of Antwerp in 1832. He eventually sailed to India, Ceylon and Singapore on board the same ship.

As a lowly boy sailor, John slept in dark, dank spaces on the ship's lower deck, the only light provided by tallow dips, whose stench mingled with the stink of bilge water and rotting food. The food was poor, the discipline harsh. The deck was dirty, slippery and wet. Despite the conditions, he lasted in the service for almost a decade, rising gradually through the ranks to become an able seaman.

In February 1833, John Capel transferred to the coastguard, enlisting as a boatman. Although it was the lowest rank in the service, the pay was considerably better than in the navy. Again, unlike the navy, wives and children were entitled to a civil pension in the event of a serviceman's death. The job also afforded the chance to settle down onshore.

Still in his early 20s, he was posted to Ireland, to the coastguard station at Ardmore. With its rows of whitewashed cottages, basin-like bay and long, smooth expanse of strand, Ardmore was one of the prettiest villages on the south coast of Ireland. Adjacent cliffs were dotted with sea pinks, purple thyme, low furze, rocky paths and charming coves. A "little hamlet," it "bursts on the view in picturesque retirement" was how the author Samuel Hayman, from neighbouring Youghal, described it.

Shortly after his arrival, John – "a remarkably steady, sober, intelligent man," according to a colleague – met Mary Fitzgerald, who lived in nearby Whiting Bay. Mary was a farmer's daughter and a year older than John. She spoke with a rich Irish brogue and had the purest Irish blood, while her husband possessed the purest English blood, Capel later remarked.

The couple were married on 28 November 1833 in Mary's local parish chapel at Grange. The ceremony was conducted "according to the rite of the Roman Catholic Church" by the well-respected and energetic parish priest Rev. Patrick McGrath, who built three churches in the area, and his curate, Rev. Jeremiah O'Meara.

The couple's first child, Maria, a future nun, was born in 1835. The following year, their son, Thomas John, the future famous cleric, entered the world. From birth, his mother called him "T. J.", using an abbreviation of Thomas John commonly employed in Ireland at the time. He would use this short form of his name for the rest of his days, signing his letters "T. J.", and employing it when interacting with family, friends and colleagues.

Their mother, a practising Catholic, raised both children in accordance with the precepts of Rome. When they were little children, she brought them to the nearby monastic settlement established by St. Declan in the fifth century, walking them from the coastguard station through the narrow streets, up to the ancient round tower, ruined cathedral, early stone oratory and holy well, pausing at the heights overlooking Ardmore with their spectacular views across the broad expanse of the bay.

She also brought them to the annual Ardmore Pattern – the word derived from "patron" as in "patron saint" – celebrating the feast of St. Declan. Penitents in their tens of thousands fastened their carts, pitched their tents, knelt, prayed and drank. "Bloody knees from devotion and bloody heads from fighting are not uncommon," the authors Samuel and Anna Hall recalled of the scene. "Every avenue teems with figures moving along to pay their devotions." It seems appropriate that one of the most celebrated churchmen in Victorian Britain began life in such an intense, fertile religious setting.

For T. J.'s father, life at Duffcarrick coastguard station, which took its name from one of the four townlands of Ardmore, was eventful. The surrounding coastline was rife with smugglers. High duties and a growing taste for tea and tobacco had inspired a thriving trade in illicit goods. John and his fellow servicemen were charged with apprehending the guilty and bringing to an end their nefarious ways. Those who were caught were subject to large fines or, even worse, to enforced conscription in the navy.

Hurricanes, storms and perilous high seas lashed the coastline, driven by weather fronts rolling in from the wide expanse of the Atlantic to the west. The Liverpool vessel *Sir Francis Burton*, which was bound for South America, foundered in the bay in 1838. Seventeen men and one woman were last seen clinging to the mast; all of them perished. Large numbers of fishing boats were destroyed in the same storm. Another boat, the *Earl Powis*, later struck a reef of rocks, two miles to the east of Ardmore Head, during a vicious snowstorm. So wild and forceful were the seas that even the coastguard station was eventually washed away.

Ardmore turned out to be a fine training ground for the novice boatman, John Capel. There was the added bonus that his wife's parents and relatives, the Fitzgeralds, ran their farms a short distance away. Although life was good, it wasn't always easy, especially for an "English" family living among predominantly Irish-speaking people. Local hostility toward the coastguard didn't help.

After four years, the family's fortunes changed. The coastguard – following the practise of relocating staff on a regular basis to avoid friendships developing with the local population – decided to transfer John Capel back to England. The family were soon packing their bags and setting out for territory familiar to the father – England's coast facing the continent of Europe.

With its isolated coves, hollow caves, rugged landscape and close proximity to France, England's south-east coast was a smuggler's paradise in the early nineteenth century. Wines, brandy, tea, spices and silk were shipped across the narrow channel from the north coast of France. Gin arrived from Holland, often in quantities so large that local families used it to clean their windows. Jamaican rum and Virginia tobacco were also illegally imported.

The Capel family's first port of call was the town of Ramsgate, Kent, where they settled into coastguard accommodation close to the beach. During the next few years, the young T. J. grew up in an area known not only for the whiff of danger associated with coastal smuggling but also for the fashionable visitors arriving at what was rapidly becoming a resort for the Victorian genteel. Whiskered gentlemen, ladies with their portable chairs and charming housemaids formed the backdrop to T. J.'s early years; they would continue to do so in later life.

In late 1839, the Capel family were again on the move, traversing for more than a decade a necklace of coastguard stations at Deal, Sizewell Gap and Hastings, among other locations. For a brief spell – 11 months – they were back in Ireland, at the East Ferry station in County Cork. There, the father was promoted from boatman to commissioned boatman, representing a rise up the coastguard scale. By then, the family had expanded and T. J. had a new sister, Mary Bridget. Three more children followed – Sarah Anne, Elizabeth and Arthur Joseph – placing further pressure on the father's meagre serviceman's pay.

The prospects for educational advancement were limited, given the family's parlous financial state. When T. J. was ten years of age, his parents addressed this issue by applying on their boy's behalf for entry to the upper school of the Royal Hospital, Greenwich. Admission was open to the sons of seamen, with entrants committing themselves to a life at sea. Records show that he never joined the school, primarily, no doubt, because he was revealing scholastic abilities far removed from a life on the ocean waves. His parents turned their sights elsewhere.

Fortune shone when the Capel family were transferred in 1851 to the popular resort of Hastings. The 14-year-old T. J. was by then demonstrating remarkable enthusiasm and energy of purpose, which was said to have been inherited from his mother. He also possessed sound sense, inherited from his father.

He did so well at his studies that he was made a pupil-teacher at his new school. In this capacity he helped with the teaching, filling a role reserved for boys and girls of high ability and with the potential for becoming teachers. His parents were so proud of the title that they insisted on listing pupil-teacher as his occupation in the 1851 census.

At St. Leonards-on-Sea – the little town near Hastings where the Capels lived – the boy's talents were spotted by the family's local curate, the Rev. John Foy. The priest, who was a polished, urbane, well-read man, college educated and with a Master's degree, recognised the new arrival's academic promise, his excellence at his studies, and his interest in religion and the classics. The cleric decided to take him under his wing.

Like many perceptive churchmen of the era – the tail end of the Industrial Revolution – Fr. Foy was alarmed by the flood of people migrating from the countryside to the cities, where they were crammed into squalid centres of industrial activity without having anyone to look after their spiritual needs. More priests were required, he believed, to teach Christian doctrine and minister among them. Encountering the bright, enthusiastic, religiously-inclined T. J. Capel on his doorstep must have seemed like a gift from heaven to Fr. Foy.

The priest quickly set about encouraging the young boy. He tutored him and provided access to his library of 1,500 books, most of them theological. Deprived of such reading matter at home, T. J. devoured the contents of the library in his spare time. He would later fondly remember those days and how influential they were in determining his path as a cleric and preacher.

Life was fulfilling and satisfying for the Capel family during their early years in St. Leonards. The father, John, was promoted to chief boatman with the coastguard, representing another move up the scale. There was further good news when the eldest daughter, Maria, decided to pursue her vocation as a nun. She joined the Society of the Holy Child Jesus as a novice and eventually took her vows.

Importantly, from the point of view of her brother, she set the pace for religious vocations in the family, which he would emulate in the years ahead. Of equal significance was that the founder of her convent, Cornelia Connelly – a Philadelphia-born convert to Catholicism, who had influential friends in the Catholic hierarchy – also took a keen interest in the boy. Like Fr. Foy, she encouraged his education and fostered his religious vocation.

Just as life seemed to be going so well, a succession of tragedies struck the Capel family. First, in 1852, when Sarah Anne was aged 11, she died from what was described as "disease of brain." She had suffered for two years before passing away. Her father, John, was present at her death, which took place at the family home. Little more than two years later, at the tragically young age of 42, the father would be dead, too.

In early October 1854, John Capel died in a drowning accident. After completing his coastguard day watch, he was persuaded by a colleague to go for a drink. At the nearby Terminus Inn, John, who was described as a casual drinker, consumed rum and water before leaving after three-quarters of an hour. "I consider that he was perfectly sober," the colleague remarked on John's condition at his departure.

John Capel never arrived home. The following morning, when he failed to turn up for work, the same colleague called to the Capel family home, where he found Mary Capel crying. "She said she had not seen her husband all night," he recalled. "I then went in search of him." He eventually spotted John's body lying in a stream near a railway bridge. The subsequent inquest concluded that he had been taking a well-known but treacherous shortcut home, slipped on the railway bank, fell into the stream-bed, became stunned, and then rolled into the five-foot-deep water, where he drowned. The jury returned a verdict of "accidental death."

While the tragedy left his wife and five remaining children emotionally distraught and financially impoverished, there was a further poignant note to the event. Earlier that day, he had told his wife that he would "hurry home in the evening, as he had some little books to read to his children." The education of his family, as ever, had been foremost in John Capel's mind. His son, T. J., would go on to fulfil his father's ambitions, exceeding them in unimaginable ways.

The 17-year-old Thomas John Capel was informed of his father's death a few weeks after starting his third-level studies in London. He had just enrolled at St. Mary's Catholic Training College for men, at Brook Green, Hammersmith, which provided for the training of teachers to work in poor Catholic areas in Britain. Having been a pupil-teacher at school and recommended for his unusual brilliance, his education at the college was provided at no cost to his family.

It was a harrowing journey home for the young man. His mother, who still had three children to feed, was badly distressed. His youngest brother, Arthur Joseph, was seven years old; his sister, Mary Bridget, had recently turned 15; in the middle was Elizabeth, aged nine. Within a day of his father's death, there was an upsetting inquest revealing the details of the tragic event. Local newspaper coverage of the drowning added to the family's misery.

Mary Capel found herself in desperate financial straits. Lacking any means of support, she composed a moving letter to the upper school of the Royal Hospital, Greenwich, seeking the return of the marriage certificate she had sent when applying for T. J.'s entry to the school. "May I beg you, Sir, if possible and convenient, to return me by next post this certificate, as I want to gain an annuity for myself and children who depend entirely on me for support, owing to the melancholy death of my husband," the letter pleaded. It is interesting to note from the handwriting that Mary, who was most likely poor at writing if not illiterate, had to enlist her son, T. J., to pen the letter.

On his return to Hammersmith, T. J. continued with his studies, immersing himself in subjects ranging from mathematics and music to astronomy and the science of education. He excelled at college, gaining a first-class certificate in his second, and final, year. His outstanding intelligence and application to his work were noted by the college authorities, who offered him the post of lecturer.

T. J. took up the position and initially taught geography and physical science. Soon after, he began to teach "method", which included everything from how to conduct a class to the art of questioning and how to secure attention from pupils – the sort of communication skills that later proved useful to him when preaching. He was also elevated to the post of Vice-Principal. At the time of his appointment, he was only 20 years old.

Capel turned out to be an excellent lecturer. The Inspector of Schools described him as "one of the ablest teachers I have ever known" and praised him for his "clearness, method, and power of illustration." Later, he described him as a "distinguished and devoted teacher." He also noted his "ability, judgement, and assiduity," for which, he remarked, "the college owes so much." Although yet to reach his 21st birthday, Capel was already catching the eye of the powers that be.

Simultaneously, T. J. studied for the priesthood. He did so for six years under the guidance and private tutorship of the Rev. John Melville

Glenie, who was Principal of St. Mary's. An Oxford graduate and convert to Catholicism, Glenie was the ideal tutor. Not only was he known as "a true friend to education," but he was also regarded as "a true and faithful priest." He nurtured Capel, teaching him theology and philosophy, just as Fr. Foy had done at St. Leonards-on-Sea, and the young student responded with energetic zeal. Of importance was the fact that the tuition was free.

On 28 August 1859, Thomas John Capel, after passing "a brilliant examination," was ordained to the priesthood by Cardinal Wiseman in his private chapel at York Place, London. It was a beautiful day, a Sunday, with temperatures in the mid-70s, continuing the brilliant weather of the previous week. Both men shared a common heritage, with Capel from Waterford and Wiseman born to Waterford parents and having attended school there for a time. They had ample opportunity to discuss matters as only two young men were ordained to the priesthood that day.

Capel was now a noted lecturer, college administrator and priest. Still only 22 years old, he was dashing from one job to the other, working overtime, burning the midnight oil, and running himself into the ground. Like the weather on his ordination day, things were about to take a turn for the worse. Storm clouds were looming, and he was soon in the throes of a physical and mental breakdown. It was decided by his superiors that a break was needed, and there was nothing better, they felt, than some missionary work in the recuperative, stress-free resort of Pau, in France.

SUNNY DAYS AT PAU

The young Mgr. Capel

The fashionable resort of Pau shared little in common with the poverty-stricken, overcrowded parishes of England where the Rev. T. J. Capel might have been expected to work after he left St. Mary's, Hammersmith. Located in the foothills of the Pyrenees, it was a winter destination for England's great and good. It boasted among its residents many notable aristocrats and their elegant wives, along with those wealthy enough to escape the harsh British winters for a more pleasing climate abroad.

Some of the visiting residents were in good health; more had arrived to recover from consumption or other ailments. All shared the sort of bond common to upper-class British communities overseas. "Here one meets with agreeable and accomplished people," Sir Alexander Taylor wrote in his book *The Climate of Pau*, published not long before Capel's arrival and which did much to popularise the resort. All the visitors – the infirm and the well – had come to avail of the wonderful climate, he remarked, yet the place offered enough variety "to please the grave and the gay."

Capel's first home in Pau – at 3 Rue Henri IV – was ideally located. It was a short walk to the elegant central square, the Place Royale, where the English Club boasted a well-stocked library of London journals and leading periodicals. Further afield were the polo grounds, lawn tennis club, golf course, and most importantly the hunt, which had become popular with the English and American contingents. There were horses for hire and walks in the nearby richly-wooded countryside – all set with a backdrop of the snow-covered Pyrenees in the distance.

Capel's plan at Pau was simple – like many of the residents, he would winter there and return to England each summer. He started with great speed, plunging into his work with the fervour of a seasoned missionary. Although initially without a base, he soon set up his mission at the chapel of the local hospice – l'Hospice de Pau – which cared for the old, the sick, the infirm and abandoned infants, and was run by the Sisters of St. Vincent de Paul. There, he conducted Masses, Benedictions, Confessions and the dispensing of spiritual advice.

He was soon devising plans to build a special mission chapel – a Chapelle du Catéchisme he called it – and he took steps to bring over from England young pupils who wished to be educated during the winter months. At one stage, the influential Catholic weekly *The Tablet* reported that his intention was to establish, under his spiritual direction, a school at Pau "for the daughters of the higher classes; combining the advantages of climate with those of a superior education."

Although he arrived in a poor state of health, Capel's energy at Pau was prodigious. He felt it needed to be, given the competition he faced from his religious opponents. He was, he pointed out, up against four Protestant churches, catering for about 3,000 souls, "wherein are respectively taught the doctrines of Presbyterians and of the High, Low, and Broad Church parties." Visiting Catholics, he warned, were "exposed to many dangers."

Capel was confident that his communication skills, powers of persuasion, and ability as a public speaker and potential converter of souls would defeat the odds. He was also wily enough to spot a popular theme for his mission. The theme he chose – the goodness, or otherwise, of God – was a hot topic following remarks made by the controversial Church of England theologian, Bishop John Colenso.

Colenso argued that the conventional view of a wrathful, angry and judgemental God was wrong. What's more, he contended, the concept of endless future punishments in the afterlife was baseless. To the contrary, he declared, God was loving, compassionate and forgiving. His proposition might sound tame today, but it threw the various churches and their flocks into turmoil in the 1860s.

The Rev. T. J. Capel addressed the controversy in his chapel at Pau. He delivered sermon after sermon on themes surrounding Colenso's views, drawing ever-growing crowds to hear him. Catholics and non-Catholics, English expats and their American counterparts, along with the royalty of Europe, sat side by side, spellbound by his fluency and eloquence. Word spread, and soon everyone wanted to hear this handsome, charming curate, with his mesmerising sermons and effortless ways.

"In the pulpit he carefully avoids being what is technically known as an orator, precision and careful illustration satisfying what he feels is needed for conviction," one commentator noted. "His sermons are singularly poetic in style, and abound with graphic word pictures, so that we may fitly term him 'the laureate of the pulpit.'" Nothing, the commentator remarked, could detract from "the brilliancy and profundity of his discourse."

Word soon reached Rome of Capel's fire, passion and skill. The young priest, who could not only win hearts and minds by his preaching but could also secure converts to Rome, caught the attention of Pope Pius IX. Impressed by reports from France, and eager to reward new talent, he elevated Capel to Papal Chamberlain, allowing him to use the title of Monsignor, and later made him Domestic Prelate of the Pope.

Back in Pau, Monsignor Capel, as he was now referred to, went from strength to strength. His audiences – especially women – couldn't get enough of him. "Half-past three found me sitting in the overcrowded chapel with the German princesses, many English people of rank, and several Americans, besides my Roman Catholic friends," a female who attended a Capel sermon in Pau wrote. "Monsignore stood on the steps of the chancel, his prayer-book in his hand, and without notes began his sermon on the sins of the tongue.

"This simple, tender, sweet-spoken lesson of charity, with the divine Golden Rule for text, sank deep into my self-accusing soul; and I sat, like many another woman in the audience, blinded with penitent tears....I shall never forget that address, or the manner and looks of the speaker. As he stood and pronounced the *Benedicite* his sad uplifted eyes, all his features, rapt, absorbed in ecstatic devotion, became purified and like the face of an angel – like the face of one who had thrown off forever all soiling contact with this world."

Monsignor Capel not only loved lecturing and sermonising at Pau, but he also loved talking to and engaging with its inhabitants. Observers described how he would sashay through the fashionable central square, the Place Royale, where two afternoons a week overseas residents would congregate. There, they would chat, drink wine, many of them reclining on wicker chairs, while listening to music described as "second only to that of the Emperor's own band in Paris."

He adored the setting: the grand hotels lining the square, the sunset glow, the nearby fast-flowing River Gave, the French soldiers flirting with attractive nursemaids in their seductive little hats. He would float in and out among the crowd, his black silk robe and purple sash gently flapping in the breeze. All eyes would be on him, with his brown hair, pale skin, large blue-grey eyes, sparkling teeth and sweet smile.

He would chat with men of wealth and substance, exchange pleasantries and jokes, and then gently walk away. He would bow to a poor consumptive, uttering sympathetic words in her ear, bringing tears to her eyes as she choked her thanks. Above all, he would charm young ladies, taking their hands, noting the warm flushes that would come and go upon their cheeks as they engaged with this handsome priest.

The women seated in the Place Royale were drawn to Capel, and he was equally drawn to them. An observer, writing in the popular magazine *The Galaxy* in 1870, described how "quickly the purple glove is drawn from his hand, and as he presses theirs, a few words are uttered in a soft low tone; and when the priest moves away the English girls are blushing bright rosy-red with delight."

Other priests would be present, the observer noted, with their "greasy, rubicund visages," walking about "like giants." Barefoot friars with their "dirty faces" would crawl stealthily along. But Capel was different. With his "almost irresistible personal magnetism," "refined, beautiful face," and "stately graceful form," he cut a god-like figure and stood out from the crowd.

Capel used his charm and charisma to achieve conversions among the ladies of Pau. His campaign was well thought out. One woman put it well: "He was thinking that women were for the most part gentle and good, prone to piety and delightfully easy to 'turn'....His experience had taught him that many women made of their religion a sentiment, an aesthetic worship, and that not one in a thousand knew or cared about doctrine." These verdant souls, she noted, were easily swayed by Capel's soft whispers.

At one stage, he explained his beliefs at a dinner party. "Women," he said, "know nothing about doctrine; they have only faith. If you bewilder an artless, loving, ignorant woman with awful doctrine, she will accept it meekly; then reading again the old comfortable words in her Bible, so easy to understand, her great mental reservation of simple, unquestioning faith will assert itself." An appeal to faith, he remarked, was the best route to a woman's conversion.

The American author of children's stories Fanny Barrow was one of his targets at Pau. He wooed her by leaving his calling card at her apartment and eventually ensured their paths crossed at a dinner arranged by mutual friends. He was the essence of charm at that dinner party. Within a minute of Fanny entering the friends' home, Capel appeared, his "stately form and beautiful face" bending over her, her hand cordially pressed. An evening of gentle yet persistent persuasion ensued.

"Eight or nine courses of fish, oysters, and lobsters, prepared in every conceivable and inconceivable style, left nothing to be desired," the author later wrote of the fare on offer that evening. "The gay gold vases, with little looking-glasses all round their outsides, were filled with bonbons and fruit; and half a dozen different kinds of wine were circulating round the table. Monsignore declined all but one or two of the simplest dishes and one glass of claret. His courteous 'Pas encore, merci' to the servants who offered him the choicest of everything, almost on their knees, meant 'not at all,' for he made scarce a pretence of eating or drinking."

Witty remarks, gay repartee, droll stories ensued, accompanied, of course, by discussion about religion and the Bible. Although he failed to persuade Fanny Barrow to convert, he came close. She was relieved she hadn't given in, yet disturbed that she had felt so open to his persuasive powers. Later, after she returned to America, she recalled her shared moments with the Monsignor at Pau – memories of a man she described as "so thoroughly good, and so magnetically earnest" and so "delightful to those not of his faith."

Monsignor Capel had better success with other foreign visitors, among them the wealthy Irish author, Alice Wilmot Chetwode. An Anglican and member of the landed gentry, she had arrived at the resort via Bagnères-de-Bigorre, in south-west France, where she had gone with a sister who was ill. Unsure of her true religious leanings, she had toyed with the idea of becoming a Catholic. The dilemma occupied her throughout the several winters that she and her sister spent at Pau.

In Pau, Alice encountered Monsignor Capel, the "gifted and zealous" young priest, as she described him. She was introduced to Capel by two ladies – a mother and daughter – who Alice knew and who had recently arrived from England. The ladies in question had been received by Capel into the Catholic Church and were devout and fervent converts. They set about ensuring that Alice would follow their example and bring her indecision to an end.

"They soon found out something of my state of mind, and charitably did their best to promote my conversion," Alice later wrote. "At their house I frequently met the priest I have mentioned, who joined his efforts with theirs." Capel bombarded the author with "a great parcel of Catholic books." He spoke to her, advised her, until she eventually "reached the home to which my steps had so long and with so many delays been tending."

On Easter Tuesday, 1866, Alice Wilmot Chetwode was received into the "true fold" in the chapel of the Hospice at Pau. The following day, she made her First Communion and remained a conscientious and single-minded Catholic until her death in August 1915. It was a major notch on Capel's belt; many more would follow.

Lady Mary Duncan became another of Monsignor Capel's early triumphs at Pau. In many ways, she typified the British gentry and nobility who flocked to the French resort. They stayed at the impressive Grand Hôtel Gassion and Hôtel de France, rode out with the hunt, played golf with their peers, and passed the time in tranquil and melancholy repose. They were perfect targets for Monsignor Capel, who engaged well with the Earls, Viscounts and Barons, and especially with their widows and wives.

Lady Duncan was a rich widow with an immaculate pedigree. Her maiden name was Mary Coutts Crawford, which to Capel, with his highly-tuned social antennae, must have had an impressive ring. Her family was related to the enormously-wealthy London banking firm, Coutts. In addition, her father was a famous Commander in the Royal Navy, who had seen active service during the Napoleonic Wars and the American War of Independence.

Her illustrious connections didn't end there. She was the widow of Sir Henry Duncan, whose father had led the British fleet in the famous Battle of Camperdown, where the Dutch were defeated in one of the hardest-fought encounters in British naval history. Not only had he ingeniously outmanoeuvred the Dutch fleet, but his battleship, the *Venerable*, had vanquished the Dutch Admiral's warship in a vicious, three-hour ship-to-ship engagement. Following a resounding victory, he was awarded a peerage.

For Capel, whose father had been a humble boy sailor and coast-guard boatman, befriending Lady Duncan, with her banking and naval connections, was a dream come true. She and her deceased husband – another former naval Commander – had lived at Eaton Place, in London's fashionable Belgravia, one of the grandest addresses in Britain. He had close connections to the Royal family, visiting the

King, attending dinners at the Palace, and for a time, acting in the prestigious role as Officer of the Household.

Following Sir Henry's unexpected death in 1835, at the age of 49, Lady Duncan, who was still a young woman, 29 years old, was left minding two children – a son, Adam Alexander, and a daughter, Anna Mary. It wasn't as if the task of rearing them was physically arduous; after all, she was assisted by a sizeable staff – a lady's maid, kitchen maid, housemaid, cook, butler and groom. She was also financially secure.

For someone so young, however, Lady Duncan had already experienced an inordinate amount of trauma in her life. She had witnessed her husband's sudden death at home from apoplexy, most likely caused by a stroke or heart attack. Four years earlier, she had lost a child, Henry Robert, shortly after birth. With a difficult time behind her and a long, uncertain road ahead, she faced decisions as to what to do with the rest of her life.

The French resort of Pau appealed to Lady Duncan as a refuge from life in London. Like many of her wealthy friends, she soon began wintering there and was already a regular by the time Monsignor Capel arrived as English chaplain. She was drawn by his charisma and magnetic appeal. In turn, he noticed her quest for inner meaning and her efforts to discover a better life. A practising member of the Church of England, she was the ideal target for conversion – wounded, spiritually inclined, in search of a greater truth. She was also refined, high profile and rich.

Lady Duncan's conversion took place in June 1865. News of the event generated enormous interest in Britain and Ireland. The story featured in newspapers ranging geographically from *The Dover Telegraph* to *The Londonderry Journal* and included most other local and regional newspapers in between. The national and religious press reported the event, too. The coverage further enhanced the reputation of Monsignor Capel, who was noted as the man who brought about the conversion and who had received the venerable lady into the Catholic Church.

Capel also received widespread publicity for his visits to the shrine at nearby Lourdes. The first time he travelled there was in late 1859, the year after the 14-year-old peasant girl Bernadette Soubirous had reported seeing visions of Our Lady. Then aged 23, Capel visited the convent run by the Sisters of Charity, where the Mother Superior arranged a meeting with the future saint. The young girl, who spoke the local dialect Gascon, was just about proficient enough in French – "very bad French," according to Capel – to engage with him.

Capel was struck by Bernadette's modesty, sincerity, honesty and quietness. Everything she said had a ring of "truthfulness and simplicity," he remarked. He also investigated reported miracles, one of which he claimed to have witnessed. It involved a lady who had lost the use of her limbs but who had emerged from the waters of Lourdes fully cured. He heard details of many other miracles, too. "On the testimony of eyewitnesses, several return home freed from their sickness," he said.

Throughout his seven winters at Pau, Capel paid frequent visits to Bernadette and became one of her greatest defenders. On his later return to England, he lectured about Lourdes and Bernadette at many venues, including the Hanover Square Rooms, where he spoke before an energetic and appreciative audience. That the setting was the principal one in London for concerts, and had enjoyed royal patronage, says a lot about Capel's growing stature at the time.

Capel especially welcomed the interest of the national press in his views. As he did with his mission at Pau, he promoted his support for the Lourdes phenomenon in newspapers as much as he could. He even commenced a controversial exchange with *The Times*, with the broadsheet expressing its disbelief over the miracles and Capel arguing in their defence.

The experience of being in the limelight was new to him, and he loved it. He was popular with the press, articulated well, aroused audiences, attracted large crowds, and was revealing himself to be a star in the making. The limelight was something he would relish and pursue for the rest of his life.

THE RISE TO FAME

Marquess of Bute

A few minutes after three o'clock, on the afternoon of Sunday, 4 October 1868, a solemn religious ceremony was held in a small town located not far from London, on the banks of the River Thames. On that afternoon, St. Peter's Church, Marlow, was packed as a huge congregation assembled for a colourful procession and to celebrate Benediction.

In the dimming autumn light, silence descended as a man clothed in the violet cassock and surplice of a Monsignor entered the pulpit. He removed his biretta, raised his eyes to the congregation, and began to speak. "What doth it profit a man to gain the whole world and lose his own soul," Monsignor Capel intoned. He was home, back on English soil, doing what he did best, with the world at his feet.

Monsignor Capel was familiar with the town of Marlow and its church of St. Peter's for some time before that solemn occasion in October 1868. Even before his full-time relocation to England, he had been visiting the area during his summer vacations. There, he had become close to Charles Scott Murray, the builder of St. Peter's, who was a convert to Catholicism and a man of wealth. Capel had agreed to act as chaplain at Scott Murray's private oratory, which was located at his nearby stately home, Danesfield.

Their friendship was no surprise as Scott Murray was exactly the sort of man Capel had grown to know and like at Pau. An Eton past pupil and Oxford graduate, he had served for a time as a Conservative Member of Parliament. A rich man, he owned another property at Cavendish Square, in the West End of London, which was described as a centre of "much pleasant hospitality." Most importantly, he had friends in high places.

Among Scott Murray's close acquaintances was the young Marquess of Bute, whose father had died when he was a baby and whose mother had died when he was only 12 years old. On his father's death, he had inherited his family's vast estates in Scotland and Wales, including coal pits, iron mines, ports, docks, shipping, and Cardiff Castle. When he came of age, a few weeks before the procession at Marlow, he formally became the richest man in Britain, arguably in the world.

During his early visits to the Scott Murrays, the Marquess, who came from a Presbyterian background, had expressed an interest in converting to Catholicism. "He shared all our home life, came to Mass and Benediction with us as a matter of course, and talked quite simply of how he longed to be a 'real' Catholic," one of the Scott Murrays wrote in a letter. Despite the family's support, Bute was unsure and postponed his conversion.

Into the picture stepped Monsignor Capel, fresh from his triumphs at Pau. He was overjoyed when he first met the Marquess at Danesfield. The tall, dark, good-looking young man was thoughtful, sensitive, self-effacing, and incredibly rich. A student at Oxford, he was already well on the road to converting to Rome, although not quite there, and was open to persuasion.

Much of Bute's hesitation was internal – the product of uncertainty over whether Rome matched his religious aspirations. He was also being held back by his guardian, General Charles Stuart, who advised him to postpone matters until he came of age. The press, having got wind of his possible intentions, exerted additional pressure by calling him "a noble pervert" and referring to his pending conversion as "a most lamentable perversion."

Through these trying times, Bute, although known to be stiff with strangers, sought help from Capel. "I knew him fairly well, and was pleased with his clear and simple way of explaining certain things I wished to know," the Marquess wrote to a close friend. "I received much spiritual help from him at a time when I was greatly in need of such help, and yet was unable, for certain reasons, to take the final step."

Bute was still uncertain when he returned to Oxford for the summer term of 1868. Capel, who was unwilling to let the Marquess far from his sight, followed him there. What he found was not unexpected. The university was, at that time, a "magnificent capital of Protestant thought," as a contributor to *The Tablet* put it, with an average of only two Catholic students passing through it each year.

But that was exactly the point – it was full of rich Protestants, many of them aristocrats, at least some of whom might be open to conversion. Unlike the poverty-stricken Irish Catholics who had arrived in Britain following the recent potato famine, and whose souls needed reclaiming, these young, wealthy Oxford intellectuals were a far more interesting and lucrative target for the ambitious Monsignor, and they were much more to his taste.

Capel reached Oxford at an opportune time. Shortly before his arrival, the university had been rocked by the tragic deaths of two students. One of them, who Bute knew well, had fallen out of a top window and died within half an hour. The following day, an undergraduate accidentally shot himself through the stomach and died almost at once. The students were "*very* sad and depressed," Bute said. "The gloom and misery of it all are excessive."

Death became the focus of conversation at Oxford. "The sight of death has awakened many from the dream of sensuality in which they habitually lie asleep," Bute remarked. "I hear men saying that they simply *dare* not die." But help was at hand: "Capel is coming next Wednesday, and I am sure his visit will do good. Indeed I think this opportunity an admirable one."

Capel, who stayed at the Catholic presbytery in Oxford, poured himself into his work. He soon made an impression as an accomplished and pious priest, hearing Confessions, distributing Communion, and conducting Masses and Benediction. He drew immense crowds and engaged well with the students. An observer remarked: "His *savoir faire*, fascinating manners, and great ability were brought to play with great effect."

He also achieved the conversion of some students and preparation of others, alarming the college authorities. One of his successes described how his Dean was outraged, told him the college was "not the place for converts," and blamed Capel for what was taking place. A potential convert, Charles Biscoe, received equally torrid treatment. "I never heard of anything so gratuitously brutal as the Dean's conduct towards him," a friend later remarked. Biscoe never converted.

Bute's spiritual advisor at Oxford, the theologian Henry Liddon, believed Capel's arrival was responsible for unsettling students and viewed him as a troublesome interloper. He hurriedly issued a mandate prohibiting undergraduates from making his acquaintance. It made no difference to the Monsignor. "All those who *want* to know me, I think, already do," he remarked.

In the end, Capel won the battle for Bute's conversion. His conditional baptism, profession of faith, and First Communion took place on 8 December 1868, the Feast of the Immaculate Conception. The event was held in the chapel of the Sisters of Notre Dame, Southwark, London – an ideal venue, "quiet and easy of access," as Capel put it, for a prominent figure like Bute. It was a turning point in the life of the Marquess; it was to prove even more transformative for Capel, who officiated at the ceremony.

News of the conversion projected Monsignor Capel onto the front pages of the national press. His role in the event was highlighted nationwide, although much of the coverage was hostile. "This perversion is the result of priestly influences acting upon a weak, ductile, and naturally superstitious mind," *The Glasgow Herald* trumpeted. What were Bute's guardians doing that enabled "their youthful and unguarded ward to be entrapped by a wily Roman Catholic Priest?" the *Oxford Chronicle & Berks & Bucks Gazette* demanded to know.

That the Marquess of Bute was brought into port by Capel "like a Dutch galleon heavily freighted with pieces of eight" was "almost too much for English patience," an Irish newspaper, *The Kilkenny Journal*, declared. Another Irish newspaper, *The Nation*, described how, in response to the news, "a kind of moral pall overspread the land – a terrible calamity, hardly inferior to the shock of an earthquake, shook our whole social system."

Capel loved the publicity and was undisturbed by its often-negative tone. Bute ignored the newspapers as much as possible. In either case, they need not have worried about the press coverage as, like two superstars, they were soon departing England, leaving a fog-bound London behind them, and heading on a five-month tour of the Mediterranean Sea.

The two men set out for Nice, where they stayed with the Scott Murrays over Christmas and into the New Year. The Monsignor performed Midnight Mass on Christmas night in the little church in their garden. All those who were assembled took Communion together, including the Marquess of Bute.

At the end of January 1869, Bute's yacht, the *Ladybird*, arrived at Nice and took the Marquess and Monsignor Capel, along with a few other guests, to Rome. There, they were received by Pope Pius IX, who administered to Bute the sacrament of Confirmation. As a token of thanks, Bute made what was described as "a munificent offering" to the Pope's personal charitable fund known as Peter's Pence.

The yacht then took the entourage to Palestine – "the continuation of my pilgrimage of thanksgiving," as Bute called it – after which they returned to Marseille, via Sicily, and headed for home. It was summer when they arrived in England.

On his return, Monsignor Capel – the man known far and wide for his "recent conversion of the Marquess of Bute" – resumed his duties as a preacher. Things had changed, however. In the wake of his newfound fame, venues were packed, often with "many ladies being present," for his talks on topics including "The Shrines of the Holy Land."

His lecture themes also covered a more pressing topic – the infallibility of the Pope – which was about to become the centrepiece of discussions at the forthcoming First Vatican Council. Scheduled to start at the beginning of December 1869, the Monsignor had his eye on attending the convocation. His hopes were realised when, later in the autumn, he was informed that he would indeed be travelling to Rome. It seemed the right destination for a man of his stature and renown.

An unusually strong sirocco blew in from the Sahara during the Monsignor's stay in Rome. The city was enveloped in a warm dampness, followed by rain tumbling down with a vengeance. The snow in the Apennines melted and the Tiber overflowed its banks. The Pantheon stood in a lake of yellow water. The enjoyment of those attending the First Vatican Council was "greatly interfered with," a visiting newsman remarked.

Capel hardly noticed the weather. In the midst of the Patriarchs, Primates, Bishops, Archbishops, Cardinals, Abbots and other Church dignitaries, he was in his element. This was the place to be, at a huge event, which opened on 8 December 1869 and for all practical purposes came to an end seven months later, on 18 July 1870, when Pope Pius IX solemnly proclaimed the dogma of Papal infallibility.

Not everyone enjoyed their time in Rome. Bishop McGill, from America, hated the Italian food. Another American, Bishop McQuaid, complained of the weather. Archbishop Manning, of Westminster, said of the proceedings: "Well, we meet, and we look at one another, and then we talk a little, but when we want to know what we have been doing, we read *The Times*." Unlike them, Capel, who was 33 years old, loved it all.

The Monsignor's reputation had preceded him, and he was recognised and admired by those in attendance as one of the rising stars of the Church. They were aware of his illustrious conversions and unique ability at delivering sermons. They also knew that Pope Pius IX rated him and was affording him a special entrée to Vatican circles. He was especially noticeable during ceremonies held at St. Peter's, where he assisted at the altar, and dressed in his scarlet robes, marched in procession down through the crowded basilica.

At that time, too, he was appointed to preach to English-speaking audiences at the churches of Santa Maria di Monte Santo and Sant' Andrea delle Fratte. The former was his favourite as it was close to Protestant places of worship and also near the Pincian Hill, which was always crowded on Sundays. Large attendances were guaranteed – especially consisting of ladies – and perhaps a convert or two might be secured.

"When I entered the church it was full. Almost all the available space had already been covered with chairs, every one of which was occupied; and within five minutes there was no longer standing room for a single soul. I fear the benches of the Anglican and American churches must have looked rather bare yesterday at afternoon service," a special correspondent for *The Evening Standard* wrote of one of Capel's Sunday afternoon sermons, which was held at three o'clock.

Capel soon appeared on the altar, dressed in a plain cassock and surplice, wearing a biretta, and ascended the pulpit. All eyes were focused on him. His voice signified culture and power. "Had you shut your eyes you might have sworn you were in an Anglican Church. The pronunciation and intonation bore the Oxford stamp," one onlooker noted. "This, added to his association with a renowned marquess, would be enough to attract an English crowd settled in Rome."

Capel's visit to the First Vatican Council enhanced his reputation not only in Rome but at home. He was praised for his "pulpit eloquence" and described in the press as "a man of peculiarly prepossessing appearance, manners, and delivery." Another report referred to him as ranking "among the best Roman Catholic preachers in our language." There was even a report in the press, on 17 March 1870, of two American ladies whose conversions were attributed to him.

As it happened, those two young American ladies – described as "sisters, of irreproachable fame" – would soon bring to light the first-known allegations of Capel's predilection for sexual misbehaviour.

Their claims are contained in an old box file stored at the Westminster Diocesan Archives, Kensington, London.

In a submission to Capel's boss at Westminster, Archbishop Manning, the sisters charged the Monsignor with having "acted with immodesty" towards one of them. They added that they also suspected him of having behaved inappropriately towards their servant, an Italian.

The sisters later visited London, where they stayed at the Convent of the Assumption, Kensington Square. There, they repeated their allegations to the Reverend Mother, speaking "very strongly" against the Monsignor. Noting during the visit that Capel was still acting as a priest, they once again contacted Archbishop Manning to complain. Nothing happened, and Capel weathered the storm.

Like the two Americans, the Monsignor had travelled to London in the spring of 1870. He was hardly home when, instead of being rebuked, his reputation received a boost of unprecedented proportions. The piece of good fortune came from the pen of author and former British Prime Minister Benjamin Disraeli, who had been quietly writing a novel since losing office in December 1868. It would become the first novel ever written by an ex-Prime Minister.

The book, *Lothair*, had a Presbyterian orphan peer as its central character. There were priests and laymen conspiring to win him to the Catholic Church, along with visits to Rome and the Holy Land. Cardinal Grandison was a paragon of devotion and asceticism, who remarks in the book "I never eat and I never drink" when refusing an invitation to dinner. There also was the suave Monsignore Catesby, a fashionable missionary whose goal in life was to convert the upper classes.

Nobody could have missed the connections with well-known personalities from the time. Lothair was the Marquess of Bute, and Cardinal Grandison was Archbishop Manning. A Duke referred to in the text was the Duke of Abercorn. An Oxford professor was the real-life academic Goldwin Smith. Monsignore Catesby was youthful, had winning manners, considerable abilities, a determined will, and possessed the beauty of the form and countenance of his family. Nobody needed reminding who that Monsignor might be, especially when he became Lothair's chief Catholic mentor.

Driving home the connection with Capel, Disraeli made an uncharacteristic error which came to light when the book was published in May 1870. On page 254, in volume three of the text, he inserted Capel's name instead of Catesby's. "Neither Monsignore Capel nor Father Coleman were present," he wrote regarding the pair's non-attendance at a dinner party. Whether his mind had strayed, his editor was asleep, or the mistake was deliberate, is unknown. In later editions, the error was rectified.

The highlighting of Capel's name created quite a stir in Victorian society. "Once that was in print the cat was fairly and irretrievably out of the bag," the compiler of the literary notes in *Country Life Illustrated* wrote. "True, of course, everybody knew all about it before, to all intents and purposes, but the little slip gave certainty to the general knowledge, and after that all denials would have been useless."

It is hard to imagine today how seismic an impact the publication of *Lothair* had in enhancing Capel's fame. It seemed that all the world read the book, and almost every newspaper and journal reviewed it. The names of horses, songs and ships were inspired by it. The book was a runaway British bestseller and sold 1,000 copies a day in America. Edition followed edition. It was translated into every European language and became the biggest publishing rage in half a century.

Capel loved the fame. The day after it was published, he was joking and laughing about his role in the book with James Macdonnell, a young and talented journalist with *The Daily Telegraph*. Over dinner, Macdonnell explained to Capel how he had started and finished the book, and had thoroughly enjoyed it. He said that it was "really clever, and very amusing."

Macdonnell believed Capel was just like his own fictional character – "a good talker, accomplished, polished, playful, a perfect man of the world." The Monsignor was far from polished, and surprisingly indiscreet, when the discussion turned to Archbishop Manning, who had also appeared in the book. "He hates Manning as only one priest can hate another," Macdonnell candidly revealed. It was an interesting observation, as time would tell.

The book and its characters became the topic of polite – and no doubt impolite – conversation during the London season. The chatter helped sales, as did a public protest registered by Goldwin Smith, the real-life professor who believed that he was maliciously caricatured in the book. The fact that he was accused of having "a restless vanity and overflowing conceit" and was "a social parasite" might have had something to do with his irritation. The publishers, Longmans, were delighted with the publicity and decided to print again.

The success of *Lothair* was hugely beneficial to both Disraeli and Capel. The former Prime Minister made a small fortune from the book. Its success also boosted sales of his previous novels. So successful was the project that Longmans paid him another large sum of money for the rights to all his works. Although Capel didn't profit financially, his name was made, and his fame spread far and wide, even to America. He owed Disraeli a huge debt of gratitude.

There is no evidence that the author and cleric ever became close in any meaningful way. Their paths crossed, however, at the wedding of Bute in 1872. On that day, the Marquess – "Lothair" – was marrying not his fictional bride, "Lady Corisande" of the novel, but the Hon. Gwendolen Fitzalan-Howard, one of the beauties of her era. And the ceremony was not being conducted by "Monsignore Catesby" but by Monsignor Capel.

Benjamin Disraeli – the creator of the characters – watched from the congregation, where he stood among the nobility, aristocrats, commoners, and clergy of all creeds. He wore lavender gloves and an eyeglass through which he viewed Capel "with marked if not devout attention." No doubt he was aware that the man he was looking at was no longer a mere rising star but, thanks to him, had become the superstar known as "Catesby of Mr. Disraeli's *Lothair*."

APOSTLE TO THE GENTEEL

The "Pro"

The Church of Our Lady of Victories, with its high-pitched crested roof and decorated spire, stood out in the early 1870s Kensington skyline. It was there, at this newly-built Pro-Cathedral, located at Newland Terrace, that Monsignor Capel consolidated his fame as a preacher following his return to London at the tail end of the 1860s.

The "Pro", as it was often called, could accommodate 1,000-plus worshippers, was lit by gas, and was frequently so crowded that the street outside would be thronged with horse-drawn carriages. That it boasted an enormous pulpit seemed appropriate as its two main preachers – Archbishop Henry Edward Manning and Monsignor Capel – were well-respected orators and widely regarded as masters of their craft.

It would be hard to find two more dissimilar characters than Manning and Capel. The former, the Archbishop, was "tall, thin, austere, reserved; the other plump, gay, handsome, and accessible," wrote the London correspondent of *The Cardiff Times*. It was unusual, the newspaper remarked, to find in close connection "two more distinct types of priest."

Manning might satisfy himself with "a biscuit and a glass of water" on the "few occasions when he goes out to dinner," the correspondent remarked. On the other hand, Capel "dines out often, and may in the height of the season be met at two or three 'at homes' the same evening, and in each is the centre of an animated and happy circle of guests." Capel, he said, was truly "the drawing-room man of the Roman Catholic hierarchy, and as such is welcomed everywhere."

The huge crowds arriving to witness Capel at the "Pro", or elsewhere, came as much to see this suave man of the world as to hear his consummate preaching. His sermons could "fix the attention of a crowded church," but people knew he could also "charm a salon," according to one news report. The style that had brought him into the drawing rooms of Mayfair was just as important as the energy and enthusiasm of his preaching.

Many who watched him speak – awestruck men and adoring women – knew they were in the presence of a lady-killer. Women found him fascinating. A profile of the Monsignor in *Vanity Fair* described his sexual charms: "He is withal, if not an admirer, at least a great controller and director of the fair sex, and he has probably made and unmade more important marriages than any man or mamma in the country."

The Monsignor was well aware of his magnetic appeal and remarkable talents by the time he began preaching to the churchgoers of Kensington. Newspapers were aware of his compelling attributes, too. "His persuasive powers are extraordinary," one commentator said. He possesses a "natural gift of voice and manner," another noted. Without any doubt, he is "the most successful proselytiser of the day," a third concluded.

"It is hard, even with his words and voice yet ringing in our ears, to define his eloquence, his power, its singular charm," a contributor to *The Galaxy* wrote, having seen the Monsignor in action. "It is, I think, chiefly owing to the utter lack of affectation, the whole-souled sincerity of the man. There is no excitement in his tone or gesture; no brilliant strokes of rhetoric. He impresses us as a man preaching Christ's words for all nations; calm, earnest, simple, but with his whole soul thrown into what he says."

The Monsignor was up against stiff opposition in London, which was full of other great preachers. Canon Liddon, an Anglican, who Capel had battled with at Oxford, was drawing crowds of up to 4,000 at St. Paul's Cathedral. The Baptist preacher Charles Spurgeon was doing even better at the Metropolitan Tabernacle, filling it to its capacity of 6,000. Add in the controversial theist Charles Voysey, the renowned Unitarian James Martineau, and the secular philosopher Frederic Harrison – all of them immensely popular – and the scale of the competition is clear.

"During the London season my father, accompanied by a bevy of daughters, would start out on a Sunday morning to discover the most exciting speaker on religious or metaphysical issues," Beatrice Webb, one of the founders of the London School of Economics, recalled. Over time, she was brought by her father to hear all the leading preachers, including Capel.

Although Beatrice enjoyed all of them "with equal zest," she had her favourites. "I went to hear Spurgeon the other day, and nothing on the earth will ever persuade me to go again!" she remarked in a letter. On the other hand, regarding Monsignor Capel, she said: "He preached *so* beautifully all against the – who do you think? – against the Protestants....I heartily agreed with him, but you know the High Church party is in such a rage at being shown up like this."

Capel knew he needed to fine-tune his technique if he was to compete in this hotbed of preaching activity. He worked hard at his sermons, spending "night and day" perfecting them, according to an acquaintance. His methodology was simple – put down on paper whatever ideas come to you relevant to the subject matter, consign the outline to your mind, and destroy the piece of paper as it is no longer of use.

He always delivered the address without using a manuscript, and he chose his style of language to suit the audience. He cultivated simplicity of speech, saying that in England there were two very well-defined languages – one belonging to the wealthy classes, the educated ranks; the other that of the common people.

"One reason why the Episcopalians – the established church – had made no progress, and the Methodists and other dissenting sects had grown so largely was because the sermons by the established clergy were couched in the fine language of the college graduate, above the masses entirely, while those of the dissenters were perfectly comprehensible to every listener," he told an interviewer.

He once judged an audience incorrectly and had to rectify matters in midstream, he said. The incident happened at Fulham, where the venue was crowded with worshippers. He assumed the audience was upmarket and "consequently to be addressed in the accustomed phraseology of the educated classes." On noticing "the unresponsive appearances" on their faces, he changed tack and used "good Saxon English." The change worked, it seems.

Although attached to the Pro-Cathedral at Kensington, where he delivered regular sermons, Capel also travelled throughout Britain to fulfil speaking engagements. He spoke in Cardiff on "The Vatican Council," in Glasgow on "Modern Literature and Art," and in Liverpool – "with a strong veneer of West-end exquisitiveness" – on the theme of "Church and State." He also travelled to Newcastle to speak at a public meeting on education.

Other sermon themes included "Conversions towards Catholicism," "Duties of Christians," "The Souls of the Departed," "The Powers Claimed by the Catholic Priesthood," "On Devotion to the Blessed Virgin," and "Our Duty to and Treatment of the Poor." Invariably, halls and churches were full, with people arriving up to three hours in advance to secure their seats and hundreds being turned away.

The same "Capel fever" was witnessed in early 1872 when he made a triumphant return visit to Ireland, the land of his birth. Huge crowds came to see him. "His presence is massive and dignified, his countenance expresses the concentration and calm strength of a mind accustomed to think deeply and to form grave, resolute convictions," *The Freeman's Journal* commented in a rave review of a lecture he delivered in Dublin.

He then travelled to Cork, where he presented a course of 11 sermons as part of an annual "retreat" at the Church of Saints Peter and Paul. A daily crowd of up to 2,000 packed into the chapel, which was "illuminated throughout by triple gas jets." A blaze of bright lights surrounded the Monsignor as he delivered his sermons. "It was impossible not to be impressed," *The Cork Examiner* concluded in yet another rave review.

Everywhere he went, women flocked to see him. It was the same in Kensington, where his female followers sought him out to hear their Confessions. Capel favoured the Confession box on the east side of the Pro-Cathedral, while the Rev. O'Connell occupied the box located at the building's north side. The majority of those arriving were young women, many from a poor background. The confessor most in demand, with the longest queues, was Capel.

Wealthy women came to seek him out, too. Some were well known. "As we tarried a great lady came, closely followed by her footman in powdered wig," author William Pepperell noted during a visit to the "Pro". He recognised the woman as a Countess known in West End circles during the London season. She looked and dressed well, and entered the church with a cheerful manner and beaming smile.

"Addressing an instruction to her servant, he went to a small side chapel near the chancel, and soon returned with a young dark official in a dingy cassock," Pepperell wrote. "To him the Countess gave a note or a card, which he deposited with Mgr. Capel at the Confessional." The Monsignor soon left the box and led her to a side chapel, where he engaged with her for 15 minutes. She then left the church, her business done.

The Monsignor also charmed young girls, as was seen during his visits to a French convent school, located near Paris, which he undertook on an annual basis in the early to mid-1870s. One of the girls, following his visit in March 1874, provided an insight to this "tall, square-built, handsome man" in a letter she sent from the school.

"He is very fascinating in private," she wrote. "He asked to see the girls, so we were assembled, Petites and all, in the *Salle des Enfants de Marie*. There he was very kind and pleasant and entertained us nearly an hour. He began by making a funny little speech in French, which he talks in the most English way possible, and got us all laughing.

"Then he asked to have the rogues of the school come up to him, and half a dozen of the Petites actually did step forward; and he made them tell all about the latest scrapes they had got into, till they were covered with confusion and the rest of us laughed till the tears ran down our cheeks." Before leaving, Capel secured a half-day holiday for the students, eliciting an inevitable round of wild applause.

Throughout his time at Pau, Capel had established friendships or acquaintances with many English aristocrats, and he further exploited these connections after returning home. He continued to seek out the noble and select of society. Each contact led to further social introductions, until it was said that he had established, or was on his way to establishing, relations with about one-half of the titled and one-quarter of the untitled aristocracy of England.

He could mix with blue bloods and the upper crust of any creed or variety. One evening, he attended a dinner party given by the Catholic convert Lady Herbert of Lea at her home in Chesham Place, Belgravia. There, he engaged animatedly with eminent, passionate Catholics such as Lady Victoria Hope-Scott and the Marchioness of Londonderry. Lady Herbert's friends, who were not there that night, included Florence Nightingale and Prime Minister William Gladstone.

On another occasion, he attended a garden party hosted by the Prince and Princess of Wales, at Chiswick, West London. At the party, he exchanged idle chit-chat with the Prince, who eventually became King Edward VII and head of the Church of England. The guests included the Duke of Beaufort, who was an Anglican and had served with the Duke of Wellington. Also present were the Archbishop of Canterbury and the Archbishop of York, both representing the Church of England.

Capel had no problem conversing with his hosts and their guests. He could theorise or philosophise with the best of them. No topic tripped him up, whether it involved the arts, science, literature, or events of the day. "He is by no means a man of solid information, but he has the happy knack of knowing how to make a big display of what he does know, and of setting it off to the best advantage," a correspondent with *The Bulwark or Reformation Journal* noted.

"He is also skilful enough never to get out of his depth; and when at all likely to be cornered – which seldom happens, as his aristocratic followers are of the same calibre – he manages either to adroitly turn the conversation, or to effect a retreat amid a brilliant pyrotechnic flare-up – a galaxy of verbiage, which effectually covers his strategic rearward movement."

While the Monsignor clearly had an unusual capacity for impressing people, he also had a remarkable ability to turn people to his point of view. His forceful mental powers and persuasive prowess were highlighted in an extraordinary experiment he undertook with the well-known English mentalist Stuart Cumberland, who was famous for his demonstrations of thought reading.

During the experiment, Cumberland asked Capel to hide a toy and then, by reading his mind, attempted to locate it. "I found it impossible of accomplishment," Cumberland said. "My 'subject,' instead of aiding me with his concentration of thought in the direction of the hidden object, was all the time (unconsciously I believe) resisting my progress. I complained of this, and said that I never professed to read a man's thoughts against his will; and that under such circumstances success was not possible."

"Exactly so," Capel replied with charming frankness, "let us, therefore, reverse the process." He then began to breathe on the mentalist's forehead and held his hands. Cumberland instantly found himself "flying across the room" and located the object immediately. Capel smiled. "Well, what does that prove?" Cumberland asked. "It proves that my will is greater than yours," the Monsignor responded.

The Monsignor put his forceful persona to good use in other ways, especially in securing conversions among aristocrats, the gentry, and the generally well off. There were many potential recruits to be found among the "dowager duchesses" and their like, one newspaper noted. Another remarked that Capel's "bland manners and brilliant eloquence" were ideally suited to recruiting them. His talents were perfect for attracting Protestants "scared by the dry arguments and serious tones of a more severe advocate," the newspaper stated.

Capel achieved many successes. By the early 1870s, he was converting three, four or five persons a week, he said. Among his triumphs was

Mary Duff, whose son owned one of the finest estates in Wales. Another was Sir Henry Bellingham, Member of Parliament for County Louth, in Ireland. A third was Zoe Shipley, one of a well-known group of brilliant sisters and who was married to an Anglican clergyman.

Lady Flora Hastings was a further convert. Aged in her early 20s, she was described as fair and bright, with an open pleasant countenance, light blue eyes, and a short nose. Following her conversion, she fell in love with the Duke of Norfolk, who was a Catholic, and they were married at the Brompton Oratory, South Kensington, in November 1877. Monsignor Capel assisted at the ceremony. Not only was her marriage a major social event, but her decision to become a Catholic created controversy and sensation in London's fashionable society.

"I also received into the Church Lord Courtenay," the Monsignor once remarked. A Member of Parliament, who came from a wealthy family with vast estates in Devon and near Limerick, Ireland, he was a spectacular catch. Unfortunately, as one of his obituaries put it in 1891, he was so addicted to horse racing "that the fortunes of the ancient race to which he belonged were considerably impaired by the losses which he sustained upon the Turf." He eventually ended up a bankrupt.

Lord Braye, an Old Etonian, who was educated at Oxford, was also a Capel convert. Not only was he rich, but he was well known in society circles. His accomplishments included military service during the South African War and for being, along with his wife, the first to travel in a motor car to a ball at Buckingham Palace. Throughout his life, he devoted himself to the interests of the Roman Catholic Church.

Away from his aristocratic converts, the Monsignor lived a busy life in those hectic years of the late 1860s and early 1870s. Then in his mid-30s, he moved in the highest social circles, sharing speakers' platforms with people like author Charles Dickens and statesman William Gladstone, and dining with the Victorian novelist Anthony Trollope and Baron von Reuter, founder of Reuters News Agency.

On one occasion, he took to the stage with Charles Dickens at the Savage Club in London, a literary, artistic and dramatic establishment that boasted distinguished men among its membership. A toast to

"The Visitors" was proposed by Dickens and replied to by Monsignor Capel. At another time, the Monsignor and Mark Twain vied with each other for audiences on the London speaking and lecturing circuit. Twain delivered humorous talks, while Capel preached at St. George's Cathedral, Southwark, only a few miles away.

He also found it easy to socialise in theatrical and bohemian circles. He attended their social gatherings, engaging with guests including the great English stage actor Henry Irving. "At these parties and 'at homes' in the 'Great Bohemia,' you meet Irving, Monsignor Capel, and others of the leading celebrities of the day," a social diarist remarked. "The conversation is animated and brilliant, and the bill of fare, in the way of music and recitations, is, of course, extremely artistic."

The Monsignor became so famous that photographs of him were displayed in London shop windows alongside those of actresses and other celebrities. His image shared pride of place with Emperor Napoleon III, Gladstone, Disraeli and Dickens. All of them were for sale. Photographs were also printed in 3-D by The London Stereoscopic Company. Those stereoscopic images were sold far and wide, from the company's offices in Regent Street to The London House, in Patrick Street, Cork.

Impressed by his marketability, the sixpenny society newspaper *The Whitehall Review* gave out free crayon portraits of him, as did the American monthly magazine, *The Galaxy*. Mark Twain was so taken by the Capel reproduction in *The Galaxy* that he remarked: "Could anything be sweeter than that?" He intended hanging a copy in his parlour, in America, alongside his own from the same publication.

Arguably the peak of Capel's social fame was reached when the prestigious weekly magazine *Vanity Fair* declared him one of Britain's great "Men of the Day." The edition, published in September 1872, included a coloured lithograph of the Monsignor, free to its readers. "In England among all the rich and well-born Roman Catholics he is nearly as popular and as powerful as he presumes to be," the publication remarked at what seemed to be the high point of his career. The power they referred to, however, was about to expand even further as the "Apostle to the Genteel" became the great "Educator of Kensington."

THE EDUCATOR OF KENSINGTON

Kensington High Street

In London, beyond Mayfair and Hyde Park, as you head towards the setting sun, lies the fashionable borough of Kensington. In Victorian times, its High Street was lit by gas lamps and bustled with horse-drawn hansom cabs and hackney carriages. At night, or on foggy days, the cab and carriage lamps lit up the streets and relieved them of their gloom. Rancid black or orange-yellow fogs often over-shadowed the borough. A smell of sulphur, from coal fires, hung in the air.

When Monsignor Capel settled in Kensington, in the late 1860s and early '70s, the landscape retained much of its old character. Established, wealthy families still lived in fine houses, with stuccoed fronts and columned porches, surrounded by squares and gardens. Rows of tiny cottages still housed the coachmen and grooms who served the rich. The slums continued to accommodate poverty-stricken families suffering from hunger, overcrowding and disease.

By the late 1860s, however, Kensington was changing, and changing fast. The Underground on High Street opened in 1868. New sophisti-cated shops sprang up, replacing the modest outlets that had once filled the streets. Department stores like Barkers, Pontings and Harrods were transforming the retail landscape. House construction was booming.

40

"Every patch of land is being built up," author Beatrix Potter, who grew up there, wrote within a decade of Capel's arrival.

The elegant, rapidly-expanding borough satisfied Capel's aspirations and dreams. He loved the hustle and bustle, the sophistication and style of the wealthy, aristocratic and populous parish. With its new Pro-Cathedral, it was the ideal place to be. It also had a fast-growing Catholic population, reflecting the migration of Catholics from east to west of the city. "London is travelling westward" was how Henry Manning, Archbishop of Westminster, put it.

Sensing the changing landscape, Capel devised plans for the future. He was, he believed, the ideal man to set up a school for boys; not just any school but a "Catholic Eton" providing high-class education for the sons of wealthy Catholic families. He had the contacts and a track record. "Teaching is my particular pleasure. I have long been engaged in the work of education, and have a passion for it," he stated, harking back to his earlier work as a lecturer at St. Mary's, Hammersmith.

He deemed Kensington to be the perfect location for the school, close to the main centres of industry and commerce but away from the hubbub and noise of London. It was also accessible to children from all parts of the busy city. "Nowadays, what with the underground railway and the omnibuses, all parts of London are very near to each other," Capel explained in an interview. He was confident the school would be a success.

First, Capel moved into an upmarket, three-storey-over-basement residential property, 2 Scarsdale Villas, located a short walk from Kensington High Street. He hired two live-in staff – Anne Collins, an Irish-born housekeeper, from Cork, and Kate Flannagan, another Irish-born woman, a general servant, who came from Limerick. With a next-door neighbour who was a barrister and a near-neighbour who was a portrait painter, the Monsignor felt comfortable and at home.

In February 1873, Capel opened his ambitious education project – a Catholic public school for "the Sons of Gentlemen," located at Warwick Road. It was modelled on prestigious public schools like Eton, Harrow, Charterhouse and Rugby, but with a Catholic flavour.

"Instruction similar to that of the Public Schools of England, together with a sound Catholic education, is offered to Boys from the age of 10 to 18," an advertisement proclaimed.

The school's Director was Monsignor Capel and its Headmaster was the Rev. J. R. Madan, an Oxford graduate. Many of the other staff members had graduated from Oxford or Cambridge in various disciplines. Two teachers – Monsieur Faribault and Herr Gaber – had been educated at the University of Paris and the University of Heidelberg, respectively. The institution also boasted "Drawing and Drilling Masters."

"With appetite whetted for teaching by his early experience at St. Mary's College, Hammersmith, Monsignor Capel has thrown himself zealously into the work of founding the Catholic public school for boys," a commentator noted. "In this, as in other departments of his work, he has spared no pains to secure a strong working staff." The school was so well arranged, the commentator remarked, that Roman Catholic families would undoubtedly gravitate there for the education of their children.

Not content with his public school for older boys, Capel set up a complementary preparatory school for male pupils aged from four to ten. It was established "in connection with" the public school, with adjacent grounds in Warwick Road. Like its senior counterpart, the school had upper-class aspirations, its principal being described as "a lady who for the past fourteen years has been preparing boys for the Public Schools of England."

The aim of the new junior school, "under the immediate personal supervision of Monsignor Capel," was to "put within the reach of families living in the neighbourhood a sound refined education for a moderate price." Monsieur Valère, who was described as a "French Professor," was a leading staff member. He was aided by trained English and German mistresses.

Further pursuing his ambitions, the Monsignor also set up The Catholic High School for Young Ladies, in Cromwell Crescent. Located a four or five minutes' walk away from the boys' schools, the girls' academy offered "to combine with home life a systematic and complete course of instruction at a reasonable expense." Its target, once again, was society's upper echelons. It was run under Monsignor Capel's "immediate personal supervision."

Soon, Capel was being spoken of as the mastermind of a thriving Catholic education hub in West London. Every time the schools were advertised or publicised, his name was mentioned. The converter of Pau and preacher of the Pro-Cathedral was fast becoming the educator of Kensington. The common denominator between all three roles – converter, preacher and educator – was plain to see: his magnetic attraction to, and fascination with, the highborn or rich.

Capel's obsession with refined society also extended to his involvement with the Catholic Governess Agency. The bureau matched governesses from a Catholic background who were young, well bred and educated, with Catholic families seeking to hire them. They taught French and Italian, piano, dancing, drawing and deportment in the homes of the Catholic nobility and gentry. The Monsignor vetted references for the agency. The centre of his activities was, once again, Kensington, although the agency's headquarters was based in Portland Place.

At a later stage, he also opened a "dressmaking establishment for the training and employment of young girls of good character" at two large houses in Kensington Square. A short stroll from his home and an easy walk from the other educational establishments, St. Anne's Home offered courses in needlework, china painting, dressmaking and millinery. It also provided temporary accommodation for convert ladies suffering from "persecution on account of their faith."

Capel's record in education was so impressive that in late 1873, when Archbishop Manning and the Catholic Bishops were considering who might run a new Catholic University College, there was only one obvious candidate to take up the position. Although lacking a university education and having no experience in high-level administration, Monsignor Capel was seen as the best man for the job.

He was the man of the moment, famed for his work in Kensington, lauded for his intellect, loved by the press, respected in Rome, and most importantly, known for his connections with those who mattered most in British society. "Never was there a stronger instance of 'the right man in the right place,'" the Catholic periodical *The Dublin Review* commented.

Capel was youthful – 37 years old – and full of passion and vigour. The intelligence and energy he was showing in his education activities impressed Manning. The Archbishop not only endorsed his candidature, arguing that he "thought him capable of beginning the College," but he also suggested him for a Bishopric. Most of the hierarchy concurred.

The Monsignor's contacts with the aristocracy were crucial. Funding was required and Capel, who knew the highest elite, could secure it. He was friends with everyone who mattered – the Marquess of Bute, the Duke of Norfolk, Lady Portarlington, Lord and Lady North, the list was endless. Many had the fervour of converts and the enthusiasm to open their pockets. They also had progeny who might attend the new college. The Catholic middle-class would be sure to follow.

The provision of a Catholic university was urgently required, it was believed in Church circles. "In the higher walks of literature, in philosophy, in science Catholics occupied a lower intellectual ground," Edmund Sheridan Purcell, a contemporary of Manning, wrote in his biography of the Archbishop. They were defeated in arguments and blundered in their writings, exposing their faith to ridicule, he maintained. For want of university training, they "let the argument against Christianity go by default."

Various options were considered, including setting up an exclusive Jesuit-run College for Higher Studies somewhere near London, establishing a Catholic College in Oxford, opening the Catholic University College at Kensington, or perhaps founding a college elsewhere.

The decision in Kensington's favour was helped by an astute purchase Capel had made in late 1872 of an old, neglected, ivy-covered, semi-ruined property known as Abingdon House. Located at the bottom of Wright's Lane, close to Kensington High Street, and situated at the heart of his education empire, he had intended to use it for his public school. It conveniently sat on a two-acre site with development potential.

The house was a short walk from the Underground and omnibuses on the High Street, and was easily accessed by the wealthy families living nearby. The decision was taken to go with the site and offer the Rector's job to Capel. He was given broad control of the project. Worryingly, he was also left in sole management of the college's financial affairs, which would later have catastrophic results.

The immediate need was for money. On 30 August 1874, the English Bishops issued a circular to be read in all the churches of England. It invited the "sympathy and help" of wealthy Catholics in supporting the venture. "We earnestly ask of those who possess wealth" to help in the undertaking, the circular pleaded. "We especially ask of you to send your contribution, if you are able, in one sum, at once, or to spread it over a number of years, or to leave it by Will to be applied hereafter."

The money raised was used to develop Abingdon House and its grounds. A temporary chapel, made from wood and corrugated iron, and large enough to hold 300 people, was built adjoining the property. Several ground-floor rooms in the house were hammered into one to form an Academical Theatre capable of holding 250 people for celebrations and graduations.

Lecture rooms, a library, science laboratory and museum were also provided. A student meeting room, tea room and billiard room were carefully fitted out, "affording many of the advantages and conveniences of a club, and obviating any pretext for wandering abroad in quest of evening amusement," *The Tablet* pointed out. Applicants could avail of board and lodging, although day students were welcome, too.

In April 1875, the Catholic University College was formally opened by Cardinal Manning, who had been elevated to Cardinal the previous month. It was a glorious event, with Bishops, nobility and other guests filling the temporary college chapel to the door. Church dignitaries were dressed in their finest, their robes coloured scarlet and purple, their pectoral crosses gold. Undergraduates, who had already begun their studies the previous October, occupied the centre pews.

Monsignor Capel delivered the sermon from the top step of the altar. He did so eloquently, we are told. Following Benediction, the assembly retired to the lecture theatre, where Capel spoke once more.

"Honours were often real dangers to those who received them," he declared. He prayed that would not be the case with him; nor would it change his life or spirit. Shortly afterwards, the company withdrew for refreshments to his new home, located in Wright's Lane, opposite the college gates – the fashionable Cedar Villa.

Reflecting his growing popularity and stature, Monsignor Capel had moved from Scarsdale Villas to the prestigious Kensington property known as Cedar Villa, where he held court throughout much of the 1870s. Described as "one of the few remaining nooks of Old Kensington," Cedar Villa and its neighbouring property, Scarsdale Lodge, were among the most prized residences in the borough.

Set in an acre of land and enclosed by walls, the properties boasted extensive accommodation, stables for eight horses, a double coach-house and grooms' apartments. The surrounding grounds were belted by thickly-planted shrubbery. Of the two houses, it was at the impressive white-coloured Cedar Villa that Capel rose to fame for the fashionable society events that became the hallmark of Victorian Kensington.

His Sunday afternoon receptions were legendary among London's artistic and intellectual elite. Everyone of note attended. The parties were held in the salon in winter, which was lofty but not too large, and on the lawn in summer, which was easily accessible from the house. The indoors were furnished in objects of art, which were scattered about, encouraging conversation and acting as a means of introduction among strangers.

At the centre of things was the Monsignor, flitting from one distinguished guest to the other, engaging in gay repartee and cheerful conversation, while ensuring that wine glasses were filled to the brim. With his intellectual countenance and commanding presence, he fitted in effortlessly, cutting an impressive figure as he conversed with artists and men of letters representing the highest order of society.

He loved showing off special guests like the celebrated American soprano Emma Thursby, whose voice was described as being "of rare purity and sweetness." A petite, attractive woman, in her mid-30s, she was in England for a season at the Theatre Royal, Covent Garden.

He arranged a lawn party and concert for her and selected guests at Cedar Villa. "The garden was filled with gay people, many of them actors and actresses, and the lively orchestral music was heard for blocks away," a newspaper reported.

"There is not a celebrity, whether belonging to the Church, the sciences, the arts, or literature, not only in this country, but of Europe and America, who has not at some time or other been seen at the Sunday afternoon gatherings," a London correspondent wrote in the *Edinburgh Evening News*. The Monsignor stood in their midst, "gay and cheerful, full of ready repartee himself, and delighting in the wit of others." It was said that he was always the life and soul of the assembly.

Cedar Villa was Monsignor Capel's pride and joy. The standout feature of the property was its broad bay window set in a cosy reception room filled with easy chairs and hung with pictures. In the window stood a bust of the master of the house, sculpted in marble. The window opened onto a rolling lawn, with a fountain in the centre. "An hour in that pleasant Kensington garden on a summer afternoon is not the least enjoyable time of one's existence," remarked *The Whitehall Review*.

Works of art lined Cedar Villa's walls, among them Raffaelle's *A Virgin and Child*, Domenichino's *The Assumption of the Virgin*, and Van Dyke's *Our Saviour on the Cross*. Books including the latest novel, a travel book, and an autobiography of philosopher John Stuart Mill were spread out on a table. What had once been a billiard room was now a richly-decorated chapel. The altar figures were by Rossi. The crucifix was a masterpiece. Richly-textured vestments were stored where the cues once stood. At one time, the smell of tobacco reigned supreme but was now replaced by the aroma of frankincense and myrrh.

Guests were greeted at the door by a tidy maid speaking with an Irish accent. Lunch was served in the dining room, which looked out on the lawn. There, Capel engaged his lunchtime guests with entertaining anecdotes, philosophical discourses and general views of the world. "But for his dress he might have been mistaken for a lawyer, or a man of the world, or a millionaire – but never for a moment did he forget that he was a Catholic, and a thoroughbred," wrote Charles Warren Stoddard, an American author who dined with Capel during a visit to England.

In the course of his lunch appointment, the author was introduced to the Monsignor's black collie, Beppo, who presented a paw and saluted with a short, low bark. Beppo, who wore a collar engraved with "Beppo, friend, protector," rested quietly by the chair of his master. He had interesting responses when German statesman Bismarck and the Pope were mentioned. "Beppo, here is a mouthful with the compliments of Bismarck," the Monsignor said to the dog, presenting him with a piece of cake. The dog refused it and turned away in disgust.

"The Pope sends it," Capel then said, and the cake disappeared in a flash. "Three cheers for the Pope," the Monsignor added, and Beppo sprang to a table under a portrait of the Pope, put his front paws on it, and barked three times with enthusiasm. Beppo became very popular, mingling with and entertaining guests who arrived at the villa. He was "a very intelligent collie," the visiting author concluded.

So proud was Capel of his home that he offered it to his sister Elizabeth for her wedding reception when she married in 1873. The ceremony was held at the Pro-Cathedral, Kensington, where the marriage and Mass were conducted by her brother, the Monsignor. Although the day was overshadowed by a dense yellow fog – "one of the densest fogs which ever enshrouded London" – the celebrations at Cedar Villa left nothing to be desired.

The wedding breakfast was lavish and tastefully presented. The delicacies were "choice and varied, almost beyond precedent," it was said. Vast amounts of ripe fruits, with their exotic colours and delicate odours, complemented the breakfast fare. Flowers of the choicest description added brightness and fragrance to the display. It was one of the finest repasts ever seen in the dining rooms of Kensington.

After her wedding, not only did Elizabeth settle in London, where her husband worked as a solicitor in South Kensington, but Capel's young brother, Arthur Joseph, also moved to the city. He, too, gravitated to Kensington, where he resided in a property located a leisurely stroll from Cedar Villa.

Arthur had done well, accumulating vast wealth as a travel and shipping agent. He had married a young Parisian student, Berthe Lorin – "a beauty with a fine figure, striking features and grey eyes" – who was boarding at the local Kensington convent, the Convent of the Assumption. Arthur was 25 years old when he married; Berthe was 17.

The couple set up home in Campden Hill Road, an affluent avenue off Kensington High Street, close to where the landscape artist J. M. W. Turner had once painted sunsets. It seemed to observers that, living side by side, the extended Capel family were fast becoming a mainstay of the newly-burgeoning Kensington social and economic scene.

Their mother, Mary, had settled well, too. She had moved into a fine four-bedroom house, St. Catherine's Villa, at St. Leonards-on-Sea. With two servants' rooms, a large drawing room, dining room and library, she supplemented her widow's pension by using her home as a boarding house. St. Catherine's was regarded as one of the most fashionable lodging houses in the area around Hastings. The Monsignor paid her many visits.

Adding to the rosy picture, a retinue of passionately-faithful women had begun to surround Capel, copying documents, dealing with correspondence, handling publicity, helping to supervise and teach at his schools, doing everything to make his life run smoothly. These volunteer helpers became known as the Pious Ladies and would feature prominently in his life ahead.

His band of devoted ladies worked tirelessly on Capel's state-of-the-art Manifold Copying Machine – "The Cheapest Wonder of the Age" – which he installed at Cedar Villa. The machine was used to prepare letters for distribution to the press and elsewhere. It was further employed when Capel published his first work in 1874 – a long pamphlet engaging battle with no less a personage than the Right Honourable William Gladstone. The publication resulted in high-profile exchanges in *The Times*, further enhancing Capel's reputation.

Things couldn't be working out better, Capel must have thought in those early years of the 1870s. Life was so good he developed a confident swagger, which could be seen daily as he strolled about the Kensington streets, heading from one part of his empire to the other.

"I hate a priest who is only a fashionable man," he once said of himself in a smug, self-deprecating manner, knowing he was at the peak of his fame and power. All too soon, however, his reputation would be ground to dust, and his empire would collapse in a ball of flames.

DECLINE AND FALL

Mgr. Capel, mid-1870s

In the summer of 1875, just ten months after the Catholic University College first opened its doors, one of its lecturers paid a visit to Rome. His name was J. P. O'Hara, a distinguished graduate of Trinity College, Dublin, who taught Political Economy, Law and Constitutional History to the student body at Kensington.

Although O'Hara found the climate in Rome very much to his taste, he wasn't in the city for the sights or the weather. Instead, at his lodgings at 43 Via di Capo le Case, he prepared for the main purpose of his trip – an audience with Pope Pius IX.

At the height of that hot summer in 1875, O'Hara travelled the three or four miles from his lodgings to the Vatican for his meeting with the Pontiff. There, he presented the Holy Father with a letter containing highly-damaging allegations about Monsignor Capel and his running of University College.

The Monsignor, according to O'Hara's statement, was habitually drinking to excess, had hangovers in the morning, and paid little or no attention to his collegiate duties. Indeed, he was scarcely ever to be seen. In his absence, the brand-new institution – which O'Hara claimed had no more than seven or eight paying students – was going to rack and ruin.

During a tour he made one day through the lecture rooms, he had encountered only one student in attendance. On discussing this with

51

the Rev. Robert Clarke, who was Professor of Natural Theology, he was told that perhaps they were all off studying physiology. To the contrary, O'Hara proposed, at least some of them were "instead of studying, amusing themselves in the Billiard Room."

It wasn't as if O'Hara had any personal gripe against Capel; in fact, the Rector had always been kind to him, he stressed. He did, however, find his performance as an administrator so badly lacking and damaging that he hoped the Pope – and the English College in Rome, to which he later complained – might do something about it.

How the Catholic University College, with Monsignor Capel at the helm, ever saw daylight was always something of a mystery. "One may wonder how the sagacious, prudent Archbishop could ever have been beguiled into so Utopian a scheme," Percy Hetherington Fitzgerald, the Anglo-Irish author and critic, wrote in 1901 about Manning's novel institution.

The college did not have the smallest chance of succeeding, he said. There was neither the money, nor the scholars, nor the buildings. "Then followed the luckless government of Mgr. Capel who was admittedly the most unfit person that could have been selected – leaving us to wonder what could have led the Archbishop to make such a choice. The painful catastrophe and collapse that speedily followed are well known."

As early as July 1874 – three months *before* the college opened – *The Scotsman* was already predicting its demise. The old, established Catholic families of England viewed the new venture with "an unfriendly eye," the broadsheet remarked. They regarded it as "a mushroom institution, started by converts" and preferred instead to send their sons to Oxford and Cambridge.

Existing colleges speckled throughout England were angry at being asked "to play second fiddle" to a new place in London, the newspaper added. Jealousies were rife. A considerable number of leading Catholics had declined several posts on offer. "No students will be found except among the personal friends of those immediately connected with it," the newspaper predicted in a remarkably visionary piece of journalism.

For its first term, a paltry 16 students were registered, generating income of £500. There were staff costs, including professors' fees, mortgage interest payments, and other outgoings to pay out of that. Capel, who had no worthwhile administrative experience or financial knowhow, was unconcerned and went wild with the chequebook. No expense was spared.

He offered Professor Barff, a chemist, £600 a year, which was an enormous salary for the time. Another £600 stipend was offered to biologist Professor St. George Mivart. The classical scholar Professor Paley received £400. Further down the scale, a lecturer, Gordon Thompson, was paid £300. The porter, Dubliner Thomas Ignatius Pickwell, earned enough to afford a three-story-over-basement town-house at 43 Pembroke Square, Kensington, where he hired two servants to look after his family and some boarders.

Student numbers increased marginally in the next two years – to 28 in the second year and into the 40s in the third – but they were not enough to underpin the college's precarious finances. The Jesuits, who wanted their own university, ignored it. The influential Churchman and theologian John Henry Newman, who had set up the Catholic University of Ireland in 1854, wanted nothing to do with it. Capel was borrowing money indiscriminately, his management was floundering, and the project was sinking with him.

To make matters worse, Monsignor Capel was failing to keep balance sheets. He was unable to produce one when the Bishops met at their annual meeting in April 1875. He assured them, instead, that all sources of income would "nearly meet" annual expenditure. A balance sheet would be on the way "in a few days," he promised. It never arrived.

The following year, 1876, Capel again failed to keep a balance sheet. He informed the Bishops that receipts were sufficient to meet expenditure and future prospects looked good. Once student numbers rose to 100 – compared to 16 in the first year and 28 in the second – the college would be self-sustaining, he predicted. "God be praised," he said, "the success in two years is so great that I now see we shall, in two more years, be well established."

In 1877, Capel was relieved of his financial responsibilities and replaced by the Vicar General, Canon Gilbert, and diocesan solicitor, Mr. Harting. In May of that year, they paid him a visit. "After long delay a ledger and cash book were produced, evidently newly written, and admitted so to be, and the books were not cast up," they reported. There was no original cash book, only various tradesmen's bills, some rough scattered memoranda, a variety of loose documents, and a banker's pass book.

Not only was it clear that University College was unable to pay its way, but it was incurring large and increasing losses. Its collapse seemed inevitable. In 1878, student numbers fell to a record low of 14. Cardinal Manning's project was crashing in flames, and the blame, he said, was all down to Monsignor Capel.

Allegations had also been surfacing that the college, since its inception, was a hotbed of poor discipline and student immorality. Students who lived in various houses of residence were free to do as they wished. "Students of University College have been seen at theatres and other places of amusement, and, in some instances, at places which, though commonly frequented, are nevertheless of a less desirable character," Cardinal Manning noted in a letter. The college was "evil spoken of," he wrote.

Especially worrying was that Lord Petre, who was a benefactor and supporter of the college, believed his son had been culpably exposed to danger. The Duke of Norfolk was worried, too. Both told Manning they could no longer advise any Catholic parent to send their sons to the institution. The Cardinal was additionally forced to concede that in one case there was evidence that a student had "deteriorated" during his residence at Kensington.

The reputation of Monsignor Capel was also plummeting rapidly. Stories were rife of his interest in and involvement with the opposite sex. Students, among others, spoke of him as "fond of women" and "the parish bull," according to Thomas Pickwell, the college porter. The Monsignor's housekeeper, who Pickwell said he had seen lying drunk on the kitchen floor in an immodest manner, was referred to as "Capel's whore."

News of Capel's sexual exploits was crossing Manning's desk with worrying regularity. He was informed how Capel, in either 1873 or 1874, had engaged in "criminal intercourse on one occasion" with a Frenchwoman who was employed as a household servant. He was also notified of a Frenchwoman, a governess, with whom he was said to have had "illicit intercourse repeatedly during a period of three years." In both cases, the Cardinal took no action, although he did raise the alleged offences with the Monsignor.

A Mrs. Showers, who knew Capel well in the early 1870s, expressed concerns that he "thought of nothing but women." One night, she said, he was drunk, and the next morning her servant complained of his improper conduct to her. Another time, during a visit to Rome, she and her son had met the Monsignor and noted that "his conduct was scandalous in regard to women." Her son had found it necessary to confront him, leading to friction between them.

A further case came to Manning's attention concerning an affair which Capel had initiated during the occasion of Confession. The charge – once again of "criminal intercourse" – was said to have occurred around 1876. In this case, the woman eventually said that she had "exaggerated" what occurred and that she was really more "the seducer than the seduced." Once more, no action was taken.

Capel's interest in young women additionally came under scrutiny. It did so after Cardinal Manning was told about a girl who had an unsettling encounter with the Monsignor. The details were revealed by her aunt, Mrs. Robert Wilson, of Phillimore Terrace, Kensington. She related how her niece was in the habit of travelling the short distance from her home to the School of Art at South Kensington.

Returning one day by omnibus, she met Monsignor Capel, who she did not know. "He talked to her, and found out that she frequented the School of Art, and after saying much on the subject, as he got out at Wright's Lane gave her his card, and asked her to call on him. When the omnibus went on, a stranger in it said to her – 'I hope you will not go to him for he is a bad man,'" the aunt revealed.

At other times, in the evenings or on Sunday afternoons, he would invite young students from the girls' school to his house. He particularly liked "two giddy young girls" and an 18-year-old occasional teacher of French and German to pay visits. They would stay for tea or walk in the garden. They often visited after High Mass on Sundays and stayed until early evening. He always insisted they come alone, without supervision.

Rumours were also surfacing throughout Kensington about the Monsignor's drinking and lavish lifestyle. He had been seen "eating oysters and drinking porter in a city supper room at 1.15 a.m., after which he said Mass in the College Chapel." The person who had spotted him was Mr. Williams, assistant to Professor Barff, of the chemistry department. College lecturer J. P. O'Hara also said that Professor Seager and lecturer H. W. Lloyd would be willing to testify to Capel's drunken behaviour.

In a further incident, Mr. Batchelor, who was a Catholic and an employee of Richard Grice's grocery and wine store at 53 Kensington High Street, met Capel following a service at the Pro-Cathedral. The event had taken place on the evening of Corpus Christi. Capel was "under the influence of drink, of which there could be no doubt whatever," Mr. Batchelor noted.

The grocer's assistant was scandalised by what he witnessed. He wasn't completely surprised as the Monsignor had been ordering from Grice's store two bottles of brandy and a dozen of sherry per week for delivery to Cedar Villa. "I always thought it a large amount for a priest's house," he remarked.

Mr. Batchelor also revealed that Capel had "a very heavy account owing to Mr. Grice," for which he was partly responsible. Because of the outstanding debt, the assistant was reluctant to confront the Monsignor. Otherwise, he said, he would have had no difficulty in doing so.

Two further incidents involving drunkenness were identified by the Kensington policeman, Sergeant Robert Ahern, who we encountered at the beginning of this book. The first related to an observation he made of Monsignor Capel at the notorious slum dwellings, Jennings

56

Buildings. The tenements, which were located on Kensington High Street, opposite Kensington Palace, housed more than 1,000 poverty-stricken, mostly Irish immigrants.

It was near there that the policeman spotted the Monsignor "unmistakably in liquor." Initially, he thought Capel might have been "attempting to keep the Irish quiet," especially given their propensity for noisily entertaining themselves and consuming alcohol on the streets. Capel's state of drunkenness made him doubt this was the case.

The second incident took place late one night or in the "small hours of the morning," Ahern explained. On this occasion, four railwaymen spotted Capel reeling along the road and said, "There goes Capel drunk!" He heard them, ran after them, severely scolded them, and then made his way to Kensington police station, where he made "a violent noise and disturbance."

Three or four days later, the Monsignor called to the police station to check if anything had been done. The police, who "knew well the character of Monsignor Capel," had taken no action as they wished to avoid creating a scandal. On discovering that the police had done nothing, he wrote to the railway company and had the men punished. The company were "afraid of opposing Monsignor Capel," Ahern said.

Meanwhile, problems were mounting at Capel's second main project, his Catholic public school for boys. It had been the understanding of Manning and the English Bishops that once University College was established, Capel would withdraw from his work with the school and devote his full attention to the third-level institution. Instead of doing so, he continued with the school and plunged himself deep into debt in the process.

Although by no means unsuccessful, the boys' school had never achieved its ambition of becoming a "Catholic Eton." Instead, it fell somewhere between an ordinary school and a prestigious institution for the British Catholic elite. Parents whose incomes ranged from £200 to £300 a year – wealthy enough to want something above an ordinary school, yet not prosperous enough to aspire to the privileges of public school education – were its primary source of support.

As a result, the school's curriculum became confused. On the one hand, it prepared boys for matriculation, entry to university and privileged careers. On the other hand, it was forced, as an American journalist explained, to supply the sort of education necessary for "those whose walk in life will, in all probability, be commercial." It additionally provided a special department called the Modern School, which readied students, aged 14 years and upwards, for the army and the civil service.

Replicating the situation at University College, Capel's behaviour was drawing adverse attention to the boys' school. Stories circulated about his drinking. "I met one of the boys and he told me that the great man went to the school very drunk one day last term, and that it was so apparent that he fell all over the place," R. Sutton Swaby, Professor of Music at St. Charles' College, Notting Hill, who knew Capel, wrote to Cardinal Manning.

Allegations also surfaced concerning immorality among the students. The Kensington-based Rev. C. Harrington Moore, who was close to Manning, revealed in another letter: "During Mgr. Capel's absence in Rome, the big boys of the 6th Form, residing in Scarsdale Lodge, under his 'personal supervision,' were entirely without surveillance, the result being that some of them were under medical treatment for venereal disease!"

Additional controversy arose over Capel's newly-established Catholic High School for Young Ladies, which he had opened at Cromwell Crescent. Since its inauguration, the new girls' institution had a damaging impact on the nuns at the Convent of the Assumption, whose girls' school was situated a mile away, at Kensington Square. Enrolments fell, debts accumulated, and the anger of the Reverend Mother reached boiling point.

Cardinal Manning must have sighed deeply when, during a visit to Rome in early 1878, a letter arrived from the convent detailing a long list of complaints. Capel "has thrown discredit on our teaching and taken our children from us. Nine are already gone," the Reverend Mother wrote. "Mgr. will not allow that it is so; but the facts are there. We are at a very serious inconvenience to pay our debts, and he has diminished our resources." She ended her long letter by begging for help.

The Cardinal must have sighed even deeper when he read Capel's views on the matter. "I am simply horrified to find that Reverend Mother has been stirring up bad feeling," Capel wrote to the diocesan administrator, the Vicar General, in a letter which eventually crossed Manning's desk. "I have not said a word, nor do I intend doing so; but as God's unworthy priest I cannot be otherwise than horrified at the misery of this." He added, once again in a long letter: "Why all this! Surely there is enough to do, and room for us all."

Further contributing to Cardinal Manning's Capel-induced headaches was the financial state of the "dressmaking establishment," St. Anne's Home. The initiative, the Monsignor once said, was part of his charitable work, which was "good as a relaxation" and "good also as a preventive against intellectual pride and hardness of heart."

Unfortunately, St. Anne's was also built on sand. "Monsignor Capel was involved heavily in debt on all sides and on the eve of bankruptcy," the Rev. Walter Croke Robinson, who intimately knew Capel having worked with him as Vice-Rector of University College, said of the founding of the dressmaking home. "It is at this time, and in these desperate circumstances, that he enters upon an undertaking on a scale so large and with liabilities so formidable! It was agreed, by all who knew the facts of the case, that never was anything undertaken more reckless and more impossible of success."

It all looked bleak for the Monsignor, especially when after only four years in charge he was forced to resign as Rector of University College. On the surface, he seemed unperturbed. His Sunday gatherings continued at Cedar Villa, where he was still regarded as the social lion of the hour. There, he cut a dashing figure in his priest's cassock, relieved by its colourful edging and buttons and his broad purple sash. Those who knew him, however, noted that his hair had become grey and his frame was tending slightly towards burliness.

Despite the chaos in his life – the debts, the affairs, the drinking, the rows, and the close shaves with his superiors – he still found time for preaching. Like any great actor, he loved the stage. He especially loved the full houses and packed churches that turned out to see him and hear him speak. It gave him a chance to air his observations and insights, as he did one night when delivering what the press described as an "eloquent sermon" in Preston.

That sermon partly concerned the sensational inquest into the death by poisoning of Charles Bravo, a London lawyer. By any standards, it was a startling inquiry, involving testimony from his well-to-do wife, Florence, who was suspected of his murder. The evidence involved details of affairs, betrayal, abuse, a possible abortion and, of course, the question of who was responsible for his death. It was, perhaps, the sort of topic the Monsignor should have avoided in light of his own sexual liaisons.

What was shocking, Capel said to the congregation at St. Augustine's Church, Preston, was that "newspapers should proclaim in the furthest part of the earth the details of an affair which was nothing less than a social degradation, and which was unworthy of a Christian country. What would it do but instruct those who knew nought of wrong in that which was wrong, encourage those who were in the lower classes of life to imitate what they heard of in the middle classes, and degenerate the morals of the community."

The role of the Catholic Church – and, of course, himself – was "to save the little ones from such degradation, and raise them to be good members of society, and religious men and women," Capel declared. Cardinal Manning, if he read the report of the lecture in the newspapers, might well have choked on his breakfast. Sitting on his study desk was a file containing material somewhat at odds with the tenor of Capel's remarks to the people of Preston.

THE MARY STOURTON
SCANDAL

Mary Stourton

The weather in London in November 1875 was generally showery, with cloudy skies spilling rain onto the streets. Hansom cabs and hackney carriages clattered about with abandon, depositing passengers at mud-spattered street corners. Smoke containing flakes of soot the size of snowflakes billowed from chimney pots.

Stray, hungry dogs, covered in mud, ran about, searching for food. Horses, too, were grimy, with muck caked up to their ears. "Implacable November weather," Charles Dickens once remarked of London and its climate at that time of year, a city "gone into mourning, one might imagine, for the death of the sun."

On one of those grey mornings, a cab pulled up outside Cardinal Manning's "palace", a large, nondescript building off Vauxhall Bridge Road, which was anything but palatial in appearance. A servant answered the door, admitting the slim, attractive young woman who had arrived, she said, to meet the Cardinal.

The young lady – Mary Stourton – was ushered into a waiting room, its walls hung with religious paintings and engravings. From there, she was led through the library to the Cardinal's study, a tranquil, cheerful room where he engaged with guests. On entering, she was greeted by a man wearing the ordinary robe of a Catholic Bishop, his scarlet skull cap and stockings the only reminder of his Cardinal's rank.

The meeting that morning was a most uncomfortable one for both parties. Manning knew she was coming; she had sent him a letter asking for an urgent appointment. He sat there, with his ascetic face, keen penetrating eyes, sharply-cut features and intellectual countenance, and listened with rapt attention to the story unfolding before him. A kind and thoughtful man, he was a good listener and a thorough note-taker.

Across from him – on the other side of a desk filled with half-written sermons, general correspondence, Latin manuscripts, and proof-sheets of articles – sat a refined, vulnerable, clearly-upset young woman whose words threatened to unravel the Catholic Church in Britain. What she said that day – and repeated over many years to come – had consequences for numerous lives in Westminster and further afield.

Monsignor Capel had sexual intercourse with her on several occasions, Mary Stourton alleged. He had groomed her and pursued her, and had left her in a vulnerable and emotional state. Although the fine details of his sexual advances have been lost to history – buried in a fog of Victorian prudery – the words "acts of criminal intercourse" were later used to describe Capel's behaviour.

These "acts of criminality," as Manning called them in his scribbled notes, had taken place in Kensington around the time when Capel was at the peak of his powers. Stourton was living in lodgings at 75 Abingdon Road, while Capel was running the new University College and residing at Cedar Villa in nearby Wright's Lane. Their residences were separated by a two-minute walk. The Monsignor was on the cusp of his 39th birthday; Mary was 23 years old.

"I am a daughter of the late William Stourton whom I believe you knew," Mary informed Manning, revealing the only details of her family history contained in the records of the Westminster Diocesan Archives. Research for this book, however, has revealed that she came from a privileged background, with a long lineage, and an extended family known for its extraordinary wealth.

Mary's father, William, was the son of the 18th Baron Stourton, of Stourton, Wiltshire, and was variously referred to as "much respected" and an "estimable gentleman." He had been educated at Stonyhurst College and had a distinguished military career to his credit. His death was recorded in November 1873. Her mother – Catherine, daughter of Edmund Scully Esq., of Bloomfield House, County Tipperary – was still living.

Mary had spent much of her life growing up in the genteel surroundings of the Isle of Wight, where Queen Victoria had a holiday home and the Stourton family resided in two fine properties, Elvington House and Ashey Lodge. While there, up to the time of his death, her father occupied himself in a number of honorary or prestigious roles, including acting as guardian to the young heir of the Tichborne estates.

The family were well-regarded in Ryde, the seaside resort on the north-east of the island. Each year, they featured in "The Fashionable List", published in *The Isle of Wight Observer*. Their travels abroad were noted, too. "Mrs. Wm. Stourton, Miss Mary Stourton, and suites have left the Gresham Hotel for Cork," reported *The Cork Examiner* concerning a trip they made from Dublin to the south coast of Ireland in 1863. Family deaths – especially the death of Mary's grandmother, the Dowager Lady Stourton – were also widely reported.

When she was young, Mary had lived the sort of affluent lifestyle that only comes with entitlement, privilege and wealth. She attended society weddings, enjoyed grand concerts run by the local Amateur Musical Society, frequented amateur theatrical performances, put in appearances at the Royal Victoria Yacht Club regatta, and as she got older, attended grand balls at Ryde Town Hall.

By the time she reached her early 20s, Mary was a bit of a lost soul. Although well-schooled, she lacked the skills and qualifications required to become a governess. Nor was she socially equipped to work in a factory or in any form of menial employment. Like many young women of her wealth and class, she drifted from one friend's or relative's home to another, killing time, and hoping to meet an eligible gentleman who might offer his hand in marriage.

She also accompanied her family to Kensington, where they resided during their visits to London. There, her family became familiar with Monsignor Capel's brother, Arthur, and his wife, Berthe, who lived two doors away. Over time, Arthur and his wife came to know Mary "on intimate terms." They knew her mother, as well, although less intimately.

The Stourtons, who were staunchly Catholic, also became acquainted with the local Convent of the Assumption, where Berthe Capel had boarded, and where they became friends with the Reverend Mother. Mary's younger sister boarded there, too. Monsignor Capel was acting as chaplain and confessor at the convent, and had been doing so for many years. Everybody knew one another. It was that sort of place, Kensington, where Catholics of a certain stature lived in a tight-knit social circle.

Not long before her involvement with the Monsignor, Mary had a brief affair with a married man from Scotland by the name of Corballis. He was infatuated with her and had pursued her for years. He had even wanted to follow her to London but was persuaded against doing so by Lord Lovat, a stalwart of the Inverness Highlands aristocracy, who knew him.

Around that time, Mary was "most miserable at home as everyone who knows me is aware of," she explained to Manning. "In a fit of desperation which I have had indeed reason to repent of," she packed her bags and travelled to Scotland to join up with Corballis. "Of course I soon found out the fearful mistake I had made and left him and came to London by myself," she remarked.

It was at this time that Monsignor Capel entered the picture in a most consequential way. There was turmoil in Mary's family. Her mother told her she was "a curse" and said that for what Mary had done "she would be ashamed to live in society." Her mother's sister – Mary's aunt, Mrs. Mary Leahy, from Ireland, who was spending an extended amount of time with the family – became involved and decided to help.

"She is devoted to the Rev. Mother and Mgr. Capel," Mary said of her aunt, who was also a fervent Catholic. "Through her all this misery began, as she induced me to get to know him," she remarked of her initial introduction to the Monsignor. On her aunt's suggestion, and "by her mother's desire," Mary was placed under the Monsignor's spiritual care. It was a calamitous move, as time would tell.

Mary divulged the details of her life story to the Monsignor, including intimate information about her affair. "I told him everything," she said. At first, he seemed sympathetic and helped her. In time, he became infatuated by her. No doubt aware of her vulnerability and conscious of the hold he had over her – not to mention the knowledge he now possessed about her liaison in Scotland – he began to pursue her.

Capel was devious in his efforts to meet her. He would call to her lodgings in Kensington and hope to meet up with her there. Aware that the landlady might become suspicious, he would talk at length to her and make it seem that she was the person he was visiting. The landlady would be thrilled at the thought that such a fine, famous, educated man was paying her a visit.

"She of course was delighted with him," Mary explained to the Cardinal regarding the landlady. "He chatted with her and spoke of my being dull and alone so he came to cheer me." The first time it happened, Mary was out, but "after a long talk he left saying he would call back about 9 as he could not get away before." Of course, he did come back, she said, leading the landlady to believe he was such a kind, considerate man.

Capel was so fatigued the next morning that he sent word to the Convent of the Assumption, Kensington Square, explaining that he was unable to say Mass. He was exhausted because he had "such a fearful lot of work to do," he said. "The poor nuns of course were pitying him so and praising him for his goodness," Mary remarked.

When Mary later met the Reverend Mother at the convent, "she of course was full of the blessing I had in having such a good kind friend as him." Everyone who became aware of her connection with the Monsignor seemed to think similarly, believing everything was above board and innocent. "My aunt who has come over from Ireland is the same," Mary noted.

As time passed by, the Monsignor became more reckless in pursuing Mary, asking her to come to his house or accompany him on social visits. One Monday morning, after saying Mass at the convent, he called to her lodgings. "I was out and he left word that he wanted to see me on business and if I would go round at once when I returned as he was going to some public dinner," she recalled. "I felt going to his house would be safe." It wasn't.

Another time, he asked her to accompany him in a cab or by the Underground to a place where he had to dine. His visits to her lodgings also became more frequent. "He has come constantly in the evening and stayed with me for an hour or so," she said. He even began to call in late afternoon. "He does not seem to care what he does," she concluded.

Mary felt that what was happening was improper. Apart from anything else, Capel was a priest: "To me it was too awful to know that last Saturday he was hearing Confessions and on Sunday that numbers were hearing him preach and firmly believing him to be so good and holy....I could scarcely imagine such things of a priest." His life, she said, "has been one of deliberate sin."

She felt trapped. "I am so in his power," she commented, referring to Capel's influence with her family and the damage he could do by criticising her to them. He knew she would be impoverished if he ever said a word against her. "God knows what would have become of me," she said, "as I have no money but what my mother likes to give me."

Neither would she have anyone to seek help from if Capel and her family turned against her. "I should not have a friend left in the world," she remarked. The Monsignor, who knew this, had made her "full dependent on him." As a result, "I dared not resist him," she concluded in her statement to Cardinal Manning.

Shortly after their discussion, the Cardinal sent for the Monsignor and "stated the whole to him." Capel defended himself by saying that Mary "had left her mother's house with a married man: and that her word could not be believed." He also produced many letters and papers.

Later, he concluded about Mary's accusation: "It is clear H. Eminence did not believe it, for not only was he satisfied with my statement, but he showed his conviction by not allowing the charge to affect either my relations with him, or my position in any way whether as confessor, preacher, or convent chaplain."

Cardinal Manning, on the other hand, held a different view. Without corroborating evidence, he said, he was "compelled to leave the case as it stood." No action was taken, and at least for the time being, Mary Stourton was forced to walk away.

The personal consequences of the Corballis and Capel affairs were ruinous for Mary Stourton. Shortly after her meeting with Manning, she was ostracised by her mother, who refused to support her. Her lodgings in Kensington ended up being paid for by Arthur Capel, the Monsignor's brother. He also arranged for her to move to Paris.

In Paris, as far away from Kensington and the Isle of Wight as possible, she settled in accommodation arranged by friends of Arthur, and there she lived with an elderly lady in relative isolation. "I see no society," she wrote in a letter to the Cardinal. "I have had nothing to do but to think of all my past folly and wickedness."

Although the scandal never surfaced in the British press, the rumour mill was soon in action. Details of the gossip reached Mary at her Parisian residence, 6 Rue Royal. "Today I am told by a person who has come from London that there I am lost and that the longer I keep away from England the better, that people say that I went there on purpose to be near Mgr. Capel, that I have written letters to you, about what I did write, and that they were not even read but laughed at," she wrote to Manning in early January 1876.

"In consequence of all this I have not received any letters from either Mgr. or the Rev. Mother at Kensington convent nor my aunt – of course they have all turned against me and I have not a single friend in the world." She added that she had written to her mother "begging her to take me back again, promising to do all in my power to redeem the past and telling her how changed I am in every way."

Eventually, Mary's mother softened: "She wrote to tell me that she forgives me all and will take me back again – her one wish is that I should go to Confession now that I am determined to make up for the past." On Mary's return to Ryde, however, the relationship did not work out.

"I came home on Xmas day and by now see how thoroughly hopeless it is for me to try and get on," she remarked in yet another correspondence with Manning. "I often feel inclined to give it all up and go on the stage, the only way I could be independent of living at home – the one thing that keeps me from doing it is for my youngest sister's sake, as it would separate me from her."

The gossip and rebuffs in Ryde were cutting and vicious. People would talk to Mary's mother when she was alone but would have "not noticed her had I been with her," Mary observed. "My mother will do nothing for me, she does not care a bit how I am talked of and is wrapped up in her prayers and the Ryde people, who are civil to her and cut me." If only her mother would leave the island things might improve, she hoped.

Capel suggested she move to Australia, where her brother lived. "I have been thinking over about Australia, and the more I do I am sure it would be a very good plan," she remarked. She pointed out that her brother "ought to be written to," and it might take a long time before she could depart.

Perhaps, Mary thought, if she told her brother how she was situated, "then he is sure on his own accord to propose my going out there." She added: "If something is not done at once it is best to give up the idea altogether." As it turned out, the suggestion was never pursued, no doubt to Capel's disappointment.

At one stage, Mary sent the Monsignor a lock of her hair. She also sent him a photograph of herself taken at the premises of Arthur Debenham, an eminent "Photographer & Miniature Painter, Under Royal Patronage," whose studio was located in Ryde. The photograph was inscribed with the words, "Forgive me." Both were kept by Capel as future evidence, should he need them. He never replied to her letters.

She met him "several times" on a return visit she made to London, according to one of Mary's old and trusted friends, Teresa Maxwell, of Houghton Hall, Yorkshire. The friend, who found Capel to be "a most deceitful and a most hypocritical man," was so worried that she wrote to Cardinal Manning, saying that Mary was "in great danger and temptation."

On one of those occasions, Mary met Capel at Cedar Villa, where he later claimed she offered him an apology for the allegations she had made to Manning. On her return to Ryde, days later, she sent to the Cardinal an unusually-constructed and out-of-character letter retracting those allegations. Apart from the structure of the writing and punctuation, which was unlike anything she used before or after, the words she chose – "consequent on" and "brooded over," for example – were not her style.

"My Lord," she wrote, "Perhaps you will remember my writing to you once about Monsignor Capel. At the time I was suffering from excitement consequent on being away from home and in my loneliness I brooded over horrible histories told me of Mgr. Capel by Mrs. Arthur Capel which at the time I foolishly believed. I am extremely sorry at having repeated them and have offered Mgr. Capel an apology which he at once accepted. I remain My Lord, Yours respectfully, Mary Stourton."

Later, in correspondence and statements, Mary denied the veracity of the letter's contents and said that the Monsignor had coerced her into writing it. "I hereby declare that the letter written by me of apology about Monsignor Capel was written by his wish and dictated to me by him – Also I never retracted what I had said and written against his morality to which I solemnly swear was the truth," she wrote in an affidavit signed for the Cardinal.

"Which is the truth?" the Cardinal asked Mary, having summoned her to his "palace" at Vauxhall Bridge Road, where she sat, once again, at his crowded desk, laden down with half-written sermons, manuscripts, and articles-in-progress. He was holding two documents in his hands – the first a letter written in November 1875, confirming that Capel had committed "acts of criminality"; the second her retraction.

"The first," she answered, staring directly at the Cardinal. "So, do you affirm this act of criminality spoken of before?" he then asked her. "I do," she replied. There was obviously something about Mary that day, as the Cardinal believed her. Action would need to be taken, he thought, but what? The decision would have to wait as a new bombshell was about to land on his desk – another dark story worryingly similar to Mary Stourton's.

THE MRS. BELLEW AFFAIR

A Hansom Cab

In the autumn of 1875 – the exact date unknown – Monsignor Capel offered to drop Mrs. Emily Louisa Bellew to her home on his way to an engagement in London. She had been visiting him at Cedar Villa, Kensington, located a mile away from her residence at Coleherne Terrace, West Brompton.

The rain fell heavily that night, it was later claimed. The hansom cab, with its driver perched on the back and passengers snug inside, eased its way through the slippery, rain-sodden streets, down Earl's Court Road, dodging other carriages, coaches, carts and wagons.

About 15 minutes into the journey, the horse-drawn cab, its curtains closed, turned right onto Richmond Road. It then proceeded the short distance towards Coleherne Terrace, with its collection of modest three-storey boarding houses and family homes with shops on the ground floor.

The fictional Sherlock Holmes would later solve many great crimes after briskly emerging from similar hansom cabs. It was a pity he was absent that night, as another act of "criminal intercourse" involving Monsignor Capel was alleged to have taken place, this time on the padded leather seats of the West Brompton-bound vehicle.

The event that night marked the beginning of a prolonged on-off affair involving Capel and Mrs. Bellew. Their sexual encounters, which were said to have occurred periodically, with some intervals lasting longer than others, continued over three years, up to the autumn of 1878. The details of the affair, although limited, were subsequently divulged by Mrs. Bellew.

On the second occasion they had a sexual encounter, she was at home and feeling unwell, she said. She had a relapse of an old illness. During the encounter, which took place in Mrs. Bellew's bed, the Monsignor was reported to have acted "in rampant manner." The "recklessness and rampancy of his passions" were "unfit for publication in a private note," according to a statement made on Bellew's behalf to the Vicar General.

That statement was made by Dr. Henry Willington, who lived on Earl's Court Road. For a time, he had been Mrs. Bellew's doctor, but more importantly he was a long-standing friend. Their respective families were friends, too, and often visited each other. The relationship was so close that Mrs. Bellew would frequently divulge the innermost details of her life to either the doctor or his wife.

Immediately after the incident in the cab, Mrs. Bellew informed Dr. Willington of what had happened. "She told me of the occurrence, either late the same evening, or it was on the following evening; but not later," he said. Willington wondered what to do. He attempted to contact the Monsignor on two occasions but was ignored. He also spoke to a friend, who advised him to do nothing. He took the advice.

Circumstances changed in December 1878 – three years later – when a clearly-upset Mrs. Bellew spoke to Dr. Willington's wife. She had a story to tell. Mrs. Willington later divulged the details to her husband. "On December 5th at 12 midnight my wife came to me in great distress about the distress of mind she had witnessed in Mrs. Bellew," he recalled. Mrs. Bellew, he said, had told his wife "all, all, everything" about the affair with Capel.

Mrs. Willington was also told that Capel had "taken liberties with" and "tried to seduce" Mrs. Bellew's servant, Lucy Stevens. The details he gleaned from his wife about the Bellew affair, allied to Capel's attempt to debauch a young servant girl, were too much for Dr. Willington. He decided that something had to be done.

Having confirmed the details with Bellew, he wrote to Cardinal Manning, saying he had information concerning a priest whose actions could cause "the largest scandal of modern times, as affects the priests and their priestly offices, in the Holy Catholic Church of England." He had enough evidence, he said, "to convict the priest in question in a Court of Law."

Manning was alarmed, having heard it all before in the case of Mary Stourton. He met Dr. Willington immediately and sent him to repeat his statement to the Vicar General. Willington explained that "Monsignor Capel had for some time past, on several occasions, criminal intercourse with Mrs. Bellew and that the lady had told him so." The revelation – just as it had in the Stourton case – would reverberate through the Diocese of Westminster and the halls of Rome for many years to come.

Emily Louisa Bellew was an intelligent woman, of modest means, who had led an interesting life. In her late 40s when she met Capel, she was both a divorcee and a widow. Her second husband was the famous British preacher the Rev. John Bellew, who she married in 1861. After converting to Catholicism in 1868, he turned from preaching to delivering public readings, for which he won widespread acclaim.

His readings, by all accounts, were riveting. *The Times* rated him along with author Charles Dickens and actress and writer Fanny Kemble as "persons who, having devoted themselves to this particular art, are the chief objects of attention to the general public." Dickens recited his own works, Kemble read from Shakespeare, while Bellew delivered readings from poets, dramatists and humorists. "In this respect, Mr. Bellew stands unrivalled," one commentator remarked.

Capel and Bellew shared much in common. Both were handsome men and featured prominently in the press. Their paths crossed at public meetings, and their careers were widely discussed by gossip columnists. Even though they no longer competed as preachers, their lectures vied with each other for public support. Their rivalry came to an end, however, in early 1874 when Bellew became seriously ill following visits to America.

Bellew died in June 1874, at the age of 50, leaving behind very little money. It later transpired that he had donated the bulk of the proceeds from his readings to charity; indeed, it was estimated that in a four-year period he had contributed £5,000 to various charitable institutions in London. Unfortunately, it left his wife in a fragile financial state. "By the early death of my gifted husband I am left almost unprovided for," she remarked.

Emily Louisa was devastated emotionally. "Mine is an intensely loving nature," she wrote after he died, "one that gives all and asks little in return, but finds its real development in companionship with, and looking up to, and waiting on the object of its affections. Such happiness was mine for a few brief years, and lavishly was my love repaid."

She felt lonely and isolated. Suffering from anxiety and sleeping difficulties, she took chloral hydrate, a popular and widely-available sedative which was used by "nervous women who found it difficult to face the world," it was said. Brandy and wine were also resorted to, no doubt to ease what she called "the loneliness of my life."

It was then she became involved with Monsignor Capel. He offered her "sensible, manly, practical advice," she wrote in a letter to him seven months after her husband's death. "I hoped to have seen more of you, and by interchange of ideas and mutual interest, have enlisted your sympathy – mine is a life which only wants an aim and an object to become kindly and useful. It was with a view to help in this matter I sought you."

Like so many other women, Mrs. Bellew became infatuated by Capel: "I knew you combined earnestness of purpose, and strength of character, with the refinement and charm of a gentleman and of a man who mixes with the world – and can enter into the perplexities and struggles of those who, weaker and less gifted, still have aims and hopes."

After 18 months in her apartment at Coleherne Terrace, Mrs. Bellew moved closer to Capel. She took up residence at 40 Scarsdale Villas, which was located less than a few minutes' walk away from his home. She brought Mary Anne Tucker, her maid servant, with her. She also employed another maid, Lucy Stevens. The affair with the Monsignor continued at Scarsdale Villas, she said.

Intricate arrangements, including security measures, were devised to ensure the servants were kept in the dark about his visits. An unlit hall lamp was used to signal it was safe to enter the house. Another arrangement – to leave the front door ajar – was also employed, until one night a policeman who was passing by "pushed it open and entered," causing "surprise and alarm," Mrs. Bellew revealed.

The Monsignor was eventually provided with his own latchkey so that he could arrive discreetly and at will. He used the key, at one stage, to make three visits in a week, normally arriving at 11 pm and staying for an hour. So often was the key referred to in their conversations that she ended up calling him "Latchkey". She once told a close friend that he was her "lover."

A Mrs. Lean later confirmed the nickname, declaring on oath that Mrs. Bellew had spoken of "a certain man whom she called 'Latchkey', who had the latchkey to her house and came in and went out at night as he chose." Dr. Willington confirmed that Mrs. Bellew had told him that the man with the latchkey was Monsignor Capel.

Capel later disputed that "Latchkey" had anything to do with him, arguing that when Mrs. Bellew spoke of the mysterious person, she must have been referring to some other lover, most probably named "Latitchka" or "Latchka", with whom she was "criminally intimate." He repeatedly asserted, somewhat unconvincingly, that "Latitchka is an individual distinct from myself."

The gossip machine in Kensington, and beyond, was soon in overdrive. Society parlours bristled with tittle-tattle. Friends asked Bellew about the nature of the relationship. One woman noted how Bellew kept a portrait of Capel which had appeared in a weekly journal. So many scandalous "hearsays" were floating in the Kensington air that Dr. Willington said they were having "a baneful effect" on public attitudes towards priests.

Anonymous poison-pen letters were sent to Mrs. Bellew at her home address. One of them referred to the damage she was doing to Monsignor Capel, "a gentleman who has never injured you, whose goodness and kindness is proverbial." She was warned that her actions were likely to cause her "some trouble."

The letter went further: "I may tell you as a fact that I know that your assertion that you were the mistress of the distinguished Ecclesiastic whom you have tried to ruin has become known, and is the subject of conversation at the London clubs." The brief, carefully-written letter was signed: "A person who knows something of your past after your divorce."

The house servants also observed what was going on. They remarked on the exchange of correspondence between Bellew and Capel, mainly because the notes had to be hand-delivered by them. They also observed the house visits, at least those made in an open and public way. The initiative – especially the sending of notes – was usually taken by Bellew, while the Monsignor frequently showed disinterest, as was his way.

Matters between Capel and Bellew came to a head following a train crash she was involved in on 31 August 1878. The crash took place at Sittingbourne, Kent, on the train's return journey from Ramsgate to London. Bellew was on her way home, having stayed with a friend at Broadstairs. The accident resulted in five fatalities and numerous injuries. Among those on the injured list was Mrs. Bellew.

Along with some broken ribs, she was badly shaken. "My nerves are terribly shattered," she remarked, "and I cannot bear the least noise or jar. I fear it will be many a long day before I recover from the shock." She was confined to bed for months, during which time Capel paid her an unusually large number of visits. He was still involved sexually with her, she said. He might also have noted the £1,000 compensation she received for her injuries.

There were two more sexual encounters between Capel and Bellew following the rail crash, according to information procured by Dr. Willington. After that, the relationship turned sour. It became even more acrimonious when Mrs. Bellew learned that Dr. Willington had met Capel to discuss the matter and the Monsignor had produced letters written by her in an attempt to show the affair was a fiction.

"You have treated me damnably, I have been true to you, but you have been false to me," she wrote to Capel on hearing what had tran-spired. Matters were about to get worse, however, when Capel was called to a meeting with the Vicar General, which was held in the presence of Dr. Willington. He denied the affair had taken place and launched a bitter attack on the character of Mrs. Bellew.

"Monsignor Capel declared that there was no foundation for, or a particle of truth in, the allegations," the Vicar General's notes of the meeting reveal. "He further added that Mrs. Bellew could not be trusted, that she drank, that Dr. May, her doctor, had spoken to him on the subject, that her daughter in law had spoken to him of her immorality, and that he very seldom went to the house."

Despite Capel's defence, the Vicar General was deeply concerned and advised Capel to suspend his public duties, at least while the matter was being investigated. Capel was appalled. "I never imagined that it was possible for the word of a woman whose character even then was known to be tarnished in no small degree to be accepted before that of a priest," he said.

Matters spiralled quickly out of control. Immediately following the Cardinal's and Vicar General's interventions, Capel went on the hunt for damaging information concerning Mrs. Bellew. He contacted her friends, acquaintances, a former landlady, previous doctors, along with house staff past and present. Digging deeply, he pulled together information about her sexual habits, use of chloral, mental health, and inner secrets. Nothing was left unexplored. The evidence, he believed, was damning.

Unfortunately for Capel, the new evidence would have to be set aside, at least for now, as his superiors were turning their attention to his alleged sexual misconduct with the servant girl, Lucy Stevens. As a result, he would soon find himself on another hansom cab ride – this time to Cardinal Manning's residence off Vauxhall Bridge Road; a much more stressful journey than the cosy jaunt he once took with Mrs. Bellew to her home at Coleherne Terrace.

THE HOUSEMAID'S TALE

Scarsdale Villas

In the spring of 1878, a bright, attractive young woman named Lucy Stevens joined Mrs. Bellew's house staff at 40 Scarsdale Villas. With her fine figure and vivacious personality, she caught the eye of those who met her. Her handsome looks were often remarked upon; her lively and energetic disposition was noted, too.

It wasn't long before she attracted the attention of Monsignor Capel. He encountered her during his visits to Mrs. Bellew's home; or at least during those visits undertaken in an upfront way. Even while the Bellew affair was ongoing, his passion for the "Protestant servant girl," as he later called her, grew by the day.

Eventually, during visits when Mrs. Bellew was unwell and confined to bed – notably after the Sittingbourne train crash – Capel made his intentions known to the housemaid. "He kissed me, called me 'dear', 'darling,' etc.," Lucy said. "He often called very late, and wanted to be let in, but was refused entrance."

Desperate to see her, he asked where her bedroom was located. Was it downstairs in the basement? Could he enter by a side door located down the steps? He also asked her to sit up after dark, await his arrival, and "let him in."

Repeatedly, after leaving Mrs. Bellew late at night, he would return an hour or two later and beg the maid to allow him to enter. Once again, she would refuse. He also suggested Lucy should "go to Confession to him." She was appalled. "What do I want with him and his nasty ways," she remarked.

On two Sunday nights, between 10 pm and 11 pm, he invited her to Cedar Villa. He did so "on some false pretence," she said. On one of those Sundays, he made drunken, immoral advances towards her, and asked her to join him in bed.

"He was standing at the door to listen for my footsteps, and let me in himself," she recalled of her arrival following the short walk from 40 Scarsdale Villas. "He opened the door before I could knock. He had no boots on and told me to pick up my dress, so as not to make a noise."

Capel was inebriated and led her into the hall. "He was drunk," she remarked, "falling about, and against the table in the hall etc." He then steered her into the dining room, where he assaulted her. "He took hold of me, and dragged me on to his knee, and earnestly begged me to go into his bedroom. I struggled out of his clasp in which he pinched my knee outside the clothes.

"He asked me why I was afraid to go to his bedroom, and said, 'you need not be afraid, there will be no baby.'" The Monsignor pleaded with her to give in to his wishes. He beseeched her and implored her: "He promised to give me a silk dress, to get me well married, a good situation etc. if I would consent to go to his bedroom.

"He called me nice, pretty, said I had a good figure, that he loved me; and used every kind of expression a man would use in trying to seduce a girl. I have no doubt he did all he could to seduce me." He ended up clumsily trying to excuse himself, saying, "It was only a lark – I thought you were fond of a lark."

Lucy recalled another visit – on a weekday evening, "probably between the two Sundays," – when she was obliged to call to Cedar Villa. On that occasion, "he treated me in a similar manner," she said. He kissed her and called her "endearing names," although he did not make improper proposals.

She later amended her remark that Capel said he would help her to "marry well." "He only said he would help me to *marry*," she said, "as he had many people about him, such as the gardener, whom he could induce to marry me."

Following the Sittingbourne train accident, in August 1878, Lucy became even more exposed to the Monsignor's sexual advances. With Mrs. Bellew confined to her bed, he had easier access to the maid in various parts of the house. He also spotted a golden opportunity when Bellew travelled to Brighton for a break.

The most significant event that took place during Mrs. Bellew's Brighton visit happened on Sunday, 10 November. Bellew had departed for the resort on the previous day – Lord Mayor's Day – which was memorable for the excitement and bustle taking place around London. There was a grand procession, accompanied by bands, state carriages, triumphal arches, elaborate decorations, and enormous crowds.

Lucy Stevens, on the other hand, remembered what occurred exactly 24 hours later, when Capel put in another appearance at Scarsdale Villas. "When my mistress went to the seaside for a fortnight, Monsignor came to the house where I was alone," Lucy recollected. He said he came to ask for Mrs. Bellew's address in Brighton. Lucy was alert to what was going on. "What did he call for – as if I did not know that he knew where my mistress was!" she later remarked.

"He kissed me, put his arms all round me, and gave me a pair of gold links. I would not take them at first, but he forced them upon me," she explained in a statement made to the Diocese of Westminster. "That was on Sunday. On the Monday morning he called, and I was not up. On the Tuesday night he called again, and asked for the wrist-links, saying that they were not so good as he thought, and that he would give me another present in a different way. This was never done: his only object in taking the wrist-links back again was to destroy what might be evidence against him."

Lucy was left with a lasting image of the Monsignor on the night he came to recover the wrist-links. "He stood on a chair, in the hall, and turned down the gas while I went to fetch them," she remarked. With the gas dimmed and the lights low, he then renewed his amorous advances. "On this occasion also, he took hold of me, and kissed me," she said. "I remonstrated in a way he did not like and he went off in a 'miff'."

During subsequent questioning, Capel vehemently denied the allegations. There was no foundation for them, or particle of truth in them, he said. The "servant girl" had occasionally called to Cedar Villa, he agreed, but her visits were to deliver messages, and he had learned of them from his housekeeper. Otherwise, their encounters were trivial and unimportant, and few and far between.

He also argued that Lucy's claim that she had been with him in his dining room could not be true as there was another gentleman located there "day and night." The gentleman was a bailiff, who had been appointed following financial difficulties Capel was encountering at the time. The bailiff had been staying in the room for several weeks to ensure that nothing was taken from the house. Lucy later amended her remarks, saying she had been confused between the dining room and the drawing room, and it was in the latter the events had occurred. Her claim was "a fabrication," he said.

As to the motive behind her "iniquitous inventions," he could only speculate that the girl was out for revenge. "This Protestant girl does not relate her story till after I had reported her for being out in the evening with a young man," he claimed. By his assertion, it appeared he had discovered Lucy at some covert activity which he had been duty-bound to relate to her mistress.

According to Lucy, this is not what had happened. Instead, it was she who had mentioned her "young man" to Capel. "He never saw me with 'my young man,'" she explained. "The night he gave me the links, I said to him 'So you would not look at me when you passed me on the street last night.' 'I never saw you,' he replied. 'But you were close enough, at all events, for you pushed against my arm.' 'I don't recollect,' he said – and I told him, 'I was with my young man.' That is how he knows of that walk."

Capel's sexual advances led to a rift between Lucy Stevens and Mrs. Bellew. The estrangement occurred following Bellew's return to

Kensington, when Lucy, it seems, informed her of two encounters instigated by Capel but neglected to mention others.

Lucy's reticence may have resulted from fear that Bellew would take
the news badly or from her own personal embarrassment. Either way,
her mistress heard of the other meetings elsewhere. She was furious
and directed remarks to the maid which were said to have been "ill
suited to a better judgement."

Lucy handed in her month's notice on the Saturday after Mrs.
Bellew's return. "I gave her notice, and said, 'I have had enough of
it, these bothers with priests, etc. etc. and your affairs,'" she explained.
She had lasted only eight months in the job.

On Sunday, 22 December, Lucy Stevens left a bitterly-cold London
and headed to the frost-covered meadows and low wooded hills of
her native Oxfordshire. It was not long, however, before she met Capel
once more in London, but this time her aggressor was fighting for his
clerical life.

The event was the Diocesan Commission of Investigation set up by
a frustrated and angry Cardinal Manning. The time had come, he
believed, to formally examine the Monsignor's scandalous and immoral
behaviour, and pass judgement on what had become a festering sore
in the Diocese of Westminster.

COMMISSION OF INVESTIGATION

Cardinal Manning

Monsignor Capel must have envied the performance of British and colonial soldiers at Rorke's Drift during the Anglo-Zulu War in 1879. A week prior to being investigated by his peers and superiors, a tiny 150-strong garrison had heroically defended their mission station against 4,000 Zulu warriors. Something similar to that victory, which was later immortalised in the movie *Zulu*, was exactly what he needed at the Diocesan Commission of Investigation.

He certainly was up against it. The panel of clergymen appointed by Cardinal Manning to the commission was formidable. Canon Richard Gell Macmullen was a Fellow of Corpus Christi College, Oxford, and had the mind and skills of a lawyer. The Rev. Edmund Pennington, with his fine bass voice, was a former Professor of Classics at St. Edmund's College, Hertfordshire, and was known for his unostentatious piety.

Also on the panel was the Rev. Robert Butler D.D., Rector of St. Charles' College, Notting Hill, and a lifelong friend of Cardinal Manning. The Rev. Thomas Barge was parish priest at St. Patrick's Church, Soho, who, according to *The Tablet*, had "a wholesome horror of frippery and tinsel," which must have alarmed Monsignor Capel. The fifth member was the genial Canon George Last, who had spent his life as private chaplain to Lord Petre and his family.

On a dull, cloudy morning, on 29 January, at 11 am, four of those esteemed churchmen – Fr. Barge was missing due to illness – stepped from their carriages outside Cardinal Manning's residence off Vauxhall Bridge Road. Joining them were the Vicar General, Canon Gilbert, and commission secretary, the Rev. Thomas Francis Knox.

Their remit was to "investigate the truth of certain grave accusations brought against the Rt. Rev. Monsignor Capel." Having bound the members to a "strict obligation of secrecy," Cardinal Manning withdrew, and Canon Last took his place as President of the Commission of Investigation.

The charges focused on four issues. The first related to "acts of criminal intercourse" between Capel and Mrs. Bellew. The second concerned "indecent liberties offered to Mrs. Bellew's servant girl." The third referred to "acts of criminal intercourse with Miss Mary Stourton." The fourth, and final, charge highlighted the issue of drunkenness, notably that Capel was "under the influence of liquor" when taking liberties against Lucy Stevens.

The Rev. Walter Croke Robinson, who was organising the case on Cardinal Manning's behalf, was worried. Documentary submissions were plentiful, but witnesses willing to testify were few and far between. Mrs. Bellew was unwilling to attend, although she did submit a statement. Mary Stourton was in the South of France. Mrs. Showers wasn't available. Many people were reluctant to speak. There were too few charges.

Robinson's worries intensified when one of the commission members told him of his concerns and frustration. It was clear from Monsignor Capel's submissions, the commission member said, that "he is fighting to the last," "declares there is a conspiracy among us," and "defies proof." It will be "no easy business," he predicted.

Those comments proved remarkably prescient as Capel, in the following days, ripped into his defence with vigour. His tactics were obvious from the start – to discredit witnesses, impugn their credibility, reveal hidden motives, identify unpleasant character traits, expose memory lapses, highlight prejudices and, above all, to rubbish the stature and standing of the main protagonists, Mrs. Bellew, Mary Stourton and Lucy Stevens.

He attacked Mrs. Bellew with venom, having identified the one-time "Protestant" as the weak link in the case against him. It was known, he said, "that her sister died in an asylum, having been detained there for eight years before her death." It was also publicly known that she was "the widow of a divorced man, that she herself was a divorcee, and that her second marriage was for some considerable time kept secret."

He additionally pointed to her use of the sedative chloral hydrate – sometimes in "large doses" – while claiming that she had used the drug, on one occasion, in conjunction with champagne, brandy and sherry. It was later revealed that the event was a most unusual one, a birthday celebration, where she had consumed two glasses of champagne at midday, a glass of sherry at lunch, and was given "some brandy and water" in the evening but "she drank only a small part of it," her maid said.

"Insanity" again surfaced at the centre of his attack on Mary Stourton. "I believe this unfortunate girl to be mad," Capel proclaimed. After her escapade with Mr. Corballis, he said, "she clung to me and my brother and sister-in-law" and told "horrible stories against me." She then cunningly "asked forgiveness of me in the hope that I would find her a husband, and thus remove her from the monotony of her home which she seems to have felt unable to endure."

As with Mrs. Bellew, he did little to disprove the alleged instances of "criminal intercourse" with Stourton. Instead, he merely denied them and upped the pace of attack: "She has attempted suicide often, I believe at least three times; has been seduced by a gentleman, has herself seduced a young gentleman while being guest of his family, has run away from home to become the mistress of the gentleman who, she says, seduced her."

There was more, he added. She was guilty of "evil doings" and was "unaccountable for her actions." She was also a "taker of chlorodyne," a compound containing both chloroform and morphine. Regarding his alleged dictation of her letter of retraction, "there is not a particle of evidence," he said. He also submitted as evidence the lock of hair and photograph she had sent him.

Unlike Mrs. Bellew and Mary Stourton, the young Lucy Stevens – the "Protestant servant girl," as Capel called her in his written statements – put in an appearance at the hearings. He seemed cowed in her presence and lacked the bravado evident in his verbal attacks on the other two absent women. Fr. Robert Butler, one of the commission members, noted his discomfort.

"He gave the commission the impression that he was afraid of her," Butler remarked. He also observed that Capel did not question Stevens on "anything but points affecting the physical impossibility of the allegations" and "did not tax her to her face with falsehood, or with motives for inventing the charges."

Fr. Butler was worried by Stevens' assertion that she had been lured to Cedar Villa by Capel at a time when a bailiff was supposedly living in the dining room. To resolve the issue, he and Canon Macmullen, accompanied by commission secretary Fr. Knox, travelled to the house in Wright's Lane. There, on 6 February, at 3 pm, they were met by Monsignor Capel and the bailiff, Henry Mothersole.

"In what part of the house have you been?" the bailiff was asked regarding where he lived and slept when protecting the property. "In this room all the time," he replied, pointing around the dining room. Canon Macmullen later expressed his puzzlement at this remark, saying "though the bailiff slept in the dining room, there was no appearance of a bed."

"Do you mean to say that you have never gone out of the room?" it was then put to him. "Only for necessary purposes," the bailiff said. He was soon agreeing that he "occasionally looked over the house," that he had "been down to the kitchen," "into the drawing room," into the Monsignor's bedroom, and "in the grounds once or twice and the balcony."

It also became apparent that he would occasionally "oblige" the Monsignor by making arrangements to suit him, or visit him in the drawing room for a chat. He had been doing all this, he explained, over a period of four months. During that time, he had always been there and was never out of the house except for just over a week the previous October when another bailiff helped him out.

"We have a contradiction between the statements of Lucy Stevens on the one side, and those of the bailiff," Fr. Butler later remarked. On the surface, he said, the evidence suggested that "the scene described could hardly occur at the time and in the manner told by Lucy Stevens." Yet, despite what the bailiff had said, he concluded that it was probable that "some criminal occurrences substantially similar did happen" at around the time they were alleged to have taken place.

Over the next two weeks, witnesses arrived, one after the other, braving the cold, unsettled weather, to present their testimony. Dr. Willington, who had initially brought to light the stories of Mrs. Bellew and Lucy Stevens, put in a star appearance. His position on Capel was clear: "If he will make such advances towards a lady's maid – who is a Protestant too – he must be dangerous, far gone, in subjection to his passionate proclivities, and will not stop."

Other witnesses testified to Capel's drinking habits, including the Reverend Mother of the Convent of the Assumption. "Have you seen Monsignor Capel under the influence of drink?" she was asked. "Twice I noticed it; once particularly before midnight Mass. His words were not coherent. It was generally observed." Her testimony was confirmed by Sr. Mary Bernardine, who accompanied her to the hearings.

Thomas Hussey, a builder – who agreed he had "lots of differences" with Capel in "matters of business" – also spoke about the Monsignor's drinking. He confirmed that he was the man who passed on Sergeant Ahern's knowledge of Capel's alcohol abuse to the Diocese of Westminster. "I begged him not to make it known," he said of his initial reaction to the policeman's revelation. Hussey eventually disclosed the information on learning that "many charges against Monsignor Capel were in the wind."

Hussey added that his coachman's wife, Sarah Wickins, saw Capel "twice drunk." Later, when questioned by the commission, she tactfully qualified those words. "I thought he had been enjoying himself over his luncheon," she said. "If I were in the same way, I should have thought I had had too much."

The high point of the exchanges at the commission occurred when Monsignor Capel questioned his fellow clergyman, the Rev. Walter Croke Robinson. Robinson was the sort of man Capel was threatened by and disliked. He was Oxford educated, a brilliant scholar, popular, humorous, a fine preacher, and had been appointed Vice-Rector of the Catholic University College, Kensington, under Capel. He was also the man who had investigated the Bellew and Stevens affairs on behalf of Cardinal Manning.

Capel spared little in his interrogation of Robinson. The questions were pointed and direct; the answers blunt and abrupt. When asked to disclose his contacts or informants, Robinson was curt in his responses. "I decline to say," "I decline to answer," "I do not remember," "I was directed by my superior" and "I decline to say who they are" were peppered throughout his replies.

"Have you seen or held any conference with any of the witnesses since their examination here?" Capel inquired. "Yes," Robinson replied. "Name the witnesses," Capel demanded. "I decline to do so," his adversary answered. "Did I understand you that you were paid for setting up the case?" the Monsignor pointedly asked. "My travelling expenses were paid," Robinson clarified.

Robinson was equally direct in his remarks about Capel. When asked by the Monsignor what he thought of him, he said: "I lost my good opinion of you about two years ago. I lost my confidence in your word, and heard many things against you as to money matters." Did I not show you great kindness at University College? Capel probed, referring to a loan he gave Robinson to furnish his house. "You advanced £100 out of my salary," Robinson witheringly replied.

Capel's brother, Arthur, also played a role at the investigation. "You are a merchant in the city of London?" the Monsignor asked him. "Yes," he replied, pointing out that his business turnover amounted to £700,000 – £800,000 a year. Arthur spoke mainly of Mary Stourton, although he agreed that he had discussed Capel's morality with the Reverend Mother of the Convent of the Assumption. "The subject was discussed between us," he noted, "but only in reference to statements which other people had made."

The Reverend Mother had a different take on her discussion with Arthur Capel. When asked if she had heard either him or his wife "speak very disparagingly" of the Monsignor, the Reverend Mother answered tersely, "Yes." The issues related to "money matters" and "immoral conduct," she confirmed. Their relationship was "not of friendship" and "they were angered with him," she declared.

Over the following week, many witnesses arrived and departed, with each contributing their views of the Monsignor. Then, on 10 February 1879, the final witness – the Rev. Robert Clarke, a friend of Capel's – was introduced. He added to the unpleasant tone of the Monsignor's defence, remarking that the wife of one of the witnesses was "a slatternly sort of woman," and that the witness had sent his child "to a Protestant school." On that note, the interrogations came to an end.

Capel's concluding remarks to the commission were combative and cutting. Bellew was a woman with "no reputation" and a "passionate nature," who, at a "hysterical age, forty-four to forty-nine," was "excited by alcohol and chloral," and ended up believing in "the impure hallucinations invented by a corrupt imagination."

Turning to Mary Stourton, he was equally scathing. She was "known to have attempted suicide, to be an habitual taker of chlorodyne, to have been while guest in a house the corrupter of the son, to have run away from home to join a married man as his mistress," he said, largely replicating his earlier remarks.

Regarding Lucy Stevens, he spoke of her "abominable charges," "inconsistencies," "improbabilities," and being guilty of "fabrication" and "gross and malicious falsehood." He continued: "Of the improbability of Lucy Stevens' whole story I say but little. She is a Protestant, a servant girl, was on her own word but eight months in the service of Mrs. Bellew." She had fabricated "a gross alleged attempt at seduction," he said.

Finally, concerning his alleged drinking, he refuted the charges, condemned his accusers, and proclaimed his innocence. He then addressed the commission members: "Permit me to tender you my regret that you should have had so painful a case to deal with, one involving the sacrifice of so much time and causing much pain. I beg to thank you for your considerate and patient care throughout this prolonged enquiry.

"Conscious of my innocence before God, and of the falsity of the abominable charges one and all now before you, I trust to the God of Justice to destroy these scandalous allegations, and to your wise and prudent judgement to examine and decide as though you were the accused."

At 10 am, on 12 February 1879, the Commission of Investigation reconvened for a final session at the Archbishop's house, Westminster. After the minutes of the preceding session were read, the members were asked to return to their homes, draw up their conclusions, and send their reports to the Vicar General. Having been dismissed, they departed into the clear, bright London day.

The commission members' private deliberations, obtained for this book, make for interesting reading. On the issue of Capel's alleged drinking, the accusations were uniformly agreed to be "disproved," "unconfirmed," "not established" and, according to one member, ought to be "dismissed altogether." By unanimous agreement, on this count Capel was deemed innocent and the charge was set aside.

Turning to Mary Stourton, the commission members accepted her version of events, even though she had been unavailable for questioning and had her veracity queried. "There is a consistency about Miss Stourton's charge which leaves in the mind an impression altogether unfavourable," Fr. Pennington remarked. Her testimony, he said, left "a grave suspicion against Mgr. Capel." Fr. Butler concurred, saying that the Monsignor's guilt was "very probable, terrible as it is."

The conclusions were equally damning of Capel in the case of Mrs. Bellew. Her testimony "cannot be disbelieved, and obliges one to pronounce the Monsignor guilty," Canon Last remarked, his verdict being supported by Fr. Pennington, who said that Capel had been "condemned by the evidence." Bellew was also praised for "coming forward, under the most trying circumstances, and incurring the hostility and anger of Mgr. Capel."

The charge levelled by Lucy Stevens was much more contentious. Although all commission members were disturbed by the inconsistencies surrounding her alleged sexual encounters with Capel, they were equally worried by the Monsignor's line of defence. He had "not been truthful," one member alleged. Why, also, did he issue so many "statements against her character, which he could not prove?" another asked. It led Fr. Butler, as we saw earlier, to conclude that "some criminal occurrences" had taken place.

The powers of the commission had to be clearly understood, Canon Macmullen pointed out. Using the finely-tuned legalistic reasoning for which he was recognised, he noted: "As the 1st Provincial Synod of Westminster instructs us, 'the mode of investigation is not a judicial process, but is to be so conducted that the truth may be arrived at in any way': and it is by weighing the probabilities of the case on either side" that decisions are to be reached.

Applying this principle, Canon Last summarised the commission's overall decision, with damning consequences for the Monsignor: "The concurrent testimony of the witnesses, Miss Stourton, Mrs. Bellew, and L. Stevens, not suspected of collusion, leaves a strong presumption against the Monsignor even where the guilt was not proved." Translated into simple English, on the three issues of morality, the commission found Monsignor Capel guilty as charged.

On 23 May 1879, four months after the hearings began, the commission members advised Cardinal Manning of the punishments to be imposed on Monsignor Capel. They unanimously agreed that the Cardinal should "withhold all faculties from him except to say Mass during the short time he may remain in the Diocese before going abroad." They also unanimously proposed that the amount of time he should be allowed remain in the diocese before leaving England should be "the shortest time possible – say a month at the outside."

They added – again by unanimous agreement – that should he remain longer in the diocese, without the consent of the Cardinal, his right to say Mass and to receive the Blessed Sacrament must be withdrawn. All hopes Capel might have of being reinstated at any future time should be denied, they agreed, before adding that if he at any time ended up "doing mischief by saying that the case against him failed in Rome or England," he should be summarily suspended from divine office.

It all seemed done and dusted. Like the Anglo-Zulu War, which by late spring was drawing to its conclusion, it appeared that the war between Capel and his adversaries was coming to a close. Any hopes the hierarchy had of emulating the British forces' pending victory were soon dashed, however, due to the avalanche of information surfacing about the Monsignor's crushing debts. Some of the stories involved details that were highly disturbing.

MONEY MATTERS

Copy of Baptismal Certificate,
from the Church of St. Peter St. Edward, Westminster.

Die 23 Junii 1878 natus et die 25 Junii 1878
baptizatus est Bernardus Alfredus Fairfield
filius - - - - - - - - - - Fairfield ,

a me
Archibaldo McDonell
Matrina fuit Maria Buchanan.

Fairfield Baptism Certificate

Monsignor Capel became increasingly desperate for money as his empire collapsed around him in the latter years of the 1870s. He sought funds everywhere, from banks and moneylenders, friends and supporters, and from people he barely knew. His finances became a tangled web of chaos and deceit, missed repayment deadlines, and threats of legal action. He plunged to dark depths, caring little for the harm he inflicted on others.

What happened to newly-born Bernard Alfred Fairfield is a case in point. It's a sad and distressing story of an abandoned baby boy, who was born in June 1878. We don't know the true name of his father – his surname, Fairfield, was given to him – and we don't know the name of his mother, although we are told she was "a lady of wealth." What we do know, however, is that Monsignor Capel was central to determining the child's destiny.

At Capel's suggestion, the baby was collected on the day of his birth from 8 Shaftesbury Terrace, Kensington. The property was a lodging house located close to Capel's boys' school at Warwick Road. Immediately after the birth, the newborn was taken to the orphanage run by the Sisters of Charity, at Carlisle Place, Westminster. Capel told the nuns that the baby's mother had immediately left for Ireland. He hinted many months later that she was still there, thereby creating the impression that she was Irish.

Tipperary-born Mary Buchanan, who was a nurse, was the person who collected the child from Shaftesbury Terrace and brought him to the orphanage. The following day, he was handed into the care of a Mrs. Casey, who was well known to the nuns and who had dealings with them over the years. The next day again, the baby was baptised at the Church of St. Peter and St. Edward, Westminster, where he was given the name Bernard Alfred Fairfield.

There are no concrete details about Capel's role in the matter, although we do know that he had preached in Ireland – in Bray, County Wicklow – during the late summer of the previous year. It would seem, however, that his visit to Ireland does not coincide, by a matter of some months, with the time of the baby's conception.

Monsignor Farrell, of Dublin, further accused Capel of having had "criminal intimacy with a young lady" in his parish "about the time of the death of Cardinal Cullen." The allegation, which was made to the Vicar General and future Archbishop of Dublin, Edward McCabe, places the affair at slightly too late a stage to account for the birth. Of course, the Monsignor might have been laying a false trail, and the baby could have been conceived anywhere, with a mother of any nationality.

At the time of the birth, Capel agreed to a proposal whereby Mrs. Casey, on the payment of a lump sum of £50, would adopt the child. Until the payment was made, he would pay eight shillings a week in maintenance. Unfortunately, he explained, the £50 was slow coming through from "the relatives of the child," and it might take some time before he received it. In the meantime, he made the weekly payments.

In February 1879, eight months later, Capel wrote to the nuns and explained that he now had received the required sum of money. "I am glad to be able to say that I have managed to secure the £50 for this purpose," he wrote, adding that he could transfer it "either as a lump sum or if you prefer in distinct and several payments to the person concerned." Mrs. Casey was happy to accept the lump sum, as agreed the previous June.

Month after month passed by, and the £50 was never paid. By late November, Mrs. Casey still hadn't received it. Nor did she receive the eight shillings a week after a last payment was made in September. "Since that date nothing whatever has been paid though I wrote many letters without receiving a single answer," the Reverend Mother of the orphanage remarked in a letter which eventually came to the attention of Cardinal Manning. She also noted that Mrs. Casey visited the Monsignor "several times" but had no success in obtaining the money.

It wasn't as if the sum involved didn't matter. As the Reverend Mother pointed out, Mrs. Casey had eight children, a disabled husband, and could not keep the child for nothing. "She has a little shop and is a very hard working woman, honest and sober and that was known since we are in London," she remarked. Her circumstances mattered little to Capel – 17 months after the baby's birth, she still hadn't received the money.

As for little Bernard Alfred Fairfield, we know from the 1881 census – taken on 3 April – that the then two-year-old was still living with Mrs. Casey. He had, in the meantime, we are informed, become "a fine little fellow." Ten years later, in the 1891 census, his name had disappeared from records.

By then, he was no longer with Mrs. Casey, who may not have been able to afford to keep him. He may have died, although no documents exist to that effect. He didn't return to the orphanage, according to official records. He may have been adopted by someone else. Either way, he ended up being a victim of Capel's malign and noxious financial dealings as the 1870s came to a close.

Somewhat luckier was a lady from Prague by the name of Marie Therese Petritzka. A stylish, attractive woman, she had arrived in England, via Vienna, aged in her late 20s. "She seems rich, is certainly very handsome, and goes a good deal into society," an acquaintance said of her, identifying the sort of qualities that appealed to Monsignor Capel. She was introduced to him through friends.

Petritzka had arrived with the authority to lodge a sizeable sum of money in a bank. She brought relevant documents with her, but she had little knowledge of where to go or what to do. Capel offered a helping hand. He was about to leave for Paris, he said, and would speak with a friend of his there. She agreed to give him the documents, and they would talk on his return.

During his absence, Petritzka, who had sources abroad, heard that he had done nothing on her behalf during his visit to France. She confronted him on his return and asked for an explanation. He had only been in the city, he said, "from Sunday morning till Sunday night," which made it impossible to sort things out. Petritzka knew he was lying. "A friend of mine saw you there on Saturday," she said.

"He dropped his eyes for a moment, and then fixed them upon her and frightened her by his manner," recalled an acquaintance of Petritzka, to whom she later told her story. As a result, "she was afraid of Mgr. Capel: that she had detected him in a lie, and was afraid of his vengeance," the acquaintance said.

She repeatedly asked for the return of her documents, but to no avail. On one occasion, Capel explained how he had incurred a great deal of expense in the matter, involving "dinners at the Club, letters, cabs, journeys and interviews." He would require compensation, he said.

Petritzka replied that if he wrote out a list of all that was due to him – and simultaneously returned the documents – her lawyer would make a payment. In response, he gave her the address of a bank in Rome. The Pope required him to reside near him for "secret services," he explained. She didn't believe a word he said.

In the end, Petritzka never received her documents, although it was said that she lost no money as a result of what had occurred. Instead, it seems, Capel had used her documents as collateral with a money-lender, and it was there they rested, gathering dust, until the financial chaos surrounding his life was ultimately resolved.

Cardinal Manning could hardly have been surprised when news of the above stories crossed his desk. At the time, numerous complaints were arriving at his office concerning Capel's financial activities. One letter revealed how Capel had borrowed £800 to pay a bill; another described a £500 loan; a further detailed a £500 debt accrued elsewhere. Yet another letter highlighted a £100 cheque which had been dishonoured by Capel's bank. An additional £92 debt had to be paid by Manning.

The Monsignor was twisting and turning in his efforts to raise money to meet debts. "Any gift will be very welcome not only for its own sake but as a token of moral support and of sympathy in our undertaking," he wrote in a begging letter to the Archbishop of Dublin, Cardinal Cullen. He earnestly hoped for a response, he said. His panic was obvious, his state of indebtedness parlous, his borrowing feral, his financial dealings beyond reckless.

Perhaps the most unlikely of Capel's victims was his old friend the Marquess of Bute, whose conversion in late 1868 had brought the Monsignor so much fame. Since 1875, cracks had appeared in their relationship. The rift emerged after Bute discovered that Capel had exploited his generosity, abused his trust, and engaged in deception. To do so was anathema to the Marquess.

Bute had been generous to Capel, engaging him as his personal chaplain on a salary of £300 a year. The post involved "very little trouble," he pointed out, and even less work. He also employed the Monsignor as his almoner, providing him with a further £300 a year to distribute among the poor, especially among those who wrote seeking his personal help.

"After some years, never finding a single pauper who has received alms at his hands, I began to have some suspicions," Bute wrote in a letter to Cardinal Franchi, one of the leading lights of the Vatican. He was particularly disturbed by what had happened – or, more importantly, what *hadn't* happened – to a gift of £50 which Bute had asked Capel to donate to the Servite Order in London.

"Nobody ever saw the money," the Marquess remarked with disgust. Its non-delivery was a grievous error on Capel's part, as the Servites were close to Bute's heart. The timing of his deception was also poorly conceived as the order desperately needed money having built a new church – the Church of Our Lady of Dolours – on Fulham Road, in the Diocese of Westminster.

Everybody who was anybody participated in the financing or opening of the church. Cardinal Manning performed the solemn opening ceremony; the Duke of Norfolk contributed money; "one excellent lady" paid for the freehold of the site; and Monsignor Capel delivered the inaugural sermon. His participation in the "elegant and abundant" post-ceremony repast, as newspaper coverage put it, and his equally "eloquent" speech must have galled the Marquess of Bute.

The consequences for Capel were enormous. Bute asked him to explain where the missing money had gone, but he received no reply. All formal connections were immediately terminated. Bute, who was worried by reports that the Monsignor might be made a Scottish Bishop, was scathing in his remarks to Cardinal Franchi: "He has not made such a success of his school at Kensington that the English would not probably be glad enough to be rid of him – but let them not do so by giving him to us."

"I can trust nobody," Bute often remarked, and no doubt he did so again after his betrayal by Capel. Unfortunately, there were many others much less fortunate – and considerably less wealthy – who would soon empathise with what he said.

THE RUIN OF MISS PLUES

A Plues Bestseller

Margaret Mary Plues was a kind-hearted woman, a true nature lover, and a wonderful writer. In the first half of the 1860s, while in her 30s, her botanical rambles around Britain were published in a series of bestselling books. These beautifully illustrated works, with titles such as *Rambles in Search of Ferns* and *Rambles in Search of Flowerless Plants*, competed with the novels of Charles Dickens on Victorian bookshop shelves.

Margaret had a deft touch with the pen. "The river Swale winds serpent-like along the valley, and when we began our exploration the morning sun was turning its waters to gold. On the hill-sides on either hand are deep clefts, worn by mountain streams, the steep banks covered with Birch-wood. In these wooded glades we began our eager search for Ferns," she wrote in the opening to her famous *Rambles in Search of Flowerless Plants*, published in 1864.

Victorians, who had a passion for ferns – "fern fever" it was called – couldn't get enough of her. For a time, she responded by releasing title after title to meet their seemingly-insatiable demand for her books. Things changed in 1866 when she converted to Catholicism. After that, she refocused her life, and while still producing books and articles on nature topics, began writing titles like *Chats about the Commandments* and *Chats about the Rosary*.

Margaret could never be described as rich. Although she made money from her writings, there was little family wealth to back it up. Her father, the Rev. William Plues, was headmaster of the grammar school in Ripon, Yorkshire, and for a number of years served as pastor of two small chapels. Described as "an excellent specimen of a good and painstaking parish priest," he had exactly the same sort of characteristics as his compassionate, caring and thoughtful daughter.

It was these highly-commendable attributes that led Miss Plues to Monsignor Capel. In the 1870s, at a time when the Monsignor was building his empire in Kensington, she decided she wanted to give something back. Spotting that he needed a superintendent to take charge of his Kensington Square "dressmaking establishment" and shelter for convert ladies – St. Anne's Home – she applied for the job and got it. No doubt her application was helped by the fact that she offered to work for free.

Although Capel was drowning in debt, he took a 21-year lease on the Kensington Square property at a rental of over £350 per annum. The owner of the house was Thomas Hussey, the builder who gave evidence at the Diocesan Commission of Investigation. Aware of the Monsignor's precarious financial position and having had "former unsatisfactory dealings with him," he refused to let the property unless two other persons signed the lease.

One of the two people the Monsignor called upon was Margaret Mary Plues; the other was Mrs. Dillon, a wealthy Catholic widow from America, who was one of Capel's financial supporters. To Miss Plues, it didn't seem like a problem, as Capel assured her that she would not be called upon to pay any money at any stage. All he required, he said, was her signature to satisfy Mr. Hussey. She duly signed the document.

Miss Plues might not have been aware of any danger, but others were. Among them was the Rev. Walter Croke Robinson, who took an interest in her case. "I knew, at the time, of the desperate state of Monsignore Capel's affairs: that he was pressed on all sides by creditors and I was quite certain that he could never pay the rent, and that therefore Mrs. Dillon and Miss Plues would have to do so," he wrote.

Robinson assessed that Miss Plues would end up paying one-half the rent for 21 years, which would be "her ruin as she was poor." He felt obliged to do something: "Being a friend of Miss Plues, and having with all her friends a regard for her goodness and excellence of character, I thought it a charity and a duty to see if I could not rescue her from ruin."

Fr. Robinson consulted with the Catholic aristocrat, the Honourable Mrs. Georgina Fraser, who was an intimate friend of Plues. Mrs. Fraser lived in Eaton Place, one of the grandest streets in Belgravia. Together, Robinson and Fraser discussed what they could do.

Mrs. Fraser immediately visited Miss Plues, asking to speak to her alone. She explained that she arrived on the authority of Fr. Robinson and that she wished to warn of "an impending danger." It was, by all accounts, a distressing meeting, with Mrs. Fraser appearing heart-broken and shedding tears.

Mrs. Fraser outlined Capel's financial position, saying that "the Home could not continue under these circumstances and that I should be ruined by being a partaker in the lease, but that the landlord 'pities me and perhaps Fr. Robinson might be able to persuade him to let me out of the lease,'" Miss Plues later explained.

Miss Plues also outlined how Mrs. Fraser said that Capel had been "judged guilty by the Cardinal of serious faults against morality extending over many years and the Cardinal was determined to suspend him absolutely, and that within a few weeks." Fraser knew this because Fr. Robinson "had been employed by the Cardinal to search out evidence both here and in Rome."

Miss Plues couldn't believe what she was hearing. "I am certain he is not guilty," she remarked. Mrs. Fraser replied: "I hope not, but the point is that he is judged to be guilty by the Cardinal and the Canons of Westminster." Plues then said: "I must go and warn Mgr. Capel for he cannot know what is hanging over him." Fraser sardonically responded: "I believe he knows quite well."

Being a kind-hearted woman – and having a warm regard for the Monsignor – Miss Plues did exactly what she had promised to do and spoke to Capel. It was a catastrophic move for everyone concerned. She explained exactly what had happened – about the visit from Mrs. Fraser and the views of Fr. Robinson.

Capel was enraged and asked her to commit to paper what she had said, which she did. He immediately dispatched a copy of her testimony to Canon Gilbert, Vicar General of the Diocese of Westminster, choosing him because Cardinal Manning was absent due to a family bereavement.

"It is simply awful to think that a priest should be allowed to act in this way," Capel wrote regarding Fr. Robinson, incensed by his actions. He was also marking the cards of the hierarchy that he had been damaged by unjust and malicious revelations – even though, as it turned out, they were all true.

Unfortunately for Miss Plues, everything that Fr. Robinson had predicted came to pass. "A crisis occurred," she explained in a poignant letter to Cardinal Manning. "A very large sum of money became due and of course I was liable. By urgent begging and by borrowing in my own name I weathered this storm but it gave me a shock."

She wrote to the Monsignor "urgently begging him to take my name out of the lease – he replied that he had good promises of subscriptions and I had therefore nothing to fear. This did not satisfy me for I know that the good man has always relied too much on promises and believes that even the money in hand can go three times as far as it can.

"So I wrote again saying that he must really withdraw my name for I would rather retire altogether than go on as we have been doing. When he answered, which was a fortnight after, I understood him to say that he did not wish me to go – but the language was not very clear and no steps were taken to erase my name."

Knowing she was facing potential ruin, Miss Plues paid a visit to Capel at Cedar Villa. What ensued was disastrous. He said that as her confidence in him was shaken it was best that she should go. Margaret was shattered. "It breaks my heart," she wrote to Cardinal Manning.

"I love the Institution, I love working with the converts – I love the two or three leading workers who have become like my own children – Two of these will find it very difficult to stay on with Monsignor Capel without me – they are both peculiar and it is hardly to be expected that a new Superintendent will understand them."

Margaret Plues was left in an impossible situation. Not only was she receiving no income from St. Anne's, but her money reserves had been exhausted and her finances were in a perilous state. She was liable for one-half the rent on the property, and was contributing a gratuity of £60 a year to the charity, which she had been doing out of generosity since she first became its superintendent. Simultaneously, through her work, she was earning for it some £80 – £100 a year.

By mid-1879, although "muddled and dazed by years of oppression and misrepresentation," as Fr. Robinson remarked, Miss Plues still remained in her job. Her reluctance to resign was down to her kindness and consideration. "She said it would be base to desert a friend just at the hour of need, and that her doing so would cause a panic among the creditors of Monsignor Capel," Mrs. Fraser said, after speaking with her.

Having finally drained her "own private purse" of all its money, Miss Plues resigned her position at St. Anne's in September 1879, and the charity struggled on for a few more months. Although deeply disappointed, Margaret's gloom was partly lifted when her lawyer contrived to have her name removed from the lease.

There still remained the outstanding sums owed to her, which she claimed amounted to £1,050 of documented debt and £158 without documentation. While continuing to be enthralled by Capel – "that truly good and great man," she called him – she instructed her lawyer to press for the money. "I only press after months of evasive promises and am still willing to wait," she said. Capel failed to respond with equivalent kindness.

"For your sake, and your sake alone, I have been negotiating for some time with a Catholic nobleman for the purchase of my property. He has been taking active steps in the matter," Capel wrote to Plues, hoping to stall her legal action. Press him, he said, and she would receive nothing as a judgement would be signed against him, and everyone with a claim would get a portion of the value of his estate.

He even got Alice Wilmot Chetwode – one of Capel's converts from Pau, who he employed as a writer and copyist – to write to Miss Plues. "A forced sale means a sale at great disadvantage," she stated in her letter. "Many others would have to be satisfied. You would get much less than is due and would be doing immense injury to all. Will you not think better of it and at least wait?"

The letter continued: "It is not like your devotion to Mgr. – and in any case to put a priest in such a difficulty! Now do get out of it. There will still be a great deal to pay." Although Miss Plues continued to press for her money – and the case did reach the courts – her claim ultimately foundered on the Monsignor's insolvency, and she was ruined financially.

The affair had other unfortunate consequences for Miss Plues. Fr. Robinson was most upset. Plues' remarks about him to Capel were turned into "exaggeration, distortion, misrepresentation" and "coloured up into 'an awful thing,'" he noted to the Vicar General. Robinson was charitable about what had happened, saying: "I have not a doubt Miss Plues never said all this, but it was extracted from her by him." Unfortunately, he concluded, it had all resulted from "the miserable infatuation and slavery of that poor creature."

Mrs. Fraser, who was the first to warn Plues of imminent danger, also became upset. Matters weren't helped when Plues wrote to her asking for a letter outlining what she had said, an initiative almost certainly inspired by the Monsignor. Although Fraser knew Plues was under "strong pressure," she wrote back "entirely declining any correspondence on the subject" and saying that their acquaintance must cease.

Mrs. Dillon – co-signer of the lease with Miss Plues – was also highly aggrieved. Now that Plues' name had been taken from the lease, she became responsible for the full payment of rent. She later claimed the total amount involved was £700, with an added £400 being paid for repairs.

Dillon wrote to Cardinal Manning concerning Fr. Robinson's actions enabling Plues to walk free from the lease: "I now write to you as his Ecclesiastical superior to ask that he should compensate for the loss he has caused me, and is causing me. The influence he offered to Miss Plues to relieve her, he can now use for me." Dillon was so annoyed with Manning that she felt prevented from "holding personal communications" with him and meeting him face-to-face, she said.

Miss Plues was dizzy from the aggravation and turmoil, the claims and counterclaims, and didn't know what to do. She was desperate for new employment and to help those she was already involved with at St. Anne's. "Can anything be found in London under regular or secular priests where I could still devote my life to teaching convert ladies to support themselves?" she asked Cardinal Manning.

"My best power is with ladies – I am too quiet with rough girls – but I have plenty of quiet resolution and that does for educated people. I teach my ladies panel and china painting, embroidery and crewel-work – and the French dressmaker, herself a well known person, teaches them dressmaking.

"If we could get a good start I believe we could make such an Institution self-supporting – only we must be within easy reach of a fashionable neighbourhood as we work principally in articles of luxury. If the Jesuits, or yourself, or the Oblates would take it up I should be full of courage – but I will attempt nothing without a clear association with a priest or priests of tried prudence. I can ensure a clientele without touching what lawfully belongs to Monsignor Capel – in fact I desire earnestly to treat him with every consideration."

We don't know if Cardinal Manning had any role in the matter, but Miss Plues did realise her dream. Within a year of her departure from St. Anne's, she had set up a School of Decorative Art, in Fulham Road, a short walk from Kensington High Street. As directress of the school, she created the designs while a group of 13 women produced crewel-work for tapestries, embroidery for house or church decoration, and paintings on china, silk or terracotta.

The school – "for ladies who have met with reverses" – operated on modest commercial principles, "asking only a fair price for honourable work." Eventually, the school folded, and Miss Plues moved on. By 1891, in her early 60s, she ended up living with her brother in Weybridge, Surrey, and had no formal employment.

In the final years of her life, this "grievously-injured, ruined woman," as Fr. Robinson called her, entered the Convent of St. Maur, Weybridge, where she became a nun. Then, in 1901, aged 73, she died, far from Monsignor Capel but surrounded by Surrey's wild meadows and heathlands full of the purple heather, rare orchids and oxeye daisies she had always loved so much.

THE MAYOR, THE MAID
&
THE WIDOWS

Peter Paul McSwiney

The alarming extent of Monsignor Capel's indebtedness towards the end of the 1870s was brought home to Cardinal Manning when further information about his reckless pursuit of money landed on his desk in London. One of the stories concerned Peter Paul McSwiney, a tough, straight-talking businessman and owner of one of the world's first department stores, McSwiney, Delaney & Co., which later became Clerys, of Sackville Street, Dublin.

Although well known for his business acumen, McSwiney was also recognised for his political and family connections. He was twice elected Lord Mayor of Dublin, in 1864 and 1875. In addition, he was related to the famous Irish political leader Daniel O'Connell, who campaigned for Catholic emancipation, and to the family of James Joyce. He ended up in Joyce's *Finnegans Wake* as the character "Peeler Pawr muckswinish", which was a play on his name.

More important, from Monsignor Capel's point of view, he had prominent religious connections. An ardent Catholic, he was a friend of Cardinal Cullen, Archbishop of Dublin, and an acquaintance of Cardinal Manning. His connections extended to Rome, where he had been bestowed by the Pope with one of the highest honours available to a Catholic layman, the Grand Cross of the Order of St. Gregory.

As might be expected, McSwiney had contacts among the Irish banking fraternity. Daniel O'Connell, his relation, was founder of The National Bank, which acted as a bank for Catholics rather than the Anglo-Irish ascendancy. O'Connell disapproved of the other main Irish banks – Bank of Ireland and Provincial Bank of Ireland – due to their "rascality" and narrow "anti-Irish" principles. His bank was especially open to business for Catholics as notable as Monsignor Capel.

The Monsignor, during a preaching engagement in Ireland in August 1877, approached McSwiney with a view to securing a loan. The amount he was looking for was £500, which he pledged to repay in three months. What happened next tells us much about his desperation for money and the state of his finances. It also reveals his indifference to repaying debts, no matter who was involved.

Capel told McSwiney he would be rendering "a great service to religion and to education in England" if he helped secure the loan. The businessman introduced him to the manager of The National Bank, Dublin, and a loan was duly arranged. The terms of the deal were simple – the £500 would be repaid, with interest, three months later, in November. McSwiney, as he later explained, was "induced to become security" for the promissory note which Capel signed and presented to the bank.

November came and passed, and the loan wasn't repaid. Capel was contacted and expressed an inability to pay until the following month. A new promissory note, pledging payment in December, was issued. December came and passed, and once again no money was forthcoming. By the following summer, the debt remained unpaid. A series of official demands including legal letters ensued but had no effect, leaving McSwiney liable for the debt.

Unlike other wealthy benefactors who swallowed hard and redeemed debts on Capel's behalf, the businessman contacted Cardinal Manning. "I trust your Eminence will excuse the liberty I take in asking your influence to obtain an immediate settlement of a debt due by Monsignor Capel to the National Bank of Ireland for which I was induced to become security," he wrote on 29 May 1878, in a letter filed in the Westminster Diocesan Archives.

"Many letters have been written by the solicitor of the Bank as well as by myself to recover the amount. The patience of the Bank having been exhausted I am now called upon to satisfy the claim which with Interest amounts to £514.15.4. Satisfied that Your Eminence will see that justice shall prevail in this matter, I beg to remain your most obedient servant, Peter Paul McSwiney."

Three weeks later, another letter – more direct and to the point – landed on Cardinal Manning's desk. This time, the correspondent was the manager of The National Bank, Dublin. The debt of £500, he said, despite many letters, "lies in my hands dishonoured. As legal proceedings may lead to injure the Very Reverend Gentleman, I will agree to accept payment of this long outstanding debt by instalments, but such should *immediately* begin."

We do not know the outcome of the appeals by McSwiney and The National Bank to Cardinal Manning. Whether the debt was settled on Capel's behalf or whether it ended up as part of later bankruptcy proceedings is lost to history. What we do know, however, is that the £500-plus was only one of many demands for the repayment of Capel's debts that were arriving in Cardinal Manning's letterbox at that time.

Another of Capel's victims was Harriet Carston, a lady's maid working for the wife of one of England's wealthiest landowners, Robert Stayner Holford. She was employed in her master's stately homes, Westonbirt House, Gloucestershire, and Dorchester House, Park Lane, London. Hers was a prestigious job, preparing her mistress for high-society events including visits to Buckingham Palace. The fact that her master was a Member of Parliament added to the importance of her position.

Harriet, who was French, acquired her surname when she married Henry Carston, who was also employed by Holford. He held a well-regarded position in the household, where he was engaged as Gentleman of the Chamber. As a long-time valued employee, he had accumulated some wealth. Older than Harriet, he died before her, leaving her a sum of money in his will.

109

Holford, who was a good employer and cared for his staff, was concerned about what had happened to the money. He feared that Capel was somehow involved. He shared his worries with his lawyer, the eminent solicitor Bartle J. L. Frere, of Lincoln's Inn Fields, London, who interviewed the maid.

Frere discovered that on the death of the maid's husband she had inherited the sum of £1,640. It was her only savings, her buffer for the future, and her nest egg for retirement. She wondered how best to invest it. It was already in the form of stock and gaining a three per cent return. She asked herself, "Could I do better?"

"In her trouble she had had recourse to Monsignor Capel," Frere later wrote. She had "taken at once" to him, he added. Capel recommended that the maid should go to Hollebone brokers, of Threadneedle Street, and cash in her stock. This she did and received the sum of £1,574. 8. 0.

She handed the money to Capel, "who promised to give her a security for it and to pay her £60 a year as interest." The agreed interest payment exceeded what she was already receiving. The deal took place in September 1879.

Monsignor Capel paid her half a year's interest in the spring of 1880. After that, he paid her no more. The maid contacted Capel, but he didn't acknowledge her. She appealed to him to pay the interest, but he took no notice. This state of affairs continued up to March of the following year, 1881, when her master brought her plight to the attention of his London solicitors.

Solicitor Bartle J. L. Frere subsequently sent a letter to the Diocese of Westminster, which was abrupt and clear. "I have mentioned the subject to Mr. Holford and am authorised by him to take such steps as may be advisable for Mrs. Carston's protection," Frere wrote.

"Having mentioned the subject to you and you having expressed a desire to inquire first the circumstances, I venture in the first place to submit these particulars to you and shall be very glad indeed if you can set things straight both regard Monsignor Capel and Mrs. Carston."

Once again, we don't know the outcome of the case, although we can imagine Cardinal Manning's shock and embarrassment when the revelations were finally brought to his attention. Not only was a grave wrong being inflicted on a humble maid, but the two gentlemen involved – the wealthy landowner, Robert Stayner Holford MP, and the solicitor, Bartle J. L. Frere – were level-headed, esteemed, influential men, and not to be disregarded. The evidence removed another plank from the Monsignor's rapidly-sinking ship.

The Monsignor's fascination with widows led him to another unfortunate victim – a wealthy resident of London by the name of Henrietta Davidson. With a personal worth of approximately three million pounds in today's money, Henrietta lived in a fashionable house in central London, and in her final years, at a prestigious private hotel in the city. She also owned a ten-bedroom summer mansion about a mile from Ascot, where she entertained distinguished guests during race week.

A convert to Catholicism thanks to Monsignor Capel, Henrietta exuded little of the self-denial associated with at least some dedicated followers of her faith. She employed an impressive retinue of staff to care for her failing health and addiction to morphine, and to look after her seven-acre Ascot property. In her spare time, she was a well-known patroness of the operatic and dramatic world. During her spells in London, her residence, Thomas's Hotel, Berkeley Square, was of a calibre where only guests like the Duke of Wellington, Baron de Rothschild, and the Earl and Countess of Coventry were invited to stay.

Mrs. Davidson had a dilemma when composing her will coming up to the final months of her life. With no immediate family to leave her wealth to, she opted instead to make bequests to people who were personally close. The bulk of her estate she assigned to Lord Courtenay, who was a fellow convert to Catholicism and at one stage had been tipped as a potential suitor in marriage for the widow. She added many bequests to her staff – including £100 and a year's wages to her coachman, another £100 to one of her servants, and a range of generous gifts to her friends.

She didn't forget Monsignor Capel, who no doubt made her aware of his needs. The sum of £1,000 was allocated outright as a gift – worth approximately £116,000 today – and he was also bequeathed a diamond or emerald ring to be chosen by the will's executor. She mentioned another staggering sum pertaining to the Monsignor, but there was a catch. "I bequeath to Monsignor Capel the sum of five thousand pounds upon trust to distribute the same among such poor and deserving persons and in such proportions and manner in all respects as he shall think proper."

Henrietta Davidson died at Thomas's Hotel, London, on 30 November 1875. Her death, aged 44, was due to exhaustion caused by a four-year addiction to morphine. "By the death of Mrs. Davidson I am informed that I come into a legacy of £6,000," Capel wrote to Cardinal Manning, ten days after her passing away. Had his incorrect interpretation of the sum been accurate, he would have personally benefited to the tune of almost £700,000 in today's values. There was one note of despondency in his letter, when he drily pointed out, "I fear the will is to be disputed."

After some legal delays, the will was finally executed, and Capel received his money and precious ring. The Rev. Walter Croke Robinson, who was suspicious, investigated the terms of the will and reported his findings to Cardinal Manning. The Monsignor, he discovered, had never distributed the £5,000 to "poor and deserving persons," as stipulated by Mrs. Davidson, but claimed to have used the bequest on behalf of University College. Whatever happened to the money, it was never used for the purpose intended but ended up in a vortex of profligate spending and disappeared like waste water down a plughole.

The Monsignor relieved another woman – Mrs. Richardson, from Wales – of substantial sums of money. She was a friend of Miss Margaret Mary Plues, the superintendent of St. Anne's Home, Kensington Square, who featured in the previous chapter and who related Richardson's story to Cardinal Manning.

Monsignor Capel first met Harriette Annie Richardson during a visit to Paris. He had gone there to seek potential donors and to raise money. Although Harriette had a wealthy husband in Wales, she was living in comparative poverty in the French capital and had no money of her own. The Monsignor, however, was instantly drawn not only by her wealthy connections but by her interest in converting to the Church of Rome.

In Paris, Capel took over Mrs. Richardson's spiritual guidance, which had up to then been provided by French preachers. After one or two sessions of counselling and instruction, he received her into the Church. Simultaneously, he asked her for money. Capel's "representations of his great suffering 'merely for want of money,'" as Miss Plues explained, made a deep impression on Mrs. Richardson. Unfortunately, she said, she had no money to give him.

Instead, Mrs. Richardson presented Capel with a ring of great value, which he took. He then asked her, "Have you no means of borrowing money?" It was an astute question as Mrs. Richardson's husband, Henry Thomas Richardson, was rich. He had accumulated considerable wealth in Wales, where together with his father he had invented a commercially successful tubular lifeboat. He lived in a mansion, Brynhyfryd, in the village of Pwllheli, which was staffed by servants. Anyone connected with him would be good for a loan.

Mrs. Richardson found means of borrowing the money and she presented Capel with £1,500. He issued a bond promising to repay it. Shortly afterwards, in November 1878, Mrs. Richardson's husband died, and before receiving any inheritance she borrowed another £1,500 and gave it to Capel. This time, she told him it was a gift and cancelled the previous bond. He was now in receipt of a handout of £3,000.

Two months after his death, Henry Thomas Richardson's will was processed, and the bulk of his estate was bequeathed to his wife. She became a very rich woman, owner of the mansion in Wales and soon-to-be owner of an elegant residence in London. News of her inheritance appeared in the press, as did news of her support for good causes. It wasn't long before the Monsignor got wind of her considerable fortune.

"The spring or summer succeeding he heard by accident that she was in London and telegraphed to her to go to him but this she declined," Miss Plues remarked in correspondence with Cardinal Manning. "She then received a letter from his lawyer asking whether she had got possession of her fortune as Mgr. Capel was much in need of further help. She replied that she had done what she could for Mgr. Capel and did not feel it right to spend more in his service."

On the face of it, the connection between the Monsignor and his convert seemed to end there. That wasn't entirely so, however, as Mrs. Richardson retained an intense veneration for Capel and remained deeply attached to him. From the Monsignor's point of view, he always spoke of her as his convert, although the bulk of the work had been done by his religious counterparts in France.

Despite no longer supporting Capel, Mrs. Richardson continued to reveal her generosity in different ways. With her newfound wealth, she established a "news room" in her home village of Pwllheli, where newspapers and books were made available to the local population. She also helped Miss Plues through her financial troubles by providing, here and there, "a little gift of money" or "some furniture," or support in other ways.

Mrs. Richardson remained a sincere and passionate Catholic in the years ahead. Although living in London, she paid for the building of a Catholic church dedicated to her favourite saint, St. Joseph. It was built in the grounds of Brynhyfryd, her residence in Wales. A first Mass was held there on Christmas Day 1879 before a packed attendance of Catholics from the local area.

She died a little over six years later, on New Year's Eve 1885, at her London residence, 7 Campden Hill Road, Kensington. Her will makes for interesting reading. Its total value amounted to over £22,000, which was a huge sum of money for its time. In keeping with her religious beliefs, she left £2,000 to the Roman Catholic Bishop of the Diocese of Shrewsbury.

A further £1,000 was left to the Hospital of St. John and St. Elizabeth, which was then located at Great Ormond Street, London. Other amounts were set aside for a hospital for incurables and for relatives and next of kin. It was the largest single bequest that caused the most surprise – she left £2,900, in trust, for Monsignor Capel, whose hold over Mrs. Richardson had clearly not diminished with the passage of time.

THE BATTLE FOR ROME

Cardinal Simeoni

The maxim "old friends are best" must have crossed Monsignor Capel's mind when he thought of Mrs. Harriette Richardson and the money he had squeezed from her at the height of his troubles in London. The most useful old friends he knew, however, were not in Wales, or anywhere else in the British Isles, but in Rome.

A long time ago, during his rise to fame as a preacher and proselytiser, he had arrived there like a conquering hero. Back then, he had caught the eye of Pope Pius IX, to whom he owed the title of Monsignor. Even though Rome had a new Pope – Leo XIII – he still knew all the right people in Vatican circles, and they occupied all the right positions of power.

Capel knew that Rome was his only hope of salvation. He travelled there in March 1879, shortly after the Diocesan Commission of Investigation came to an end but before it issued its recommendations. Facing the distinct possibility of losing some or all of his priestly faculties at Westminster – or, indeed, being dismissed altogether from his role as a priest – he travelled to Rome in the hope that something could be done on his behalf.

On his arrival in the city, one of his first ports of call was Propaganda Fide, a department whose function was to propagate the Catholic faith throughout the world and to bring about "civilisation among barbarous and savage nations," as Carlo Botta, the nineteenth-century Italian historian, indelicately put it. Formally titled the Sacred Congregation for the Propagation of the Faith, it was housed in an imposing palazzo situated outside the Vatican, in the Piazza di Spagna, where it flew the Vatican flag and claimed diplomatic status in the Italian state.

Propaganda, as it was commonly called, was one of the great power-houses of the Catholic Church. Its tentacles reached far and wide, into all missionary lands. With its own seminary, chapel and printing presses, it was a hive of activity, buzzing with Cardinals, Bishops and Monsignors, along with *minutanti*, *scrittori* and *protocollisti* preparing, copying, stamping and registering documents for worldwide distribution. It justifiably had the reputation of being an independent seat of power.

Since the Reformation, when the old bonds with Rome were severed, Propaganda was a major focus of attention for British Catholics. Regarded at the time as missionary territories, Great Britain and the United States fell under its control. Most matters of a religious nature in those territories – including the removal of a priest – lay within its powers. It was no surprise that Monsignor Capel made haste to Propaganda as he sought to clear his name.

When Capel arrived in Rome in 1879, the Prefect of Propaganda was the handsome, charismatic, sallow-skinned, former Vatican Secretary of State, Cardinal Giovanni Simeoni. Capel had already been in touch with him by letter, just after Christmas, complaining that he was a victim of the financial chaos at the Catholic University College – a state of affairs created entirely by others, he claimed. No mention was made in the letter of the imminent examination of his sexual encounters with women or his alleged drunkenness. They were not part of his narrative.

Simeoni, who was a wily and experienced operator, prepared himself for Capel's arrival. Shortly after receiving the Monsignor's letter, he spoke for a considerable time with the Rev. Joseph P. Palmer, who was visiting from London and who told him everything about the Monsignor's conduct in Kensington. Palmer "frankly answered" all the questions put to him, the Cardinal said.

When Capel eventually met Simeoni, his line of defence was fanciful – that Cardinal Manning was jealous of him as a preacher and of his success in securing converts, that he resented his social popularity, that he had acted towards him with passion and prejudice, that he had been let down in his running of University College, and that there was a conspiracy against him at the Diocese of Westminster. Simeoni was unconvinced. Neither he nor the Pope found Capel's version of events believable, he later said. Nor would they ever do so, he added.

Capel paid visits to other departments of the Vatican seeking a more favourable response. He flitted about, full of energy and action, engaging with one high official after the other, bamboozling those he met. "It has struck me how very defenceless in one way these high officials are against a bold, bad man," Fr. Robert Butler, Manning's friend, who later analysed the Monsignor's tactics in Rome, remarked. He is "almost in their presence before they have time to think."

Butler, a former member of the Commission of Investigation, noted how Capel spent his time "working on the traditional hesitation and timidity of nearly all" and embarrassed people by his "downright audacity." One senior Vatican figure, who was close to the Pope, complained to Butler how impossible it was to acquire "necessary knowledge" from Capel because he behaved in this way. He clearly was a man who had "lost his shame" and used every "means of deceiving," Butler concluded.

Another senior official at the Holy Office, Archbishop Sallua, had good reason to rue Capel's devious tactics. At one stage, Capel suggested to Sallua that he would like to hear the Confessions of two people he knew who were about to be received into the Church. Ever a courteous and mannerly man, Sallua said to Capel that he could go right ahead, presuming that he had already secured general permission to hear Confession from someone else. He hadn't. Capel took Sallua's agreement to mean that he could now hear Confession in Rome.

Soon, Capel was claiming that Rome had not only given him faculties to hear Confession, but they had informed him that faculties conferred on him in Rome could be used elsewhere. Simeoni, when he heard that Capel had attributed the latter remark to him, vigorously denied he ever said it. He also pointed out that at no time was Capel given the right to hear Confession, apart from the "mess" that had arisen with Archbishop Sallua.

Capel also asserted that the Pope had given him a "present", but Simeoni stressed that the claim was "a pure invention." In addition, the Monsignor publicly declared that Rome had decided in favour of his innocence. Not alone was this untrue, Simeoni said, but he pointed out that he had spoken to the Pope on the issue, and on hearing of Capel's transgressions, he had said that he could not be innocent given the "many distinct charges coming from such different quarters."

The issue of what to do with Capel became a thorn in the side of Propaganda during the Monsignor's two-month stay in Rome. The department initially stepped aside as Cardinal Manning – who came to Rome to settle the matter – attempted to strike a deal with the Monsignor. The discussions were fraught and prolonged. Eventually, under pressure from Cardinal Simeoni, Capel caved in and agreed to quietly leave England "for such a time as shall render your return free from danger to others and to yourself."

It was the ultimate climbdown by Capel. The sentence avoided the inevitable publicity of further proceedings and allowed for the matter to be hushed up at Westminster. The United States of America was suggested as a possible destination, and to sweeten matters, Simeoni proposed that Capel should be permitted to preach there. All seemed neatly wrapped up, but by no means was the matter concluded.

Capel returned to London in May, acting like a victorious general fresh from battle. His first act on reaching the capital was to speak at a benefit for the Newsvendors Benevolent Association, which provided pensions and financial assistance to newsmen in need. Journalists and their editors in attendance were delighted with the upbeat news he brought back from Rome. It was a story they were only too happy to share with their readers.

The Catholic world "has been rejoicing during the past week on his return, triumphant, after complete exoneration from all blame, and higher in esteem than ever," a correspondent with *The Evening Telegraph* declared in her London gossip column, reflecting the tone of the general coverage. "The numerous visits of congratulation he has received upon his return to his administration have kept the neighbourhood of Cedar Villa in a state of the greatest excitement," she added.

Bishop William Clifford, who had been in Rome at the same time as Capel, was far from impressed. "In Mgr. Capel's present conduct I cannot (I am sorry to say) see any sign either of a penitent priest, or of a priest who knowing himself to be innocent seeks to remove the false impression which calumny has made on the minds of others. I see nothing but the efforts of a man to keep up appearances before the world. If this be so, a clever man with a bold tongue will not be very scrupulous as to what he says or what he does....I think you have a dangerous person to deal with," he wrote to Cardinal Manning.

Within a few weeks, Capel announced that he was remaining in Kensington. He had decided, he said, to continue to run his public school for boys, which was still operating at the time. He had also returned to preaching. He did so at High Mass at his school on Trinity Sunday, after which he announced that he would preach again on ensuing Sundays. He additionally revealed through the press that he would continue with the work of St. Anne's Home, although that institution, too, was in its final days.

"He cannot be stopped," the Rev. Walter Croke Robinson remarked in exasperation. Another colleague of Capel's, the Rev. Robert Clarke, added that he had spoken to the Monsignor, who told him the Holy Father had quashed the case against him, that he would certainly remain in London, and that his various works would continue on their former footing.

Capel will bluff it out, Fr. Clarke predicted, "trusting that the ecclesiastical authorities will not continue for many months to insist on his doing what they see he will not do, and that they will prefer to let the matter drop if he goes on without further scandal." Meanwhile, he pointed out, everything was back to normal at Cedar Villa. The visitors were returning, luncheons were being held, and most importantly, the Sunday afternoon parties were once again in full swing.

Cardinal Manning, not for the first time, must have placed his head in his hands and wept. He wrote to Capel, warning him that he had reached "this most perilous moment" of his life and threatened "certain inevitable consequences." He also convened a meeting of the senior hierarchy in the Diocese of Westminster, which resolved that "Mgr. Capel should be interdicted at once from saying Mass and from all ecclesiastical functions whatsoever within the limits of the diocese." The meeting resolved that action should be taken immediately.

Unfortunately for Manning, there was another storm brewing which needed his urgent care. News was crossing his desk that Capel had become involved in a new affair – this time with a woman named Mrs. Rutherford Smith. The resulting scandal would match those involving Mary Stourton, Mrs. Bellew and Lucy Stevens, and engulf Westminster and Rome in yet another agonising controversy.

MRS. RUTHERFORD SMITH

Golden Cross Hotel

The Golden Cross Hotel, opposite Charing Cross Railway Station, was a busy commercial establishment popular with travelling salesmen and country visitors to London. Noted for its clean rooms and moderate prices, it had once been a famous staging post for the horse-drawn coaches that criss-crossed the highways and byways of England. The hotel gained an added lease of life with the opening of the nearby railway in 1864 and the Underground in 1870.

It was at the Golden Cross that Charles Dickens' fictional David Copperfield stayed during his first visit to London. He was initially allocated room number 44, "a little loft over a stable" which "smelt like a hackney-coach." The hotel was also featured by Dickens in *The Pickwick Papers* as the location where Mr. Pickwick alighted from his cab to be greeted by Mr. Tupman, Mr. Snodgrass and Mr. Winkle. The hotel Dickens wrote about had been demolished to allow for the construction of Trafalgar Square, but a new version had been built nearby in the 1830s.

Monsignor Capel entered this updated yet sombre-looking Golden Cross Hotel fresh from his "triumph" at Rome. He passed through the building's recessed porch and heavy front doors on his way to meet an attractive woman, in her mid-20s, named Mrs. Rutherford Smith. Recently separated from her husband, she had arrived in London seeking work. Anyone meeting her would have noticed how similar she was to the Monsignor's previous conquests – good-looking, vulnerable, lonely, and in search of a meaningful life.

It was during that visit to the Golden Cross in 1879 that the first act of sexual intercourse took place between Capel and Mrs. Rutherford Smith. She was ill at the time and staying at the hotel having left her husband following the recent breakdown of their marriage. Ironically, it was her husband, a convert to Catholicism, who had asked the Monsignor for help out of concern for his wife's vulnerable state.

John Hoadley Rutherford Smith had been particularly worried about his estranged wife's intention to go "upon the stage" in London. "I had specially requested Mgr. Capel to see my wife and to use his influence to prevent her entering a profession to which I objected," he later wrote. Although the Monsignor agreed to meet her and dispense spiritual comfort, he ended up having an affair involving numerous sexual encounters stretching over a period of three years.

Mrs. Rutherford Smith later admitted to the relationship, saying that she and Capel had engaged sexually "numberless times," and that, at one stage, he had expressed his intention to marry her. He had given her money, which was frequently sent by letter post, and had promised that he would secure apartments for her in Paris and Brighton. He additionally asked her not to go to Confession, no doubt in an attempt to ensure their affair remained secret.

The relationship was noticed by family and friends who spent time in Mrs. Rutherford Smith's company. Among them was her sister, Emmie, who was also staying at the Golden Cross when the liaison was blossoming. "From my own observations and from what my sister has frequently told me, I have not had a shadow of doubt that the past three years there has been a continual criminal intercourse between my sister and Mgr. Capel," Emmie wrote in 1882.

Emmie's fiancé, Dr. Coppinger, who was another resident at the hotel, shared her suspicions. "Dr. Coppinger to whom I was engaged and who was staying with myself and sister at the same hotel, was from his own observations equally convinced that a criminal intercourse was going on between my sister and Mgr. Capel – the effect of this knowledge has been such that I have given up the practice of my religion," she commented.

Sarah Munden – Mrs. Rutherford Smith's maid – also revealed details of the affair. She had been, she explained, her mistress's "confidential maid" for nearly seven years and had frequently seen her with Monsignor Capel. Every time he visited, her mistress would "warn me to keep out of the way," she said.

An astute observer, Munden noted the state of the bed linen after his departure. "I used to put out clean linen when ever Mgr. Capel came to see my Mistress and I always had to wash it privately after he had left her," she remarked. "My Mistress [sic] linen should not be in that condition unless her husband came to see her which he did not." It was clear that Capel was "constantly committing adultery" with her mistress; she had often confirmed that fact to her, she said.

This faceless, almost anonymous woman, Mrs. Rutherford Smith, had a colourful history. Although invariably mentioned without reference to her character or past, our research has unearthed a complex background of privilege and poverty, of youthful happiness cruelly curtailed, of an escape to the bright lights of London, and of disappointing involvements with men, including Monsignor Capel.

Clara Dolman, which was her maiden name, was born in 1853, in Stockwell, South-West London. Her father, Frederick, who was a "gentleman" and "fundholder," later moved his family to the village of Sampford Peverell, Devon, where he was "respected and esteemed by all who knew him," a report in *The Taunton Courier* noted in 1877. He raised his large family in a seven-bedroom home, with three substantial reception rooms, a coach house, stable, and walled garden, set in an acre-and-a-half of ground.

Frederick Dolman was sufficiently wealthy to send Clara to Newland House, an expensive boarding school for young ladies in Sherborne, where fees were set at 30 – 60 guineas a year, depending on age. Not long after she completed her education, she met John Hoadley Rutherford Smith, a "gentleman" and banker's son, who she married at the age of 21. It seemed the perfect match. Unfortunately, it soon turned to tragedy.

The couple's two children died soon after birth. A short time later, Rutherford Smith's finances went into freefall. Friction developed with his father-in-law, who he called upon to help settle his debts. The conflict between the two men resulted in Frederick Dolman inserting a notice in the local newspaper which declared: "I will not be responsible for any debt or debts incurred by any member of my family without consent of myself or wife in writing."

The newspaper notice, published in January 1879, coincided with the breakdown in the couple's relationship. Not long afterwards, Clara, who was then in her mid-20s, left her husband and headed for London. There, she lived off small family trust funds, residing for a time at the Golden Cross Hotel and at houses where she rented apartments. It was at that time that she met Monsignor Capel.

Reports soon surfaced of the relationship, prompted by Capel's easily-recognised features and the growing gossip surrounding his lifestyle. Two Brothers of the Little Oratory delivered accounts of him entering Mrs. Rutherford Smith's ground-floor apartment, which was located in the same house they were living in at Montpelier Square, Knightsbridge. The Monsignor visited several times a week, arriving in the evening at around 9 pm and staying until 11 pm or 11.30 pm, they informed Cardinal Manning.

Mrs. Rutherford Smith's husband – the couple were still formally married – was made aware of the rumours. He received two notes by post, both of them anonymous, alerting him to what was going on. "I caution you as I have had to caution others against allowing your wife to go to luncheon so often at Monsignor Capel's. Her friendship with Monsignor Capel is more than of an ordinary character and you had better come to London to sever the acquaintance," he was warned by one of the correspondents.

He initially ignored the communications – one was a letter; the other a postcard – before eventually deciding to travel from his home in Southampton to the capital. What followed had consequences for all concerned – for Monsignor Capel, Mr. and Mrs. Rutherford Smith, the Diocese of Westminster, the Rev. Walter Croke Robinson, and even for Propaganda Fide in Rome and the Holy Office. It would also make the Rutherford Smiths well known in the clubs, parlours and tea rooms of London.

John Hoadley Rutherford Smith arrived in the capital in the autumn of 1880, where he heard "evil reports" about the activities of Monsignor Capel. Two or three acquaintances, he said, informed him of what was taking place. He subsequently spoke to his wife, who "thought it only just to admit to me her adultery with Monsignor Capel in order that I might if I thought proper take steps with the view of obtaining a divorce."

He then went in search of evidence to use in court. He did so by visiting his wife's previous landlords. "I have communicated with the landlord of one of the houses where she had apartments who tells me that although he could not actually prove the deed, his suspicions had been frequently aroused in consequence of Monsignor Capel's constant visits at all hours added to the fact that he (Mgr. Capel) paid her account there which was £25 (twenty-five pounds)," he wrote after one of those visits.

One Saturday, towards the end of November, Rutherford Smith went to Confession, to the Rev. Walter Croke Robinson, at the Pro-Cathedral, Kensington. In the course of his Confession, he happened to mention his troubles of mind. Robinson, who had investigated Capel on Cardinal Manning's behalf and who was still collecting evidence concerning his behaviour, was most interested in what he heard. He first advised Rutherford Smith to talk to Cardinal Manning, but he was reluctant to do so. Fr. Robinson then suggested he should call to his private residence on the following Monday, at ten o'clock.

On Monday, Rutherford Smith arrived at 79 Abingdon Road, Kensington, at the appointed hour. He repeated all he had said two days before. It was during that discussion that the seeds of conflict and misunderstanding were sown. Robinson regarded this second conversation as being outside the scope of the Confessional and therefore no longer subject to its rules of secrecy. His visitor later claimed that he believed the conversation to be a continuation of his Confession; otherwise, he remarked, "I would not have repeated what I had said."

Afterwards, Fr. Robinson spoke to Cardinal Manning and to the Rev. C. Harrington Moore of the Pro-Cathedral about the new information he had gleaned about Capel during his Monday meeting. As far as Manning was concerned, it was the ultimate betrayal by Capel, who was not only ignoring the agreement reached in Rome but was flagrantly continuing his sexual activities in London. When Rutherford Smith was made aware of the meetings, he claimed the *Sigillum Confessionis*, or Seal of Confession, had been broken.

Capel was outraged when he heard of Fr. Robinson's involvement in what was soon to become known as "The Kensington Confession Case". Not only was he shocked that his adversary was continuing to accumulate evidence against him, but he also saw an opportunity to take revenge against a priest who had become such a personal and professional threat. Memories of Robinson's role at the Commission of Investigation must have haunted him as he sat down to communicate his anger to the Diocese of Westminster.

"I charge the Revd. Mr. Robinson with having maliciously maligned me during the past four years and at last with having used the confessional for this purpose," he wrote to Canon Gilbert, the Vicar General, sarcastically using the title "Mr." to diminish Fr. Robinson. The priest, he added in another letter to Gilbert, "leaves the impression that he is authorised by ecclesiastical superiors to get up a case against me." He protested that he "ought to have protection at once against the malevolence of Revd. Mr. Robinson."

Following a meeting with Capel, Rutherford Smith charged Fr. Robinson with having divulged what he had told him in Confession. The complaint went to Manning along with Propaganda Fide and the Holy Office. It was a serious accusation which, if substantiated, could have resulted in Robinson being forbidden to exercise his ecclesiastical functions. The issue was publicised widely, causing the priest much embarrassment.

Capel simultaneously launched an attack on Robinson through the press. Not wanting to identify himself as the source of the attack, he turned to one of his Pious Ladies, Mrs. Annie Gomess. Handing her a manuscript on which he outlined the case against Robinson, he asked her to copy it in her own hand and to send it to the newspapers pretending to be a "poor Protestant outsider" baffled by what had occurred.

Referring to Fr. Robinson, who was a convert, as an "ex-parson," the letter described how he had heard a man's Confession and then told him "to call at a private address" where he "asked him to repeat what had been said." That he had later divulged what he had been told would surely sit badly with "born Catholics," the writer claimed.

The ex-parson was clearly trying to "get up a case" against another priest, the letter alleged. The phrase "get up a case" was exactly the same as the phrase used by the Monsignor in his earlier correspondence with Canon Gilbert. Mrs. Gomess later confirmed that the letter had been drawn up by Capel and rewritten by her at the Monsignor's request, to be furthered to the press.

What followed was a shambles of major proportions. Rutherford Smith threatened to name Monsignor Capel as co-respondent in a divorce action against his wife. His solicitor, George Lewis, although convinced that "criminal intimacy" had occurred, was reluctant to pursue the action because of the scandal that would ensue. The Vicar General and Cardinal Manning were no doubt relieved to hear the news of the solicitor's reluctance. Capel, too, must have breathed a sigh of relief.

Clara Rutherford Smith embarked on another affair – with a Captain Graves, who lived in St. John's Wood, London. One day, her husband spotted the couple in Bond Street, where they were entering a cab. He followed them in another cab and watched as they alighted at a house in Hamilton Gardens. He found out that they were residing there as man and wife. A court action followed in 1885, and the couple were formally divorced that December.

Not long afterwards, in 1886, Mr. Rutherford Smith married again, to Edith Mary Place, in Somerset. By then, he had withdrawn the breach-of-secrecy case against the Rev. Walter Croke Robinson who, although he escaped censure, had his name dragged through the halls of Propaganda Fide and the Holy Office. Robinson was also threatened with court action by Capel, but that never materialised, either.

The biggest loser turned out to be the Monsignor. His attempts to turn the spotlight on Fr. Robinson weren't quite as successful as he had hoped. Instead, the spotlight shone on him. Tongues wagged and jaws dropped as mountains of tittle-tattle surfaced in Kensington and elsewhere. Unfortunately, to paraphrase Capel's contemporary Oscar Wilde, many of those "monstrous" bits of gossip muttered behind his back had the ring of being "absolutely and entirely true."

INFAMY AND DISGRACE

Victorian Gossips

The High Street Kensington Railway Refreshment Room was a flourishing centre for gossip in Victorian West London. Run by the caterers Spiers and Pond, the venue, with its floral displays, spindly coat stands, upholstered seats and fine tablecloths, attracted travellers and locals alike. They came not only for the moderately priced quality food but to hear news of actress Sarah Bernhardt's financial troubles, socialite and actress Lillie Langtry's affair with the Prince of Wales, and details of who was – or who was *not* – invited to the latest garden party or society ball.

With the sound of shrill whistles, hiss of steam, slamming of carriage doors, and clatter of rushing feet as a backdrop, it was at the "Kensington Railway Restaurant," as Capel called it, that Mr. Rutherford Smith "indiscriminately" divulged details of his wife's affair. He repeatedly did so, the Monsignor alleged. "In this way he has proclaimed the matter, and it is not surprising that the papers have got hold of it," he said.

Victorian gossip columnists loved hearing news of Capel's exploits and misfortunes. "The greatest mystery still prevails with regard to the ruin, public and complete, which has so suddenly overtaken that spoiled child of the Roman Catholic Church, Monsignor Capel," the compiler of a popular London gossip column commented. Another hinted at his womanising. "Monsignor is very popular with the ladies" was how the writer delicately put it.

A further columnist wrote of the "busy tongues and malevolent imaginations" which were ripping apart this "drawing-room man of the Roman Catholic hierarchy." Notable detractors included *The Whitehall Review* which, having described Capel as a priest whose troubles had made his hair "prematurely silvered," remarked: "A clerical wag once said of him that he had 'made many converts, but not one Catholic.' There is a spice of truth in this joke, for strange fish have come into Monsignor's net."

Titbits like these helped pass the time in London clubs – among them the Reform, Garrick, Carlton, and the Union where a member once described how, sitting by the fire before settling into haunch of mutton and apple tart, he would converse with lawyers, merchants, MPs and gentlemen at large, and "if Lady Harrington happen to drive past our window in her landau, we compare her equipage to the Algerine Ambassador's." The news of Capel's adventures with women was like gold dust among these gentlemen, the finest of London society.

Apart from idle gossip at clubs, soirées, ladies' afternoon tea parties or below stairs among servants, the Royal Mail helped keep the Monsignor's notoriety alive in the early 1880s. Up to 12 mail deliveries were made each day in London, with letters arriving shortly after being posted, replies returning within hours, and news travelling fast. Nowhere was the impact of the postal service – the email system of its day – more profoundly felt than at Cardinal Manning's office.

"Cannot you by some means arrest the fearful scandal that has fallen upon our blessed Church thro the disgraceful conduct of Monsignor Capel," T. O'Grady, one of Manning's numerous correspondents, wrote in January 1880. "The tales circulating and daily multiplying of his reckless extravagance, of his profligacy with Catholic women (one even followed him to Rome last year) whose money and presents have mainly supported him for years, is distressing....His removal from London would greatly assist in quieting these matters."

Capel is an "arch-swindler and liar," the Rev. George Angus remarked in another letter to Manning. "What a pity to see an able man ruined by ambition, drink, and etc. etc. This I hear on all sides – everywhere," he said. A further correspondent was equally exasperated. "I have on more than one occasion seen females issuing from his Confessional with a smile on their faces, which was far from edifying," he remarked.

Barrister and future MP James Carew also wrote to the Cardinal: "In conversation some time ago with a solicitor of high standing and acknowledged prudence, he stated that if your Eminence had known as much as he did, you would have been 'bound' not merely to refuse to renew his faculties but to suspend him....only on Monday last, a member of my profession and a Protestant told me that his conduct has been, and is, freely discussed in many circles."

Even the Rev. Walter Croke Robinson entered the fray, writing that "innumerable enquiries on all sides have been made as to why the scoundrel is not suspended? Why is the agony prolonged?" Capel is "so utterly lost to all that is good, that kindness is thrown away upon him," he claimed. Although he is "fighting and threatening just as much as ever," Robinson assured Manning he would bring him "one or two more scandals before long." He was, he said, "on the scent."

Robinson need not have worried about finding new evidence as two of Capel's closest allies – both from his inner coterie of Pious Ladies – had lost faith in the Monsignor and were revealing his darkest secrets. Mrs. Annie Gomess and Mrs. Fanny Geldard were the ladies in question. Each had inside knowledge of his late-night trysts, dubious financial dealings, underhand methods, and self-aggrandising publicity campaigns. If it was gossip you wanted, they had it.

No one was more damning of Capel than Annie Gomess, who had supported him during his rise to fame and who had written letters to the press on his behalf. In a formal interview with Vincent Harting, solicitor to the Diocese of Westminster, she disclosed details about the Monsignor's "criminal intimacies." Apart from listing nine affairs, with names supplied, she said there was a previously-unknown case involving a woman he had made pregnant and a subsequent abortion he had arranged.

Around Christmas 1881, Gomess explained, Monsignor Capel had come to her "in great agitation" and disclosed that "a lady was with child, and said it was by him." The pregnancy, which was two-and-a-half months old, would be "the utter ruin of her and of himself," he said. In the course of their conversation, Gomess mentioned that when she lived in India a physician had told her that if she ever again became pregnant she could die.

The physician had given her a prescription "to be taken in the first month," she remarked to Capel, who immediately insisted on acquiring it. She refused to hand it to him for some time, but eventually she did so. "He returned the prescription a few days after saying he had acted on it," she noted. He added ominously that "now she was as much implicated as himself."

It wasn't the only threat Capel issued to Gomess. At another time, he stood over her and forced her to write a letter to the Pope by using "great violence, holding a poker in his hand." The letter complained about the behaviour of Cardinal Manning, the Vicar General, and Mr. Harting, the diocesan solicitor. She wasn't even aware of what she was writing as the letter was dictated to her in French. Later, she retracted the remarks, saying they were forced from her by Monsignor Capel.

Gomess also described how Capel took an interest in her 18-year-old daughter. Every time he visited her house, he would kiss her. One evening, on arriving at the house, he found she was alone. He locked the door and blew out the light. Her daughter immediately stood up and unlocked the door again. Her two sons, who studied at Capel's school, were so annoyed with his behaviour towards their sister that they threatened to "thrash" him.

She additionally revealed that she had copied letters written by the Monsignor and sent them to the newspapers. The letter concerning Rutherford Smith and Fr. Robinson was one of them; others condemned Cardinal Manning. The purpose of the latter, she explained, was "to show that Catholics ought to put their confidence rather in him (Capel) than in the Cardinal." She had a boxful of these letters, including articles, which Capel was trying to get his hands on.

By the early 1880s, both Mrs. Gomess and her Pious Ladies colleague Mrs. Geldard were simultaneously distancing themselves from Monsignor Capel. Each had her own way of doing so. Gomess remained on intimate terms with the Monsignor while condemning him to others. Geldard, on the other hand, made her feelings outwardly known, with the result that the Monsignor threatened legal proceedings against her. Indeed, she said, he threatened to indict everyone who spoke against him, including Cardinal Manning.

Geldard was disgusted by Capel's "iniquitous and scandalous career." She identified numerous affairs, previously unknown, which he had indulged in. One involved a woman "of light reputation," another was an aristocrat "of similar fame," a third a convert he had "seduced." There also was a Mrs. Franklin, whose home he visited "almost every evening remaining very late." More worrying was another woman, also named, whose "child from this year was Monsignor's," she was told.

Geldard also knew the 18-year-old occasional teacher who Capel would invite to Cedar Villa and who we briefly heard about earlier in this book. Her name was Mademoiselle Ackbar, and she taught at his girls' school in Kensington. Ackbar, who was described by another Pious Lady as "very light and fast in manner and dress," informed Geldard that Capel had "often called her into his room to sit alone with him" and that once "she offended him, for he asked her to stay and have some wine with him in his room....and she refused."

Ackbar further told Geldard that, on one occasion, she had gone to Confession at the nearby Carmelite Church in Kensington and was upset by what the priest had said. She mentioned this to Capel, who was clearly alarmed. He asked her what she had been questioned about and what she had answered. On hearing that the confessor had told her to avoid a certain priest, he said he presumed the remark referred to him.

Capel then warned Mademoiselle Ackbar that "she was to consult him as to her Confessions, and that he would tell her what it was necessary to say." He would "direct her," he said. He then kissed her and petted her, and laid her head upon his chest, saying "he would not have his darling child worried by any priests."

Geldard was also concerned by the chaos at the girls' school in Kensington, which Capel had asked her to help superintend. She ended up taking charge of the two senior classes, as there was no Head Mistress. She also assisted Capel with his personal affairs. In addition, she was obliged, due to staff shortages, to "run backwards and forwards" to one of the boys' school residences, where she would prepare their meals. Discipline was non-existent at the schools, she said, and she decided to leave.

In retaliation, Capel refused to issue her son a certificate which he was due to receive from the public school. The matter caused an acrimonious and lengthy battle between Geldard and the Monsignor. It wasn't the first time he had used this tactic, she discovered – he had also refused another boy, Percy Hughes, his certificate because he had chosen to attend the Carmelites on Sundays and not Capel's private Mass. The boy was distraught and begged his father to take him home.

Tired of the mayhem and madness, the scandal and deceit, Fanny Geldard finally departed the service of Monsignor Capel. "It is all so awful that I seem to be in a dream," she wrote in a letter. "Nothing that Mgr. Capel attempted would astonish me, he is daring, unprincipled and insane enough for anything," she added. "He is so bold, and shameless, I have no doubt that he must be insane."

Throughout the period from 1880 up to early 1882, Monsignor Capel suffered reputational meltdown in the eyes of the British public and press. The glowing media tributes of a few years earlier were replaced by news of his financial problems, loss of priestly functions, and disappearance from the pulpits of Westminster and elsewhere. Former friends shunned him. Patrons and sponsors, who had once bankrolled him, disappeared. He was forced to live off funds provided by Sarah Parish Dillon, his American-born benefactor who was one of the few remaining people willing to support his lifestyle and activities.

His family were also affected by his fall from grace. His brother, Arthur, and sister-in-law, Berthe, wished for him to baptise their new son, Arthur Jnr., who was born in September 1881. "I write humbly to ask your Eminence the favour to allow the child to be baptised by my brother-in-law Mgr. Capel and to allow the baptism to take place in my brother-in-law's private oratory at Kensington," Berthe wrote to Cardinal Manning, shortly after the birth. The reply was immediate – permission was refused.

Denied his rights to practise as a priest, Capel turned his attention to unusual pursuits, including inventing and patenting a flying machine. The machine was like a cab on wheels, with a light, strong mast rising from the centre, and wings that could be inclined according to whether the operator wished to ascend, descend or remain horizontal. It was to be fitted with propellers and driven by steam, gas or electric engine. The contrivance was very much "in nubibus" – up in the clouds – according to the popular weekly illustrated newspaper *The Graphic*, "but we hardly think that it will ever rise to those regions in reality."

A further favourite occupation of Capel's – attending social occasions – was no longer as it once had been. In earlier times, he had graced the stateliest mansions and finest dining rooms of London; now, he was reduced to guest appearances at publicity launches and minor commercial events. One of them involved travelling on the trial-run sailing of a new passenger steamboat, the *Glen Rosa*, from London to the watering places of the east and south-east coasts, including Clacton-on-Sea.

Another concerned the launch of a new Pullman car train – "with compartments for luggage and servants" – which travelled from London's Victoria Station to Brighton. It was on that rain-drenched trip that he met Boston-born newspaper correspondent Arthur Warren, who filled Capel's mind with stories of the wonders of America. "As we parted at Victoria, he invited me to dine at his house, making an appointment for the following week," Warren recalled in his book, *London Days*.

A week later, the two men sat together in Capel's study, with the fire-glow playing over the room as the twilight faded into darkness. On the left wall was a large photograph of Pope Pius IX featuring members of his household, including Monsignor Capel. Other walls were decorated with a dozen or more photographs of celebrities. Although Capel, who was dressed in his cassock and biretta, looked dignified, Warren remarked that his star was clearly fading.

Many matters were discussed, including Capel's obsession with Cardinal Manning. Warren wondered why the Cardinal "had thrown his influence against the captivating Monsignor." Whatever the reason, he mused: "When the Cardinal was against a man in his flock, that man's chances for preferment, and even for holding his own, were not worth discussing." The conflict between the two men, of course, had multiple roots. Soon, those of a financial nature came into sharp focus as Capel faced ignominy in the London Bankruptcy Court.

BANKRUPTCY

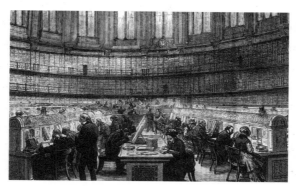

British Museum Reading Room

The Reading Room of the British Museum became a popular haunt for Monsignor Capel during his bankruptcy proceedings in 1880 and 1881. He could be found there regularly, hard at work, surrounded by a motley assortment of scholars, researchers and eccentrics, some of whom were equally busily occupied, others sleeping, snoring, coughing, wheezing, or chattering with their friends.

With his manner "as suave and as refined as ever," Capel fitted in with the Reading Room's atmosphere and clientele. Fellow readers included Mark Twain, Charles Dickens and Oscar Wilde. The impoverished Karl Marx had spent long days writing *Das Kapital* at seat G7. Lenin, seated at J8, studied and wrote there later on. Capel was another of its famous readers, visiting while sorting out details pertaining to his fall from financial grace.

Revealing "a tinge of care and anxiety in his manner," as one observer noted, Capel set about unravelling the dire state of his personal and professional finances. Matters looked bleak. According to information presented at the opening day of his bankruptcy proceedings, his secured personal debts amounted to £18,556 and unsecured debts were £7,295. On the other hand, his personal assets were given bluntly as "nil."

When translated into a rough equivalent today, the size of his personal indebtedness – in excess of three million pounds – was substantial. That figure, of course, excluded most of the debts outstanding on his education projects, which were even more alarming. Add in that he had kept no proper accounts and the challenge he faced in the London Bankruptcy Court was formidable.

Capel might have been wise to reach up his hand and take from the shelves of the Reading Room a copy of his old acquaintance Charles Dickens' relatively recent work, *David Copperfield*. "Annual income twenty pounds, annual expenditure nineteen nineteen six, result happiness. Annual income twenty pounds, annual expenditure twenty pounds ought and six, result misery," Mr. Micawber advised the young David Copperfield. Take the latter path, he concluded, and "you are forever floored."

It was a pleasurable half-mile walk from the British Museum, past Bloomsbury Square, down to Lincoln's Inn Fields, where Monsignor Capel, then aged 43, put in his first appearances at the London Bankruptcy Court in the summer of 1880. Those pleasant strolls contrasted sharply with the grim decor and dour atmosphere of the court itself, where the Registrar, William Powell Murray, and a cluster of barristers in tired, poorly-powdered wigs, awaited him.

"What we note on entering the court while business is doing, is a lack of everything agreeing with one's ideas of the dignity and majesty of justice, and a general aspect of wear and tear, not to say shabbiness, about the denizens of the place, and also of the place itself. The court room is small and inconveniently crowded, and it is with difficulty that we are able to edge in sideways and take post against the wall," wrote a correspondent for the popular Victorian-era periodical, *The Leisure Hour*.

Victorians loved reading daily courtroom reports in the press, especially those concerning Monsignor Capel. He was, after all, no ordinary merchant – no shopkeeper, tailor, pawnbroker or cheesemonger – but a notable luminary. Everyone was obsessed with his bankruptcy. Newspapers obliged with details of his negligence and extravagance, and with hints of his dishonesty. The bleak particulars, involving his failed mortgage repayments, loans and gifts from star-struck female admirers, were read with relish in parlours and public houses.

There was a surfeit of unsavoury information to digest, including mouth-watering testimony provided by Capel's near-neighbour Sarah Parish Dillon, the rich American widow who featured earlier in this book. She had known Capel since 1866, she said, when her late husband had advanced him money. In March 1874, Capel had asked her for more – a loan of £500 – and she met his request. She could not say if the loan was made for private or Church purposes; it was made to him as a friend.

Capel looked for additional money in August of that year, when she gave him a further £100. She took no receipt for it, she explained, as "Catholics were not in the habit of taking acknowledgements from priests." She loaned him a further £550 in March 1877 and was unsure for what purpose it was intended. She had also, as we saw in an earlier chapter, acted as one of the guarantors for the lease of St. Anne's Home and was out of pocket as a result.

By the end of her summation, Mrs. Dillon had tendered proof that Capel owed her a total sum amounting to £5,924, of which £3,848 was admitted. That final sum of £3,848 translates to approximately half a million pounds today. Capel, in evidence, accepted that this figure referred only to loans, adding that there were also many gifts. In return for the money she had given him, only the sum of £50 had been repaid, Dillon revealed.

Another of the Monsignor's dedicated followers – Alice Wilmot Chetwode, who had been converted by Capel at Pau and had later worked for him in Kensington – also turned up at the bankruptcy hearings. She was soon in deep trouble. Suspected of making a fraudulent claim against Capel's assets, which resulted in the impounding of her documents, she avoided a substantial legal penalty by the skin of her teeth.

In an effort to be a first-ranked creditor against Capel's property, Chetwode had submitted a falsely-dated deed for a £1,000 loan she had made to Capel. The date under her signature was eight months earlier than the date on the legal stamp verifying the signature. It was clear to all who subsequently viewed the document – including the judge – that the date beneath the signature had been falsely inserted in an attempt to establish her as the leading creditor and the first in line to be paid.

"So suspicious did the Master in Chancery think the matter that he ordered the deed to be impounded," the Rev. P. Fenton, a priest who closely followed the case, informed Cardinal Manning. It was also suggested that Monsignor Capel must have been involved in, or was at least knowledgeable of, the scheme. Both Chetwode and Capel were at one stage threatened with prison as a result of the attempted fraud. Chetwode immediately relinquished her claim, and in return, imprisonment was avoided.

It took eight months to resolve Capel's personal bankruptcy, which was largely due, the judge said, to his failure to keep proper accounts. The lack of proper financial details resulted in interminable rows over the admissibility of debts and the value of assets. In the end, Capel was made bankrupt for £28,000, "on his own reckless speculations," as Cardinal Manning remarked.

What occurred at the London Bankruptcy Court was only part of the picture. The Cardinal was also in direct receipt of demands for repayment of more than £6,000 worth of Capel's debts which had accrued in London and Dublin. In addition, Capel demanded £6,000 from the Cardinal, arguing that he had invested that amount of his own money in University College, and it needed to be repaid.

In the end, Manning compromised by paying Capel £3,000 while also forgiving him a debt of £1,000. "He could have proved nothing against us," the Cardinal remarked, yet he received a total of £4,000. The whole affair cost Manning £10,000 – about one and a quarter million pounds in today's money – leading a Bishop to comment that the Cardinal was now "poorer than a Church mouse and drained to the last farthing by Mgr. Capel's affairs at Kensington."

"This was a heavy cross, a grave scandal, a grave hindrance to the work of Catholic education, and a postponement of any College for

Higher Studies to an indefinite future," Manning commented on the implications for his University College. For a time, the institution limped on but was shut down in 1882, as was the boys' public school, bringing to a close the grand schemes of the "Educator of Kensington", Monsignor Capel.

Capel's ownership of his beloved Cedar Villa also came to an inglorious end. The unravelling of his tangled financial affairs revealed that in November 1878, in his scramble to raise money, he had mortgaged the property for the sum of £1,200. He had also mortgaged for £600 the adjoining property, Scarsdale Lodge, which he had been using to house students.

Mortgage payments on both properties had fallen into arrears, resulting in judgements being obtained against him for Cedar Villa, which he lived in, and also for Scarsdale Lodge. His last remaining benefactor, the wealthy Mrs. Dillon, sorted out the Cedar Villa problem by acquiring the property when it came up for sale in 1880. She immediately moved in, employing five staff to cook and perform general housework.

Meanwhile, Capel, who was forced to live next door in Scarsdale Lodge, refused to recognise a court order requiring him to leave and barricaded himself inside. Dillon sorted out this problem, too, by taking over the house and allowing Capel to remain in residence. The 1881 United Kingdom census shows him residing there along with his Irish-born housekeeper, Anne Collins, and domestic servant, Margaret Collins, a Londoner. In that census return, Capel described his occupation as "Prelate of the Pope."

In the meantime, his household effects and personal belongings – which had been guarded for some time by a bailiff at Cedar Villa – were presented for sale. London was enveloped in a dense, freezing fog as the sale, by court order, got under way. The city had rarely seen such bad weather. Footmen carrying burning torches led carriages down Fleet Street. Regent's Park was covered in ice. Theatres were half empty; the streets were mostly deserted and silent. The city, as one newspaper put it, was under the rigid sway of Jack Frost.

Despite the dismal weather, London's society queens and their distinguished husbands, along with ordinary citizens, crammed into the dining room at Cedar Villa, where the auction took place. The room was "crowded to suffocation," it was said. It was noted by one observer that those present were, in the main, coldly indifferent and just plain nosy, and their objective was not the desire to buy.

"There is always something inexpressibly sad in the dispersion of the familiar objects of a household," one newspaper columnist remarked. In the case of Cedar Villa, this sense of heartbreak and regret was even more pronounced, he wrote. Not only was Cedar Villa decorated under Monsignor Capel's personal direction, but the sense of sadness at its demise was increased "by the knowledge of the extreme pride and pleasure the house and all its surroundings had afforded to its reverend occupant."

Up for auction were the paintings, furniture, sculptures, and various other antiques and literary curiosities. There were several ecclesiastical items, including the elaborately-painted altar in Capel's private chapel, a mother-of-pearl reliquary representing the Stable of Bethlehem, a beautifully-modelled statuette of the Virgin Mary in Italian Carrara marble, and a marble bust of Christ by the famous American sculptor, Edmonia Lewis.

Other items were of a more personal nature, including 30 dozen bottles of wine, the marble bust of Capel which had stood in the reception room window, and a large presentation album of unique design and with mechanical movements which had been presented to the Monsignor as a gift. The album had an inscription on the silver plate fixed to its walnut stand: "Presented to the Right Rev. Monsignor Capel by the masters and pupils of his school, on the anniversary of his birthday." That gift had been handed to him only three months before the auction.

"It is not without a feeling of regret that one sees so unique a collection scattered to the winds," commented one newspaper which took an interest in the sale. "The library in itself was large and wonderfully interesting. The paintings comprised gems of the greatest masters. In the private chapel there were wondrous shrines and ecclesiastical ornaments of the rarest workmanship. There were exquisite pieces of sculpture, and there was furniture the value of which depended no less on its tastefulness than its antiquity. The residence was at once a museum in interest and a home in comfort, and that is what can be said of few men's houses."

Another newspaper remarked: "One can understand now why Cardinal Manning, who eats dry biscuits at a wedding party and toys with a crust of toast when all others around him are feasting their full, did not number himself among the admirers of the brilliant and eloquent man of society who attempted so unsuccessfully to found a Roman Catholic university in the midst of liberty-loving and free-thinking London."

The prices secured at the auction were surprisingly low. The marble bust of Christ by Edmonia Lewis sold for £3, the Stable of Bethlehem reliquary reached £6, the bust of Capel went for £7, the mechanical presentation album brought in three guineas, while the Carrara marble statuette of the Virgin Mary did somewhat better, selling for 24 guineas. A number of watercolours, drawings, engravings and photographs fetched only small amounts.

The money obtained for the paintings was even more disappointing. Raffaelle's *A Virgin and Child* was knocked down for a mere £3. 10s. Domenichino's *The Assumption of the Virgin* went for 20 guineas, while Van Dyke's *Our Saviour on the Cross* also secured 20 guineas. The low prices were attributed to doubts about the authenticity of the paintings. Overall, the three-day sale realised about £1,700, which was helped by the 200 guineas achieved for the altar.

The most poignant and heartbreaking moment arrived with the announcement of the sale of Beppo, the black collie dog who was once the light of the Monsignor's life. This was the dog who would refuse food supposedly given to him by Bismarck but would scoff it when it was said to come from the Pope. He was always a favourite with visitors to Cedar Villa.

"The poor animal, friendly as ever, has, like everything else, been allowed to get out of condition," an observer to the sale recalled. "He is looking fat and old, as if he would not growl at Bismarck and wag his tail for the Pope much longer." He, too, had to go, bringing to completeness the ruin of a man who had not only squandered his empire but had lost a companion who was his closest friend of all.

As Capel surveyed his shattered life, he identified the one last place he could turn to for redemption. He had been badly wronged, he believed, and demanded that his "honour as a priest of God" should be "vindicated against the malicious calumnies and false accusations of evil people." Where else could the "fullest investigation" take place than in that great seat of ecclesiastical power, the Vatican? There, he hoped, his case could be finally brought to rest.

THE RECKONING

Rome, 1880s

S hortly after arriving in Rome, in February 1882, Monsignor Capel visited Cardinal Jacobini, Vatican Secretary of State, who was effectively the Pope's Prime Minister. He climbed the straight, seemingly-endless staircase to the Cardinal's top-floor study, where the statesman – of imposing appearance but unimposing manner – received him cautiously. Capel had arrived without a letter of introduction, which put Jacobini on guard.

The Monsignor presented the Secretary of State with a copy of his freshly-published pamphlet, *Great Britain and Rome*. The slim volume – just 70 pages long – argued for re-establishing diplomatic relations between the two jurisdictions, which had been broken since the Reformation. After declaring his devotion to the Holy See and explaining his great influence in England, "especially with the English priests," Capel made a bold proposition.

"What about using my influence to further diplomatic relations with Britain," he suggested to Jacobini. The Secretary of State replied "civilly but cautiously" and pointed out that there was a British MP, Mr. George Errington, already performing the role of intermediary. He would continue to use Errington as his "interpreter with the English Government," he stated, and declined "to employ any other." He later checked with visiting English priests, asking, "Who is that man, Monsignor Capel?"

Always feeling at home and protected in Rome, Capel based himself in the city for much of 1882 and the first half of 1883, only returning to London on a brief visit. While claiming through the press that he had been officially summoned by the Pope – who, he said, commanded him not to leave – the truth was that he was there of his own volition, partly drawn by the bustle of the city's streets, the deep-blue sky and bright sun, the prospect of meeting friends old and new, and the fact that he was broke.

Rome was awash with money, which Capel was desperately short of. Luckily, he had contacts. One of them was Mrs. Linden, the wife of a wealthy American banker, who helped finance his visit. Another was a rich American lady, Madame Reggio, who was happy to pay for his accommodation at the elegant Hotel Quirinale, situated on Via Nazionale, one of the most fashionable streets in Rome.

The Quirinale was ideally located close to Propaganda Fide and not far from the Vatican. It was expensive, costing Capel's benefactress 4,000 francs for his stay. As it turned out, on departure, an extra 700 francs was added to his bill largely for wine and spirits delivered to his room. Madame Reggio was far from pleased and wished she had known "enough of her guest to be on her guard."

Of course, Capel was also in Rome for a purpose. He had arrived to finally discredit Cardinal Manning and his fellow "conspirators" and "calumniators," to overturn the negative outcome of the Diocesan Commission of Investigation, and to secure help in having his faculties as a priest fully restored. Ideally, he hoped to return to the Diocese of Westminster, although that seemed unlikely. A new role was needed – something suitable to his intellect and abilities – and nothing could be better than the position of international mediator between two great powers.

Never one to miss an opportunity for publicity, Capel contacted his newspaper friends at home to inform them of his imaginary assignment as diplomatic intermediary. One British broadsheet reported that the "Roman Correspondent" of *The Standard* – who they knew to be none other than the Monsignor – had announced that "communications between the Vatican and Great Britain will be maintained by flying visits of Monsignor Capel."

In Paris, the coverage – no doubt also written by Capel – was similarly upbeat. *Le Soir* reported that the Monsignor's "recent visit to the Eternal City has produced considerable sensation there in political circles, on account of his lengthy and frequent conferences with his Eminence Cardinal Jacobini." The visit to Rome of this "staunch advocate of the propriety of the English Government being represented at the Vatican and *vice versa*" was "not without political significance," the newspaper remarked.

Fanny Geldard, who knew the Monsignor's methods all too well, was angered and bemused when she read the news reports. "They bear the mark of Mgr. Capel's style, and can only emanate from his pen," she wrote to the Vicar General in London. "I have heard that he states among his entourage that he is the accredited 'Roman Correspondent' to the English papers....I fear he will do as much harm in Rome, or even more than he did here."

Cardinal Jacobini, when he was informed of the press coverage, was furious. He assured the Diocese of Westminster that not only had he "never authorised Mgr. Capel in any one way to act as his agent or interpreter," or act on behalf of the Vatican, but that "those paragraphs in the papers were entirely unauthorised by him or, as far as he knew, by anyone in Rome." It was a devastating putdown of the Monsignor's new claim to fame.

The rejection of his diplomatic initiative didn't deter Monsignor Capel. He set about preparing his appeal to Rome, determined that a Vatican tribunal would investigate his treatment by Cardinal Manning and the Diocese of Westminster, and in doing so clear his name. He "called on everybody," it was said, spent innumerable hours at Propaganda Fide and the Holy Office, and left his calling card behind him everywhere he went.

He also entertained extensively. He particularly engaged with visitors from America and England, and with people who were "least respected," it was noted. At one stage, he claimed, "Why, there is not a diplomat in Rome that has not called on me," although that assertion may not be entirely true. His friendship with the press was often commented upon. He was also seen at evening parties, on one occasion being reported as drunk.

Up against Capel, representing Cardinal Manning, was the Very Rev. Robert Butler, the London-born Rector of St. Charles' College, Notting Hill, who was familiar with the Monsignor's history following his role on the Diocesan Commission of Investigation in 1879. A slim, energetic man, with a doctorate in divinity, Butler was a close, trusted friend of Manning and was referred to as his "spiritual son." His personal self-assessment – "I pray hard and work hard" – summed him up. It was no surprise that the Cardinal, who was suffering from a prolonged bout of illness in London, should send him to Rome to act on his behalf.

Unlike Capel, who stayed at a prestigious hotel, Butler took a room at the more modest English College. Again, unlike Capel, he was often short of cash. At one stage, he borrowed 100 francs from the Rector of the college to cover the cost of vetture, the Italian hackney coaches that transported him across the city. He used the money well, repeatedly visiting Propaganda Fide and the Holy Office, engaging with almost every senior administrator in Rome.

Inevitably, the two sparring partners – who had both been born in 1836 – crossed paths on their travels. They were adversaries, so relations were tense. The first time they met was in the anteroom at Propaganda Fide. "We at once exchanged friendly looks and bowed to each other," Butler remarked. The second time was more strained: "We exchanged salutations as before, we were even accidentally left alone, but we each had our own books or notes." The third and final time, they "did not speak" and barely bowed on departure.

Dealing with the Holy Office almost drove Fr. Butler mad. He was hugely unimpressed by one senior administrator, Archbishop Sallua. Another official, Cardinal Laurenzi, irritated him when he expressed the view that "gentle treatment" might work on the Monsignor even though he had a "clear sense of Mgr. Capel's guilt." That viewpoint, Butler remarked, was "sheer ignorance!"

Fr. Butler got on better with Pope Leo XIII, who he met in a private audience. "I had him all to myself," he later remarked. He had been worried in advance about taxing the Pope's patience by dwelling too much on the Capel affair. Deciding to pick his steps carefully, he first presented money donations to the Pontiff, making him "very much pleased." He also presented him with a book.

Butler built up to the burning topic of the day. He started by talking about Cardinal Manning, explaining that he had been ill, suffered a good deal, and would never wish to trouble His Holiness with his anxieties. He continued by explaining how the Cardinal worried about his clergy, the pressure they were under, and how certain decisions had been a trial. "You're talking about Capel," the Pope kindly interjected, breaking the ice. "Yes," Butler replied.

Pope Leo XIII, who was said to "know everything about everybody," focused his keen, bright eyes on Butler and said that Capel's proponents had asked that he should be allowed to preach in Rome. "I would not allow him," the Pontiff stated emphatically. He went on to say that he had decided to send him to Florence, and he could do his preaching there. The Capel case was a delicate one, he remarked, but he would speak to Cardinal Laurenzi about it and "tell him to see into the matter."

When Capel requested a similar private audience, the Pontiff remarked: "I won't see him." Somehow, he managed to secure one. As ever, the Monsignor was nothing if not devious. "There are two or three people in process of conversion, may I hear their Confessions?" he asked. The Holy Father replied: "Yes, you may hear them and them only." The Monsignor took the reply to mean his Confessional rights were restored. He also took the permission to preach in Florence as meaning that his preaching rights were reinstated.

In the end, it wasn't the Pope but 13 Cardinals who adjudicated on the guilt or otherwise of Monsignor Capel. The Monsignor rose to the occasion. He argued that Cardinal Manning was jealous of him; that he was a victim of financial mismanagement by others, was falsely accused of immorality, stopped from teaching by an act of authority, and in consequence he was ruined. He went so far as to claim that "when he was driven to let his effects be sold by auction the Cardinal actually bid for some of them."

This "highest tribunal on God's earth," as Capel called it, considered the case during the unusually wet and stormy month of September 1882. An insider later explained that without Cardinal Manning's presence, the case of Westminster was fatally weakened. Documentary evidence without distinct proofs was dropped, some evidence mysteriously disappeared, and the impression was created that Manning had exaggerated Capel's notoriety.

The resulting decision was an unimpressive compromise. The verdict, as described by Cardinal Laurenzi, was that Capel was "not condemned, but not innocent," with the condition that he must live a good life and demonstrate the possibility of being trusted once more. The finding was neither here nor there. Instead, to many, it was a Jesuitical outcome – a bit like being told: "We accept you are innocent, but don't do it again."

Once more, Capel, the consummate news spinner and publicist, sprang into action. With little concern for subtleties, he contacted London, where the Press Association released details of his "triumph" at Rome. He has been "successful in all the points of his appeal to the Pope," one newspaper subsequently reported. "His trials are over," another broadsheet proclaimed.

He even wrote to a lady friend in Cork, claiming victory: "God be praised, Rome has patiently heard and judged my cause." The "triumph" was also noted in Capel's local newspaper in Waterford, the county of his birth. "The victory is most complete," he was quoted as saying in their report.

He also wrote to his friend, the Rev. Robert Clarke, in London: "My calumniators are beaten along the line at every point. Let me ask you to thank God Omnipotent, and Our Lady of Sorrows." He concluded by pointing out that he could now preach again, had done so "last Sunday," and planned to "do so again next Sunday."

Fr. Butler, writing from Rome, was enraged by the authorities' willingness to consider a one-sided case. Accepting "the word of a guilty man, who's allowed to give testimony for both sides" is "a strange phenomenon," he remarked. Perhaps, he reflected, "there exists a system in Rome which hides bad men." He also wondered why Rome so often left "a great deal to the individual responsibility of the offenders, and after a certain point even abandon cases to the direct control of God."

Although Capel openly expressed jubilation at the verdict, he recognised that his future was most uncertain. Without priestly faculties at Westminster, and with no hope of returning there, he faced the dilemma – after 16 months in Rome – of what exactly he could do. As far as the Vatican was concerned, he was troublesome, time-consuming, and the controversies over his battles with Manning were attracting bad publicity in the press. Cardinal Nina, former Vatican Secretary of State, declared him to be "not a suitable man for holy employments."

"Why doesn't he go and hide in America?" Pope Leo XIII finally said in exasperation. The deal devised by the Pontiff was simple – in return for a letter of recommendation from the Vatican, and being allowed to preach "as far as possible," the Monsignor should depart for America for at least six months, hoping no doubt he might stay there forever. Keeping matters quiet and hiding – "nascondersi" being the Italian word used by the Pope – was to be the basis of the agreement.

The letter of recommendation, which was obtained for this book, makes for interesting reading. In it, Cardinal Simeoni briefly outlines how Monsignor Capel was leaving for America with "the consent of Propaganda" and with the intention of lecturing in different parts of the country. "He is a talented speaker," the letter explained, who would "do good" through his preaching. No mention was made of his troubles at Westminster or the findings of the Commission of Investigation. Nor was any reference made to his sexual misbehaviour or his drinking.

Capel tried for one last concession. He wanted to conduct a "mission" in America on behalf of the Pope, hoping it would enhance his prestige and boost his reputation. The mission he suggested was to collect funds for the Pontiff's Peter's Pence. "Faccia pure" – go ahead – Cardinal

Simeoni told him, but solely with the permission of whatever Bishop whose diocese he ended up in and "let him have the money." It wasn't exactly what the Monsignor wanted to hear, and the proposal was dropped.

At the end of June 1883, Capel packed his bags and bade farewell to Rome. Travelling to the city's Stazione Termini, he passed by sun-drenched sidewalks lined with eucalyptus trees and filled with clerks, bawling newsboys, solemn priests and tourists going about their merry ways. Overcrowded tramway cars and omnibuses rattled through the streets, heading like Capel's carriage to the Piazza dei Cinquecento, facing the railway terminus. A long journey lay ahead – across Europe, through winding tunnels, past lakes and wide rivers, all the way to France, and onwards to England and America.

The Monsignor stopped over in Paris, where he officiated at the funeral of John Ryan, correspondent with *The New York Herald*, who he knew from his visits to the city. He then travelled to London to collect his belongings. While there, he told the press that he was going to America to lecture and preach, and "to transact some business in connection with the Propaganda." Then, without permission, and in a final act of defiance, he said Mass on the high altar at the Carmelite Church, Kensington. He was, as the Rev. Walter Croke Robinson remarked, "bold, insolent, and hard to the last!"

AMERICA

Steamship Arizona

The massive hull of the *Arizona* – the fastest ocean steamship afloat – slipped from Liverpool docks at 3 pm on Saturday, 21 July 1883. It was a dull, leaden, overcast day, but that didn't matter. Instead, Monsignor Capel was invigorated as he stood on deck watching the vessel clear the pier with a rush, shoot into midstream, and head westward for America.

The steamer sailed past Ireland's Hook Head, slid by Capel's birthplace at Ardmore, paused at Queenstown, and then headed off on its nine-day voyage to New York. He was travelling first class, and the 25 guineas ticket was worth it. The ship boasted smoke rooms and ladies' lounge rooms on deck, bath rooms below deck, along with ballrooms, library and piano. The voyage was the finest available on the Atlantic.

There were colourful characters on board. The son of the great robber baron and multimillionaire Jay Gould – notorious for his unscrupulous practices as a financial speculator and railroad magnate – was a first-class passenger. Imre Kiralfy – the famous stage producer who, it was said, could swear in English, German, French, Italian and Hungarian – was in first class, too.

A lesser-known passenger, Mr. Tomkins, was planning to join the Salvation Army and convert America to godliness. He confided the purpose of his visit – a secret – to everyone on board. He even gave a recitation in his cabin for Kiralfy, but the producer wasn't impressed. Joining them, of course, was Monsignor Capel, aged 46, fleeing the chaos left behind in England but explaining that his visit was for rest, recreation and observation.

"We had a delightful passage," Capel later remarked. He described Mr. Tomkins, the prospective Salvation Army recruit, as "a very worthy man" and "very amusing." He particularly enjoyed the company of another guest, Lord Bennett, who was off on a shooting expedition and who he said was "a very pleasant fellow." Young people were also present; he found their antics highly entertaining.

The Monsignor performed priestly duties on the trip. He preached twice to the steerage passengers on the Sunday. There were many Irish emigrants in that part of the ship, he remarked, and they formed the bulk of the congregation. "They looked as though with a fair chance they could do well in the world," he said. Hebrew, theatrical and many poor people were also travelling steerage. Together, they formed "a most mixed congregation," he noted.

On Sunday evening, the *Arizona* arrived off Sandy Hook, the spit of land enclosing the entrance to New York Bay. Guests lined the decks, viewing the hills of New Jersey, Long Island and Staten Island growing purple in the cloudy sunset. The ship's destination, New York City, lay not far away. Early on Monday morning, the vessel was piloted into New York, where it docked at the foot of King Street at 9.30 am.

Relatives, friends and well-wishers crowded the quayside, greeting the new arrivals and travellers returning home. There were hearty farewells on leaving the vessel. The Monsignor was the centre of attention. "He was surrounded by the passengers who had been won by his genial and affable manners during the voyage, and who were desirous to pay their respects to him on parting with such a pleasant companion," a newspaper reporter observed.

Capel looked well as he stepped ashore. "Those who braved the discomforts of early rising in order to meet and greet their friends at the Guion Line pier, saw a tall and exceptionally handsome man, clad in priestly dress," a journalist with *The New York Tribune* noted.

"Time has dealt gently with the Monsignor," another reporter, with *The New York Herald*, remarked, having met him many years earlier at Pau.

Newsmen huddled around Capel, listening to how his journey had brought him from Rome to Paris, to London, to Liverpool, and onward to the dazzle and excitement of New York. "I have been planning this visit to America for ten years," he explained, "but it was not until about a month ago that my affairs and work were in such a condition that I could leave them. I can't tell how long I shall remain here, but it will probably be for several months. It is my intention to deliver a course of lectures on secular and religious subjects, but I have no idea when or where I shall begin."

Waiting for him on the quayside were the wealthy banker Townsend Burnet Baldwin and his wife, Mary. Mary was the daughter of Mrs. Dillon, who was Capel's last-remaining benefactor in Kensington. Her mother had arranged for the couple to meet him off the boat. The Baldwins were doyens of New York society, and they owned a mansion in New Jersey. It was there that Capel planned to rest for two weeks following his lengthy transatlantic journey.

First, the trio took a horse-drawn cab to the fashionable Brunswick Hotel, which was popular with visitors from England as well as wealthy young men about town, and there they had breakfast. After a short rest, the Monsignor paid a visit to Cardinal McCloskey and Archbishop Corrigan, the two senior churchmen of New York. The Cardinal received Capel "with his usual courtesy and prudence," Corrigan wrote to Cardinal Simeoni at Propaganda Fide in Rome. The restrained tone of the letter indicates that the churchmen's welcome might have been less than warm.

Capel and the Baldwins then travelled by the Pennsylvania Railroad to their mansion at Edgewater Park, New Jersey. On reflection, the Monsignor must have been satisfied with his day. His fellow churchmen aside, the reaction had been enthusiastic. "The charm of his manner is his complete naturalness," one news commentator remarked. "He is apparently the most unaffected of men. Americans will note in his

conversation a rather pronounced English accent. That he would himself describe as his misfortune rather than his fault. He will doubtless
encounter much curiosity....a man that no one would be apt to pass
without asking: 'Who is he?'"

It took only a week before the American public got their first taste
of Monsignor Capel's ability as a preacher. For the prelate, the date – 5
August 1883 – was historic. For New Yorkers, the event was historic,
too. On that Sunday morning, he delivered his first public lecture at the
Church of St. Francis Xavier, New York. A crowd of more than 6,000
people arrived at West 16th Street to see him.

The crowd came to a standstill outside the church, where they
jostled to get inside. Half an hour ahead of time, the venue was packed
to capacity. Latecomers lucky enough to gain entry had to stand in
the aisles, their crowded lines extending from the entrance doors to
the space in front of the altar. Hundreds were left outside.

The unusually large crowd had arrived that morning with one
purpose in mind: to witness the phenomenon known as Monsignor
Capel, an orator billed by one New York newspaper as "Rome's Great
Revivalist" and by another as "The Noted Proselytising Priest." That
he was speaking on the relatively dry theme of the legacy of St. Ignatius
of Loyola mattered little to the congregation, who were determined
to see and hear this extraordinary man.

It wasn't as if they had nothing else to do or no alternatives to turn
to. Buffalo Bill and sharpshooter "Doc" Carver were performing their
Wild West show down the road, at Coney Island. The much-maligned
but hugely-popular play *The Rajah* was packing them in on Broadway.
The great unconquered, never-knocked-out world boxing champion
John L. Sullivan was arriving in town for a world title fight at Madison
Square Garden. Even those attractions found it hard to match the
Monsignor's compelling appeal.

Among the more than 6,000 people present were many Irish
Catholics, although well-known Protestants also attended. Banker
Henry L. Hoguet was there; so also was noted lawyer Algernon S.
Sullivan, and Alexander Sullivan, President of the Irish National League

of America. Congressman Samuel S. Cox turned up, too. "Monsignor Capel's fame as a revivalist and a preacher had evidently aroused a widespread interest among the members of the Romish Church in this city," *The New-York Times* commented.

Monsignor Capel had lost none of the style and verve he was known for in Europe. He arrived on the altar wearing a black biretta and the purple great cape – the cappa magna – of a Monsignor. The congregation was hushed; there was a perfect stillness. As he marched across the sanctuary on his way to the pulpit, he raised his biretta when passing the celebrant of the Mass and saluted him with a bow of courtly grace. Nobody had ever seen such a poised and dignified gesture before.

As he mounted the pulpit, he looked "slightly flushed in the face and apparently somewhat awed at the vast multitude gazing on him," one newsman reported. His broad English accent, with its soft tones, wooed the crowd. "In his reading of the Epistle and Gospel he uttered each word with a distinctness and a richness of expression that could not fail to excite admiration," another newsman noted.

"When he laid the book down and began to preach he became magnetic," *The New-York Times* commented. "With no oratorical display whatever he succeeded in holding the close attention of his listeners chiefly by the force of his strong personality." His voice was rich and strong, his manner graceful, his gestures limited, his language unadorned, his delivery energetic. "The Monsignor spoke for nearly three-quarters of an hour, and the large congregation would undoubtedly have been pleased had his sermon been twice as long," the broadsheet remarked.

Capel's performance that day won widespread praise. The congregation admired his spontaneity – he spoke without notes – and they were charmed by his mannerisms and turns of phrase. They loved how he pronounced "knowledge" with the emphasis on the "o", making the word sound like "no-ledge". He also pronounced "perplexity" as if he were saying "par-plexity". They weren't familiar with English spoken like that.

His accent was less "English" than the posh tones of "our American young men who come back from English schools with an accent which they have managed to acquire somewhere and somehow," one person remarked. His peculiar style, another person commented, allied to "his rich, soft voice, his rapturous clasping of his hands as he appeals to his listeners; his handsome, candid face, his small, white hand, and the grace that governs his every movement, these and many characteristics serve to rivet one's attention."

The Monsignor was well pleased with the response to his first lecture in America. There were, however, signs that not everything was going quite as smoothly as he had hoped. Despite the glowing reviews, much of his subsequent postbag was poisonous. Some letters condemned the makeup of his audience, accusing them of being "drunken Irish." Others attacked the falsity of his historical statements.

The criticisms hit home. "There is one thing which I wish you would ask of the public for me, and that is to restrain themselves from writing me anonymous letters," he complained to a journalist. Even the way people were pronouncing his name irked him. "I wish you would inform people that my name is not Cappelle, but Cay-pel. You don't talk about Cappelle Street, Dublin, do you? It's an old Norman name, the family name of Lord Essex, and has been in the country long enough to be pronounced rightly."

Capel put his annoyance aside as he prepared for a tour through the East Coast and Midwest of America. Coming at a time when the 19th century lecture circuit was at its peak, the prospects for such a tour being a money-spinner looked good. The omens were especially promising for visiting Europeans, most notably those from the British Isles. All Capel had to do was look to Oscar Wilde for inspiration.

Wilde had arrived in New York shortly after the Monsignor. His ill-fated play, the peculiarly named *Vera; or, The Nihilists*, was about to open at the Union Square Theatre on Broadway. He had made a fortune the previous year from his 140-date tour of the United States and Canada. He hoped that his new play, and some selected lectures, would replicate that success.

Monsignor Capel had aspirations similar to Wilde's. Like Wilde, he hoped to complete 100-plus speaking engagements, using many of the venues where the controversial poet and playwright had lectured in 1882. They included New York's Chickering Hall, Boston's Music Hall, San Francisco's Platt's Hall, and Brooklyn's Academy of Music.

The money would accrue from admission fees paid at the door or through the advance sale of tickets. The general pricing system was simple – a fee of 25 cents per lecture would draw in clerks, artisans or mechanics; 50 cents would push the clientele further upmarket; while $1 or more would restrict admission to the professional classes. Capel opted for an absolute, and only occasional, minimum of 25 cents, a normal admission fee of 50 cents to $1, and upped the ceiling to a steep $1.50 for selected events. Reserved seats would cost more.

Like Wilde, Capel was a colourful showman. He planned to appear in a long cassock with scarlet silk buttons, short cape with cord-trimmed sleeves, and long crimson silk cloak similar to a Roman toga. Wilde presented himself with white gloves tucked into his opera hat and a red handkerchief hanging from his waistcoat. Just like the ring-master of Barnum & Bailey's circus, with his bright-red tailcoat, black top hat and riding whip, the two visitors from England fitted their roles to perfection.

They both employed impresarios, or tour managers, whose purpose was to organise logistics, secure venues, arrange publicity, and ensure that fees or other monies were paid. Wilde was handled by Richard D'Oyly Carte, the famous English talent agent who brought Gilbert and Sullivan together, and who built London's Savoy Theatre and Savoy Hotel.

Capel, on the other hand, employed a young man named George Bradshaw, who he described as his "courier, secretary and factotum." Often noted for his "silk travelling cap" and "commercial traveller" appearance, his job included dealing with paperwork, minding the cash, and handling queries when Capel was unavailable. Looking ahead, this "man of business," as he was called, declared that the tour would be the "biggest thing of the kind" on record.

Although the Monsignor and secretary would stay at the same hotels, instances where both turned up at important events proved to be rare. They seldom appeared together at celebratory dinners, and Bradshaw never accompanied the Monsignor when he was a guest of notable families. On those occasions, the secretary had to fend for himself.

Bradshaw was fortunate that new communications technology was evolving rapidly in America at the time of the tour. By the 1880s, there were more than 50,000 telephones in use across the country, allowing for the easier booking of hotels and venues. Telegraphy – and especially the use of telegrams – was also extensively employed. Railroads, of course, proved essential.

The new technology made it possible for places like Butte, Montana, to contact Bradshaw in the hope that the Monsignor might pay them a visit. Back then, Butte was a small town, having been established only two decades earlier as a mining camp. On learning that Capel had reached America, the manager of their newly-built Grand Opera House hoped "to make things lively this winter" by securing a date with the Monsignor. The plan never came to fruition.

As with any modern rock tour, the star performer, Monsignor Capel, and his assistant hoped to make money from the sale of merchandise in the cities they visited. Among the products was a range of photographs of the Monsignor priced from $1 to $3. Supplies were provided to shops such as James B. Dodge & Bro. in Pittsburgh – one of the oldest booksellers in the city – where sales were expected to be brisk.

Photographic promotion cards were also printed, which Capel planned to sign and present to people he met along the way. The cards, featuring the Monsignor in full regalia, turned out to be useful for presenting to his fans. One newspaper in Idaho featured a lady who met Capel on a train. "He graciously gave her his autograph and photograph," the broadsheet noted. She said he was "as courtly a gentleman as she ever met."

Looking ahead, Capel knew it was going to be a tough tour from a preaching point of view. In New York, he was up against skilled competitors like Monsignor Preston, pastor of St. Ann's Church. A former Episcopalian clergyman and convert to Catholicism, he was a formidable preacher and attracted enormous crowds. On occasions, carriages lined East 12th Street from Second Avenue to Fifth Avenue, ferrying the wealthy Catholics of New York to hear him speak.

Numerous other pulpit orators lined the Monsignor's planned route through America. Well-known Presbyterian, Methodist, Baptist and Episcopalian speakers were everywhere to be seen, delivering their messages in church halls and on the streets. But Capel wasn't worried. He knew he could turn heads, charm audiences, and earn vast sums of money while doing so. It was only a matter of getting the show up and running.

ON THE ROAD

Midwest Steam Express

For the next two years, Capel lived like an upmarket itinerant preacher, travelling by steam train through the East Coast and Midwest of America, staying at the finest hotels or in the white clapboard mansions of the rich. He dined at the best restaurants and was entertained at lavish dinner parties held by his hosts in his honour. At times, when there were no willing hosts available, he would turn to the local Archbishop for support.

His fame preceded him, and he drew huge numbers to his much-anticipated events. It wasn't only Catholics who attended; Protestants, Unitarians and other denominations were present, too. Guests at his lectures paid for entry at the door. He also availed of collections made inside on his behalf. In addition, he lived off wealthy benefactors who lavished him with money or provided loans.

American women loved him and were drawn by his personality and good looks. No matter where he went – Boston, Philadelphia, Chicago, Detroit, Washington DC, or elsewhere – they flocked to see or meet him. They stood around him four deep. "The number of fashionable ladies who were present was remarkable, for a lecture, and most of them kept their opera-glasses fastened on him during the entire evening," one newspaper remarked.

Another newspaper, in Chicago, dryly noted how his female fan base waved their perfumed handkerchiefs at him as he arrived on the platform to speak. They also brought "their kidded palms to meet in applause of his beautiful sentiments." These were the people who sustained clergymen like Capel, the newspaper asserted, hoping by their actions to "make their way heavenward as best they can."

Capel chose his hosts well. Their common denominator was wealth. In Washington DC, he stayed with Frank Riggs, owner of Riggs Bank, which was known as "The Bank of Presidents". Another of the city's bankers, William Wilson Corcoran – a multimillionaire and noted art collector – also provided accommodation. Yet another host was Mrs. Benjamin Ogle Tayloe, whose husband was once the richest man in America and whose home was situated across the street from the White House.

A further famous banker, the Irish-born Eugene Kelly, who had initially made his fortune on the back of the California Gold Rush, also wined and dined Capel. Kelly was an ardent Catholic and one of the founders of the Catholic University of America. He and his wife entertained the Monsignor at the opulent Oriental Hotel, Coney Island, which catered only for the very rich. Capel was already familiar with the hotel and on a previous visit had "attracted no small attention," it was said.

Capel also caught the public's eye when he stayed at the summer residence of John Lee Carroll, former Governor of Maryland. The house, in Newport, Rhode Island, was surrounded by the villas of numerous millionaires. Carroll was an influential man and noted for his skill as a lawyer. The Monsignor regarded him as a valuable contact and source of support.

Although Capel stayed in the plushest hotels when touring, including the luxury Grand Pacific in Chicago, he always looked forward to returning to his favourite establishment, the Brunswick Hotel, New York. He stayed there on many occasions, using his elegant suite of rooms as a base in the city. There, he drank Lacryma Christi wine, a bottle of which always sat on the table. Visitors noted the vast collection of invitations to dinner stuck to the mirror. His rooms seemed more appropriate to a person fond of sensuous luxury than the asceticism of priesthood.

The Brunswick suited the Monsignor's desire for exclusivity. Everyone knew that only the rich and famous stayed there or dined there. After dark, when the six great lamps in front of the door were lit and the illuminations from nearby Fifth Avenue were glowing, visitors from out of town were "wont to peep over the blinds at the prosperous-looking people in the opulent dining room," *The New-York Times* remarked.

The main restaurant's cuisine at the Brunswick was among the finest in New York. Its wine rooms and cafes were of an equally high standard. When Capel tired of the hotel's gourmet dishes, he would cross the street to the famous plush restaurant Delmonico's, whose chefs had only recently invented Baked Alaska and Lobster Newburg. Like Capel, Mark Twain was drawn to Delmonico's; he, too, loved the restaurant and referred to its cuisine as "the perfection of dining."

Delmonico's and the Brunswick were frequented by the most fashionable ladies in New York. These dashing women came from good families, held their heads high, carried their shoulders well back, and moved briskly, one commentator noted. They lunched in the middle of the day, while their husbands worked downtown. The youngest of them were "rapid," or fast, the commentator added.

There were ample opportunities for wrongdoing. Sometimes, the women were single and young. In that case, if a scandal came to light, the news spread fast and "the maiden is shipped to a convent, or sent abroad with a dragon of an aunt. Of course nothing is done to the man in these cases," the commentator remarked.

Although the opulent lifestyle on tour was to his liking, it was increasingly becoming clear to Capel that the underlying hostility towards him, which had first become evident after his inaugural lecture in New York, was growing. In Chicago, he was accused of using clever but false arguments, and that he was underestimating the intelligence and understanding of American audiences. Some people said they even preferred their own pastors to him, which must have stung him greatly.

He did little to ingratiate himself with Bostonians, claiming they spoke the worst, most stilted, least melodious English in America. He also irritated residents of Wisconsin when he recalled a meeting he witnessed between Pope Pius IX and a prominent Wisconsin politician. The politician, who came from Oshkosh, "walked right up to the successor to St. Peter," Capel remarked, "and, seizing his Holiness by the hand, exclaimed: 'I am glad to meet you, Pope, because we have often heard of you out in Wisconsin.'" Residents of the Midwest state were far from amused.

Nor did all Americans take kindly to his intermingling with the rich. "His proudest moments are spent in telling of the socially distinguished persons he has won for Rome," *The Chicago Tribune* acidly remarked. "He probably thinks, as many others of his cloth do, that the church will always have the poor with them, or that the poor, the ignorant, and the lowly are not worth much trouble or effort, their souls being hardly worth saving."

He was likewise getting up the noses of some women, most notably the formidable orator and lecturer, Anna Elizabeth Dickinson. The Monsignor's views, she said, were diametrically opposed to the "advanced views and liberal thought" of many American women. "I understand he is an entertaining man," she added. "I can comprehend how certain Americans are blinded by his social charms. But that does not matter. He makes certain remarkable assertions. Since slavery days no subject has stirred me as does this."

A more serious attack was directed at Monsignor Capel when a tall, stout, somewhat bald man, with black whiskers and moustache, ascended the pulpit at the People's Church in Clermont Avenue, New York. The man was Dr. Justin D. Fulton, a member of the Baptist Church and a renowned preacher. He was an orator with a dash of carelessness to his manner and a heart that ruled his speech. "He is like a Frenchman – all passion, rushing in a whirlwind of words all on fire" was how a fellow churchman described him.

Dr. Fulton had two passionate hates – Roman Catholicism and Monsignor Capel. On that day, in September 1883, he went for Capel's jugular. Quoting "reliable sources," Dr. Fulton alleged that Capel had misappropriated funds intended for the college at Kensington. He was even more specific, stating that those funds had been provided by the Marquess of Bute. As a consequence, he said, Monsignor Capel had been banished by Cardinal Manning, and his decision had been subsequently upheld by Rome.

Fulton went on to claim that Capel had fallen from favour in England, where he was the subject of unpleasant talk. He added that contrary to the way he presented himself, he was of humble origin and without prestige. What's more, he said, "a silly section of our fashionable society gave their guest the greatest consideration here about the time he seemed to be in the least esteem at home." It was a blistering attack, timely, powerfully delivered, and perfect for the newsmen in attendance at the event.

The Monsignor was on tour when the allegations surfaced in the press. He was "exceedingly angry and showed it plainly," a reporter who confronted him in Baltimore wrote. Capel knit his brows, and having read the charges, indignantly said: "That whole statement is a wicked, libellous invention, made for too transparent a purpose. In my country the speaker as well as the publisher could be civilly as well as criminally prosecuted. I will ascertain how I can be protected by the laws of America from such inventions of a minister of the Gospel."

After initially threatening legal action, within days Capel softened his stance. He said he would soon be returning to Brooklyn, where, he intimated, he would counter the "calumnious fabrication" from the pulpit or in the press. He eventually softened his position further, remarking about Fulton: "My slanderer is a stranger utterly to what truth and justice demand of honourable men. I cannot notice him further." He was clearly fearful of exposure in court. He was also hoping that the matter might disappear and be forgotten. At least for the present, his judgement was right.

Monsignor Capel received better news when one of his targets for conversion, George Bliss, who came from a well-known Puritan family, was baptised into the Catholic Church. As converts go, Bliss wasn't exactly the catch of the century. Financially, he was little league and certainly no Vanderbilt, Astor or Mellon. Nor was he a great celebrity like cowboy Buffalo Bill or Shakespearean actor Edwin Booth.

He was, though, a noted lawyer, and was particularly known for his role as prosecuting counsel in a prominent corruption case involving the awarding of United States postal delivery contracts. In what was referred to as "The Star Route Scandal", he proved to be lenient – to put it mildly – in his prosecution of those involved. There were few convictions.

Capel met Bliss shortly after his arrival in New York. The introduction was facilitated by Bliss's wife, who had once been a member of the Episcopal Church but had converted to Catholicism. After her conversion, she had installed a private chapel at the family residence on West 39th Street. A devout Catholic, Mrs. Bliss hoped that one day her husband would share the same faith as herself. At her suggestion, Monsignor Capel undertook the job of conversion.

The Monsignor, whenever he was in New York, visited the Bliss family home, where he was welcomed as a guest. He said Mass in the little oratory, invited his potential convert to his lectures, and battled hard to win him over. "It was not a matter of persuasion," a Church colleague of Capel's later said, "but was a fight of mind and argument." The Monsignor persisted, and after much labour, Bliss was baptised into the Catholic Church on 9 June 1884.

A flurry of speculation about other conversions followed in the national press and in the society rooms of America. At one time, it was suggested that the widow of publisher Frank Leslie – famous for his *Frank Leslie's Illustrated Newspaper* – had been converted by Capel. At another time, it was said that the unscrupulous businessman Jay Gould – whose son had travelled on Capel's ship to America – was in his sights.

The rumour even did the rounds that Carrie Astor – the young heiress from the enormously-wealthy Astor family – had been sent to Europe to escape Capel's clutches. The action was justified, one commentator noted, as the Monsignor was "a charming man" with a "potent missionary's influence." None of the speculation was true. Capel's conversion pickings were slim in America, although another rumoured success was appearing in the news.

To bring about the conversion of heiress Lily Hamersley would have been a triumph for any clergyman in mid-1880s New York. She was the widow of a real estate millionaire in the city who had died in 1883. A young woman, in her 20s, she was tall and fair, with light hair, beautiful eyes, and possessed a wonderful figure.

She also happened to be one of the richest young women in America. A multimillionaire following her husband's death, she lived in her inherited property at 257 Fifth Avenue. There, she held elaborate dinner parties and musical events. In her spare time – of which she had plenty – she frequented the opera. Her full name, Lilian, didn't rhyme with million for nothing, people said.

Although an Episcopalian, Lily Hamersley was known to have attended the lectures and sermons of Monsignor Capel. He was also known to have visited her at her Fifth Avenue residence. The rumour mill was soon in overdrive. Before long, word was out that she had become a Catholic. "A Convert with Millions," one newspaper headline declared. "Four Millions Converted," another headline trumpeted, referring to that broadsheet's understanding of the extent of her wealth.

Capel was suitably coy when asked to confirm or deny the rumoured conversion. He would do neither, he told a reporter, saying he regarded the matter as a professional secret. The reporter asked a prominent Catholic priest if he knew the truth. "The whole thing would never have been circulated but for one rash priest in this diocese," the cleric responded. Although he wouldn't reveal the name of the priest who had leaked the story, the reporter was left feeling – or, more correctly, *knowing* – it was the same clergyman who had allegedly baptised Mrs. Hamersley: Monsignor Capel!

The truth, as it later transpired, was that Mrs. Hamersley hadn't converted at all. Four years later, she married the Duke of Marlborough, uncle of Winston Churchill, moved to England, and lived at Blenheim Palace. After the Duke's death, she married again, this time to Lord William Beresford, brother of the Marquis of Waterford. Someone quipped that she had achieved a remarkable three-in-a-row – her first marriage for money, her second for a title, and her third for love. She died in 1909 and was buried at Curraghmore, County Waterford, Ireland. The service was conducted by a Church of Ireland clergyman.

Despite the Hamersley setback, Capel's celebrity status continued to give him access to the finest events in New York. Since he arrived in the city, he craved invitations to the best social gatherings. He dreamt of one involving millionaires, billionaires and America's social elite. Luck came his way in February 1885 when he was invited to a reception given in honour of the enormously-wealthy attorney, David Dudley Field.

Capel arrived an hour late at the Gramercy Park mansion owned by Field's brother, Cyrus, where the reception was being held. In dramatic style, the Monsignor entered the brownstone building at the foot of Lexington Avenue with a swagger, wearing, as one observer remarked, "some sort of official jigger of gold and red – the robe of the Pope's household, I suppose."

The rooms were filled with whiskered, long-coated men, sporting cigars, exuding quiet personal confidence and economic success. These were the patriarchs of New York's finest families, most of them business tycoons, barons of industry, great men of finance, eminent lawyers, all of them figures of enormous wealth and stature.

Frederick Vanderbilt, the railroad magnate and in today's terms a billionaire, was there. Jay Gould, another railroad magnate and billionaire, was also there. The great American financier Russell Sage, yet another billionaire, was present, as was financier August Belmont, lame from a duel fought 50 years earlier and who was a mere multimillionaire.

Thomas Edison, inventor of the light bulb, put in an appearance, looking as if he had "gained thirty or forty pounds in the last four or five years." Even the President of the Senate and the Speaker of the House of Representatives were in attendance, as was the Mayor of New York and three of his predecessors.

"The assembly at the reception was far the most distinguished I have ever seen," the author and poet William Augustus Croffut, who was present, later wrote. "Well-known heads loom everywhere, many of them familiar from their caricatures." An estimated 1,000 – 2,000 celebrated guests put in an appearance.

The Monsignor felt at home. He stood there, back to the wall, close to the man of the evening, David Dudley Field. "He is an uncommonly handsome man, tall as a grenadier and graceful, with blue eyes, red cheeks, and a symmetrical mouth," Croffut said of Capel, as he observed him holding court.

"A score of people are taken up and introduced; he smiles on them blandly, gives them pleasant words and lets them go. Friends he slaps on the back familiarly, and one or two he embraces, after the manner of Central Europe, in spite of the scarlet collar that spans his shoulders stiffly."

Capel was delighted when introduced to Henry Ward Beecher and Thomas De Witt Talmage, the leading pulpit orators in America. When presented to Beecher, he said: "Ah, Mr. Beecher, this is indeed a pleasure. Do I at last see the world-renowned apostle of America? It has been the ambition of my life. This is the proudest moment of my existence."

"The pleasure is mutual," Beecher replied. "Your intellect I have admired, but you are a much more handsome man than I had imagined." "What!" broke in the Monsignor, with a low laugh, "getting jealous of me already?"

Just then, the Rev. Dr. Talmage joined the two preachers and received his dose of "the oil of flattery," an observer noted. They were barely engaged in conversation when the billionaire Russell Sage was brought forward for an introduction.

The introducer whispered in Capel's ear the extent of Sage's wealth. At that instant, the Monsignor was said to have turned his back on both Beecher and Talmage and "vainly tried to fascinate the big-tailed fox of Wall Street." The prelate knew whose friend he most wished to be.

The reception ended at the stroke of midnight, and the great and good of New York headed to their homes. There is no evidence that Capel achieved any conversions, or secured any loans or contributions, from those he met. By all accounts, however, he seemed to have enjoyed the occasion, which was a good thing, as disastrous news about his drinking and general behaviour was about to explode in the press.

FAREWELL NEW YORK

Delmonico's, New York

A round the time of David Dudley Field's reception, Monsignor Capel disgraced himself at a gala dinner at Delmonico's, New York. Given the nature of the event, and the setting, what took place was nothing short of shocking. For a start, he was guest speaker at the Police Inspectors and Captains banquet. He was also among distinguished company in a classy venue known for its fine food, silver chandeliers, frescoed ceiling, and panoramic views of Fifth Avenue.

As many as 600 bottles of wine were consumed that night by the superintendent, captains, inspectors, and a couple of hundred guests of the New York City Police Department. Teetotaller and ex-Senator Roscoe Conkling, who was there, didn't drink. We don't know what the other guests, including top railroad lawyer Chauncey Depew and New York's first Roman Catholic mayor William Grace, knocked back. But we do know that Capel overdid it.

The New York Star reported that the Monsignor ended up in "an intoxicated condition" at Delmonico's. The newspaper further alleged that, after the dinner, some of the guests, "with a poor idea of what constituted practical joking," brought the clearly-inebriated prelate to the home of a woman of low morals and doubtful reputation. There, they spent some time in social enjoyment.

"How long he would have stayed is a matter of conjecture, but a servant girl, who had not the highest regard for her mistress, called him out into the hallway and whispered to him that the mansion was no place for a Catholic clergyman," the newspaper reported. Suddenly sobering up and "thoroughly frightened at the dilemma in which he was placed," Capel hurriedly departed.

Unfortunately for Capel, the incident came to the attention of Cardinal McCloskey, Archbishop of New York, who was not amused. He became even less amused when one of his informants, hotel employee Henry C. Olds, who knew all the local gossip, outlined Capel's exploits to his assistant, Archbishop Corrigan. The fine details went even further than the story in *The New York Star*.

Capel had "drunk to excess" at the banquet and was "quite paralyzed thereby," Olds explained. He departed in the company of two young men and three young women from Philadelphia. They headed initially for the St. James Hotel restaurant, where they ate and drank until 11pm. They then took two carriages to a brothel on West 28th Street.

There, he alleged, the Monsignor "retired with a lady" – a detail omitted in the newspaper report – and arrived back at the Brunswick Hotel at one o'clock. The brothel owner was so pleased that she later boasted to all and sundry that Capel had been a guest at her establishment.

Following the event, the Monsignor feebly wrote to Archbishop Corrigan, hoping to explain away the disaster at the banquet. "Mine was the last speech of the evening," he wrote. "And when I stood up, the room was full of the fumes of tobacco smoke. At all times tobacco painfully effects [sic] me. And on this occasion the heated atmosphere reeking with smoke simply took away my memory and made me feel dizzy, and my speech was in consequence spoiled."

Capel's letter was safely filed away by the Archdiocese of New York, in whose possession it remains to this day. Interestingly, it is accompanied by another letter – this time containing an eyewitness account – explaining that the Monsignor, that night, was "the drunkest man" the person ever saw. "He was under the influence of liquor at the beginning of the banquet, and kept drinking all the time," the eyewitness reported.

Although Capel may not have known it, his drinking was well known to those who encountered him during his early years in America. Despite being regarded as "a genial man of the world and the best of company when out of the pulpit," his consumption of alcohol was often noted. One newsman remarked on the "sad failing which the eminent divine has in common with many other men of genius – a partiality for the fluid which inebriates as well as cheers."

People who met Capel referred to him as being "flushed in the face" or "red-faced," and commented on how his "potations became more frequent as time went on." A woman who spoke to him and found him conceited and ill-mannered was overheard in conversation with a friend. The friend said: "I am surprised that he is ill-mannered. I thought he was the pink of perfection in that regard." The woman laughingly replied: "Most of the pink has gone to his face."

In time, more Capel escapades appeared in the press. One of them concerned an event at West 30th Street police station, where he was seen behaving in a bizarre and erratic way. The Monsignor, who was wearing a black overcoat turned up around his throat and a silk scarf, was intervening in a row between two prisoners. The couple, a husband and wife, were described as "fair specimens of the toughest class."

The prisoners, who were intoxicated, had been involved in a domestic dispute. With his sleek silk hat tilted off the back of his head, Capel was lecturing them and trying to restore marital harmony. The desk sergeant, captain and several policemen in front of the desk were shaking with suppressed laughter. Eventually, peace was restored, and the couple "rapturously kissed each other to the great amusement of the select party of spectators," a newspaper reported. The couple then left for home, accompanied by great laughter.

Prior to that event, Monsignor Capel had been involved in another unedifying occurrence, where he was relieved of a large sum of money. It appears that the notorious "bunco" operator "Kid" Muller, who was a genius at scamming victims of their cash and possessions, had relieved the Monsignor of a $260 cheque and $60 in cash.

The scam took place in "Kid" Muller's rooms on 21st Street, in the presence of an accomplice. There, the Monsignor handed over his money on the promise of a substantial return on his investment. Having departed from the house, he had second thoughts about the nature of the deal.

Capel returned to the rooms and demanded that his cheque and cash be returned. Muller, fearing police intervention, agreed to give back the cheque but not the $60 in cash. The story came to light after Muller went about town "boasting of a brilliant, though not very profitable, piece of roguery," a newspaper report explained.

All these stories, at one time or another, ended up in the press. The revelations did little to enhance the Monsignor's reputation, especially at the Archbishop's house in New York. The diocese's achievements in expanding the number of New York parishes, developing Catholic education in the city, and completing the reconstruction of St. Patrick's Cathedral after it had been gutted by fire, were being usurped and undermined by this rogue priest.

Bad news kept flooding into the Archbishop's residence on Madison Avenue. "Grant me an interview of a few minutes today," hotel employee Henry C. Olds wrote to Corrigan on 10 February 1885, adding, "I can communicate to you something of great importance." The Archbishop's scribbled notes of their conversation were damning. They describe Capel's activities with a widow at the St. James Hotel, Broadway, to which Olds was connected.

The notes read: "Dinner ordered in private room at St. James....Lady in deep mourning....All delicacies of season....Rhine, Amontillado, Quart of Champagne, Chartreuse, Bottle of Brandy....Domestic dismissed about ten....Withdrew a letto [Italian for "to bed"] till 12 when servant knocked and requested guests to withdraw....Bed disarranged, as if used....And Mrs. N, handsome widow....in very bad order when leaving Hotel."

Capel's impact on the families he stayed with also featured in letters to the Archbishop. One wealthy woman described the havoc he caused in her daughter's home. While staying there, he asked for a gift or loan of $5,000 and was given $1,500. In addition, the family were obliged to pay for his printing and advertising, as well as his wine and carriage bills of $150 a month.

After a while, he suggested to the daughters of the household that they should cash in a recent inheritance and join him in Europe. One of those daughters, he suggested, "could make her fortune on the stage." Eventually, he was asked to leave but begged for three extra days' grace. After his request was granted, he remained for the best part of two more weeks. "Did you ever hear of such bold attempts to rob a family of money and reputation and peace?" the woman asked. "Can you not get him out of the country?"

The desire to expel Capel from America featured in another letter, this time from no less a figure than William George McCloskey, Bishop of Louisville, Kentucky. "Will you kindly tell me, so far as you can remember it, the exact purpose of Mgr. Capel's letters of introduction, (or whatever else you please to call them), from Rome, and who signed them," he wrote to Archbishop Corrigan. "I wish this man were safely out of the country and I would cheerfully join in a letter to Cardinal Simeoni to say so. I would be glad to have an answer by return mail."

Archbishop Corrigan, too, reached the same conclusion – that Capel had to go. The breaking point for him was a remark Capel had made in a speech. "He says the laity of this district is like a good ship without a pilot," Corrigan wrote. It was shocking, he remarked, how Cardinal McCloskey had been so publicly insulted. "The sooner he leaves America the better," he concluded, sealing the Monsignor's fate. Contact was made with Rome, and a speedy reply was received. "I send power to expel him," the telegram baldly stated. The date was 17 March 1885.

Cardinal McCloskey was quick to take action. In a devastating note to Monsignor Capel, Corrigan wrote: "His Eminence, the Cardinal Archbishop instructs me to say that the time which you are supposed to spend in this Diocese has already been exceeded, and that he deems it advisable you should now report to the proper authorities elsewhere. He accordingly hereby restricts your use of all faculties in this Diocese." The termination date was given as two weeks hence.

Capel had no choice but to pack his bags and go – and go he did. He didn't leave America, as many had hoped; instead, he headed west, to Iowa, Nebraska, Kansas and Colorado, among many other states. His route wound its way through mountain ranges, rugged terrain, valleys and basins, rolling hills and tallgrass prairies. He lectured in the major cities en route, and traversed the continent in railroad day coaches and overnight sleeping cars.

Then, in June 1885, after lecturing in Salt Lake City, Utah, he travelled to the railway hub of nearby Ogden and took the train to San Francisco. He arrived on 16 June 1885, hoping, like the gold prospectors who had arrived there three decades before him, for a fresh and lucrative new beginning. Unfortunately, things didn't quite work out as planned.

CALIFORNIA

Grand Opera House, Los Angeles

At 8.20 pm, on Friday, 10 July 1885, Monsignor Capel walked onto the stage at the Grand Opera House in Los Angeles. He was dressed in a black soutane edged with red, with red buttons, and wore a red silk cloak. He waved away a formal introduction from the priest who was with him and proceeded at once with his lecture.

The audience that night was reported as being very small. The size of the attendance undoubtedly had something to do with the topic, "The Dignity of Woman." It wasn't the wisest of themes for a state with one of the most vibrant women's rights movements in America. There was a danger that he might not go down too well.

The Monsignor didn't pull his punches. His words were controversial. "The positions of women's rights are so absurd that I think every intelligent person will be willing to cast them aside," he declared. "It is a reversal of nature. I have been among women who stand for women's rights. I have noticed that they haven't beauty – or, if they have beauty, it is within. They lack delicacy and refinement. They are like men who say there is no God – 'cranks.'"

The response of the press was scathing. "It is evident that Monsignor Capel is a good ways behind his American brethren on the question of women's rights," an editorial in the *Santa Cruz Sentinel* remarked.

Women, the newspaper said, are the most moral and sober Americans, the natural educators of the race, and they and their children are the chief victims of drunken men. Instead of denigrating them, it is time to give them the right to vote, the newspaper argued.

Eleven days later, Monsignor Capel delivered another version of his lecture, "The Dignity of Woman," at the Germania Hall in Oakland. The audience was at best moderately large and a shadow of the vast queues in Chicago and New York. Insensitive to the mood out West, he again dived headlong into his ill-chosen theme of women's rights – an issue which he said would "take the breath of our grandmothers away."

"Men have certain qualities and characteristics which fit them for the great struggle of life," he remarked. Women, to the contrary, "possess rapid seizure of thought, but they are lacking in energy." Their role, he said, is to provide companionship to men at home, "lighten their burdens and soften down all their troubles."

The husband is the natural "head of the wife," he argued, just as Christ is the head of the Church. The Book of Genesis declared that men are to be "rulers of the earth" and are to "increase and multiply." It follows, therefore, that women are intended to be wives and mothers. In that role, they can bring comfort to their husbands, he added.

Monsignor Capel failed to turn up for his next lecture on "The Dignity of Woman." He was ill, it was said, allegedly suffering from diphtheria. Those who arrived for the lecture found the doors closed. Soon, he was missing other engagements, causing much disappointment. He had arrived in California "with a flourish of trumpets," as one newspaper remarked, but his star was fading fast.

West Coast audiences were giving him the cold shoulder. Only one-half of the seats were occupied for his lecture at the Avon Theatre in Stockton. The same proportion of seats – one-half – was filled for his speech at Platt's Hall in San Francisco. The upper tiers were empty at the Metropolitan Theatre in Sacramento. An audience "very limited in numbers" turned out for another lecture in Sacramento, largely, it was said, because an earlier lecture "did not fill the measure of public anticipation."

Church leaders were also turning their backs on Capel. A solitary priest and a layman were the only people to greet him from the train at Oakland. Archbishops looked coldly on his presence and failed to turn up at his lectures. They also neglected to offer him invitations to their residences, a courtesy normally extended to visiting Church dignitaries. Instead, Capel based himself at the prestigious Palace Hotel, San Francisco, where he rented two rooms and received visitors.

He soon found himself embroiled in controversies. One of them involved a well-known British visitor to California, the Marquess of Queensberry, who was famous for the boxing rules that still bear his name. The Marquess, who was a committed agnostic, and the Monsignor argued publicly, and bitterly, over the existence of miracles. His views on the "Irish Question," where he took a pro-English line, also gave offence; as did his views about the care of orphans.

Further controversy surfaced when the Monsignor's brother, Arthur Capel, made a disgrace of himself on a visit to New York, and news of the event ended up in the Californian press. He had engaged in what *The Record-Union*, of Sacramento, referred to as an all-night and following-morning "excess of conviviality" at the city's Union Club. Badly inebriated, Arthur fell asleep in one of the club's lounges and had to be lifted to a cab with much difficulty. The unpleasantness of his condition resulted in his pass for the club being revoked.

News of the death of Capel's mother in England added to the Monsignor's misery, as did news filtering through from Cardinal Simeoni in Rome, via Archbishop Corrigan in New York, instructing Capel to return to Europe. Find him, the letter instructed, wherever he might be, and inform his local Bishop or Archbishop of the instruction. Corrigan sent the letter to Archbishop Riordan of San Francisco.

Coming on top of a bout of malaria – an affliction endemic to California, characterised by high fever and shivering – it seemed that the years 1885 – 1886 were the worst of Capel's life. Topping it all, however, were revelations that exploded in the press towards the end of that period. Within weeks, the Monsignor's reputation lay in ruins.

Something extraordinary happened in the month of October 1886. As if out of nowhere, a succession of newspapers, from New York to the West, investigated the Monsignor and revealed details of his murky past. Every morsel of gossip, every quiet whisper, every little-known fact was collected, written down, and published in the nation's press. What happened was a bit like a perfect storm. By the time things settled, the Monsignor's credibility was shattered.

The revelations were devastating. The *New York Star* alleged that in San Francisco Capel was doing exactly what he did in New York – borrowing money whenever he could, from whoever would lend it, and not repaying it. "He had not kept his word in returning large sums of money he had borrowed," the newspaper remarked.

The report added: "He tempted and almost succeeded in persuading two or three young ladies of excellent family whose guest he was, over whom he exerted an extraordinary influence, to yield up their inheritance. The scheme was detected just as it was almost consummated, and the Monsignor was shown the door. The story soon spread among the elite, and after that he was coldly greeted on all sides, and eventually ostracised from society."

Another newspaper – *The Omaha Daily Bee* – revealed how the impecunious Capel had borrowed the price of his fare to America from the wealthy Henry F. Gillig, who ran a company in London known as the American Exchange in Europe. The company, which was based on the Strand, provided steamship and railroad tickets, currency exchange and other services to Americans overseas. The Monsignor paid back the fare soon after his arrival, but only after relieving the money from ladies in New York.

"Friends of mine were written to from the other side to have nothing to do with Capel when he came over here, as he was in disgrace in his own Church, and he was a man who, aside from his personal fascinations, had a very poor reputation," the columnist with the *Bee* wrote. "If New York society had taken the trouble to inform itself about Mgr. Capel it would have learned enough to let him severely alone."

Throughout the month of October, newspapers intensified their battle to expose the hidden, sordid details of Capel's activities in

America. Press reports were issued from, or reprinted in, all parts of the country, revealing infamous events including the Monsignor's drunken soirée at Delmonico's and his strange, intoxicated behaviour at New York's West 30th Street police station.

A further episode at the West 30th Street station – to which the Monsignor seemed to have taken a bizarre liking – was recalled in *The Washington Post*. The event was witnessed by one of the newspaper's reporters, who published his account at the height of the Capel controversy. It concerned a bout of horseplay between a police sergeant, Sergeant Schmittberger, and the Monsignor, which took place in the presence of other members of the force.

Sergeant Schmittberger produced his police club and flourished it in front of Capel, jocularly offering to demonstrate how he would disable him in the event of an incident. Capel said there was no way he could do so if he chose to resist. He even offered to bet that he could take the club from Schmittberger. The sergeant, who was large and seasoned, smiled at the idea of the smaller clergyman prevailing, and he accepted the bet.

The Monsignor flung down his hat and coat and rolled up his shirt sleeves. "In two minutes Schmittberger was on his back on the floor," the reporter recalled, "and, as the Monsignor flourished the captured club over the prostrate form of the big policeman, he said: 'Gentlemen, this is the Church triumphant!'"

Newspaper editors, reporters and columnists responded to these events by pointing to Capel's alcohol consumption as their likely cause. One newsman wrote of the Monsignor's "degradation through the love of liquor." Another described him as "a drunken vagabond." Yet another said he was "a man of bibulous habits and a high liver."

The *New York Star* also addressed the Monsignor's fondness for drink. "It was noted with some concern, even in his early days, that he was developing a taste for the wine cup. No great harm, however, came out of it until about the time he established the great Catholic public school at Kensington....The school did not prove a success, and the matter so preyed upon his mind, it is said, that he partook heavily of wine," the news report concluded.

The revelations created ripples as far away as Shreveport, Louisiana, a town at the juncture of the Red River and the Texas Trail, which boasted its own newspaper, *The Shreveport Times*. In the late afternoon of 13 October, the newspaper's editor, Charles McDonald Puckette, sat down to write his editorial for the next day's edition. An able newsman and a writer of force and elegance, he chose the tragedy of Monsignor Capel as his theme.

"Our readers will remember that a few years ago a certain Monsignor Capel came to this country on a lecturing tour," he wrote. "He was the feted and pampered pet of the grandest of the land, and he numbered among his converts to the Roman Catholic faith many of the most prominent names in literary, political and business life."

The scene had changed, he noted. Capel had "too great a fondness for the wine cup," was guilty of the "fraudulent obtaining of money," and was charged with numerous liaisons with distinguished and hand-some women. "He rose and he fell," he concluded. "His reputation is gone forever." Although the editor didn't know it, Capel's reputation had even further to fall.

The story of how Monsignor Capel had procured money for a charitable purpose yet used it for his own personal ends hit the news-stands in October 1886. The details had been doing the rounds in society circles for some time but had not been publicly exposed. All that changed when a succession of broadsheets, including *The New-York Times* and *The Philadelphia Inquirer*, brought the infor-mation into the public domain.

The story involved the wife of a leading light of Cincinnati society who was so impressed by the Monsignor during his visit to the city that she gave him a substantial cheque. The cheque, for $1,000, or about $25,000 today, was expressly intended for the Pope's Peter's Pence, to be spent in accordance with the Holy Father's charitable intentions. Instead, the cheque was cashed by Capel at the luxury jeweller Tiffany's, in New York, and used to buy a diamond bracelet.

The donor of the money, Alice Bowler, of Clifton, Cincinnati, was in her late 20s and the wife of a wealthy and successful local attorney. Her husband, Robert B. Bowler, would later be appointed to high office as Comptroller of the Treasury in Washington DC. She lived in what was variously described as a "beautiful" and "hospitable" mansion, where she entertained lavishly. Her act of kindness to Capel was inspired by his apparent dignity and integrity when she encountered him while lecturing in her native city.

"The Monsignor was shown attentions by some of the best families here, and delighted all who met him by his culture and his wit," *The New-York Times* remarked from Cincinnati in its report which, it pointed out, revealed a story never before seen in print. "Mrs. Bowler, of Clifton, it has since been learned, was so much pleased with the Monsignor that she entrusted him with a check for $1,000, which she designated as Peter's Pence.

"Some time afterward the check was returned to her in the regular way, with the endorsement of Tiffany upon it. Curious to know how that name came to be upon the check, Mrs. Bowler, it is stated, wrote to that house inquiring how the check came to be presented to them. The reply she received was that they received it in payment for a diamond bracelet.

"The indignation of Mrs. Bowler at the diversion of her gift of Peter's Pence to the purchase of such an article, evidently intended as a present to some woman whom it was no credit for the Monsignor to know, was shared by her friends, and it is stated that it resulted in a curtailment of contributions to the church by one lady who was previously benevolently inclined."

The story spread far and wide after it was first published. Not only did it appear in *The New-York Times* and *The Philadelphia Inquirer*, but it also surfaced in numerous prominent newspapers from California to Washington DC. The headlines, which included "The Ecclesiastic's Disgrace" and "Capel's Cincinnati Exploit," had a crippling effect on the Monsignor's efforts to raise further funds. The charges were, indeed, "ugly," as one newspaper remarked.

Monsignor Capel was outraged by the disclosures. One newsman who called on Capel in California found him "seated at a table on which was spread a mass of law books and not less than 1,000 extracts from newspapers reflecting on his character. The papers were an odd lot – papers from London, New York, Berlin, Rome, St. Petersburg, Hong Kong, Ceylon, Australia, France, Scotland, Ireland, and in fact from every country where the Romish church has a footing."

Capel promised simultaneous legal proceedings in California and in the Eastern United States. "The prosecution will be directed only against such journals as have shown marked animus," a prominent attorney close to him revealed. The obvious inference was that newspapers which had been relentlessly pursuing Capel – and their numbers were growing – would be made to pay, while those which merely republished material would be left alone.

There is no evidence that legal recourse was ever pursued by the Monsignor. No doubt, he thought it better to let matters lie. There were other stories waiting in the undergrowth: stories which one newspaper said were "of a kind that won't bear printing." On that count, the newspaper was wrong – these stories would soon appear in the national press.

MRS. VALENSIN

Alice Valensin

In early December 1885, Monsignor Capel entered one of the redwood-panelled hydraulic elevators – known as "rising rooms" – and descended to the lobby of the Palace Hotel in San Francisco. He passed the grand staircase and walked through the foyer of the largest, costliest, and most luxurious hotel in the world. The opulence of the establishment was not only to Capel's taste but to the taste of other esteemed guests including Mark Twain, Jack London, Sarah Bernhardt, and a long line of American Presidents.

Shortly after emerging on the street, Capel had a chance encounter with an attractive woman and familiar face from the past. Her name was Alice Mary Valensin, daughter of a rich Californian land owner and married to Count Giulio Valensin, who came from a prominent Italian banking family. Many years earlier, Capel had met Alice when she was studying in Europe and living there with her family. By all accounts, Capel was delighted to renew the acquaintance, no doubt drawn by Alice's good looks, slender frame, stylish appearance, and considerable wealth.

The Monsignor, who was battling malaria and tired after delivering over 100 lectures on his American tour, was only too happy to accept an invitation to recuperate at the Valensin ranch. Located 22 miles from Sacramento, the Arno ranch was situated in an area where, it was said, "perpetual summer exists, skies are blue and the sun ever shines" and was therefore ideally suited for health restoration. Capel, no doubt, was also encouraged by news that Alice and the Count were no longer living together.

The spectacle on Capel's arrival must have gladdened his heart. A rippling sea of emerald grain, intermixed with beds of orange poppies, stretched to the far distant horizon. The ranch grew figs, grapes and olives, and had an orchard full of oranges and lemons. The large wood-frame home was well stocked with champagne and wines; the stables housed driving, riding and trotting horses, and had stablemen to care for them. "The living at Arno farm was as good as could be had in the country," it was said of the 4,000-acre ranch.

The place did have its drawbacks. Mrs. Valensin had six people living with her on the property – her ageing father, John F. McCauley; her mother, Caroline McCauley; her brother, George, and his wife; her young son, Pio; and a ranch manager who was a former Sacramento lawyer. Capel made short shrift of the manager who, according to a press report, "became so jealous of the priest and raised such a continual disturbance over the matter, that Mrs. Valensin induced him to leave the place."

The father – a gruff, hardy pioneer, in his late 70s – was a different matter. With Capel happily settling in, McCauley became suspicious of "the remarkable intimacy which had sprung up between his daughter and the priest," according to the *St. Louis Globe-Democrat*. "He did not like the looks of things, and naturally conceived a dislike for Capel, which very quickly increased into an absorbing hatred." That issue, too, was resolved when the wealthy gentleman passed away shortly after Capel's arrival.

Soon, Caroline McCauley – Alice's mother – was also departing. "It was only a short time before a severe quarrel occurred between the reverend gentleman and that lady, which led to the prelate receiving a sound slap in the face," another newspaper, *The Omaha Daily Bee*, discovered. "After this quarrel, Mrs. McCauley left her daughter's house and went to Missouri." Mrs. Valensin's brother, George, and his wife likewise departed, having experienced marital difficulties.

The only person still in residence, apart from Capel and Valensin, was young Pio, to whom the Monsignor became tutor. "At present the situation is this," *The Omaha Daily Bee* concluded in October 1886. "Mgr. Capel, Mrs. Valensin and young Valensin are living alone at the ranch, with no other company than the servants. Besides the ostensible post of tutor, Mgr. Capel acts as the manager of Mrs. Valensin's property, and, as the land is all rented and otherwise tied up, the position is very much of a sinecure."

There were occasional visits by Count Valensin, mainly concerning issues relating to farm stock. Those who knew the Count described a dapper little fellow, addicted to stylish clothes, patent leather shoes, fast horses, and who was "never so happy as when exchanging confidence with a jockey or horse trainer, or watching the blackboard in a pool room." With his diamond-studded shirts and emerald rings – and the fact that he once fought a duel out of jealousy with a man who sought his wife's affections – Capel wisely kept out of his way.

The "Count," as he was invariably called – he wasn't a real one – had strong opinions of the Monsignor. When interviewed, he expressed the view that the relationship between Capel and his wife had become one of an improper nature. "I am thoroughly satisfied that Mgr. Capel has taken my place with Mrs. Valensin in everything but name," he commented. "I cannot say that I know it of my own knowledge, but I am as certain of it as I can be of anything. Any man of common sense can judge of the matter for himself by looking at the existing state of affairs."

There was no man with more common sense than Patrick William Riordan, Archbishop of San Francisco. He soon got wind of the Valensin affair, and like Cardinal McCloskey before him, decided that Capel had to go. A friend of his, Cardinal Gibbons of Baltimore, outlined Riordan's state of mind in a letter. Riordan hoped the Monsignor would "soon return to Rome," although he feared that he might never do so. In the meantime, he was battling to keep the Valensin affair quiet. He "had to use all his tact to keep the scandal out of the papers," Gibbons remarked.

Unfortunately for Riordan, the news leaked out, and the nation's press went into overdrive. The coverage from coast to coast referred to "rumors of a disgraceful character" and "charges of scandalous conduct," noted how the Monsignor had been "behaving very naughtily," and forensically scrutinised his "unseemly career." "The Valensin Scandal," "A Great Churchman's Fall," "The Charges Against Capel" and "No Longer a Catesby" are examples of the numerous headlines that surfaced.

Newsmen had a field day. The *Streator Free Press*, from Illinois, alleged that Capel had "debauched" Mrs. Valensin, "the daughter of one of the richest families" in California. *The New-York Times* wrote of the Monsignor's "doings on the Sacramento river" and how his actions had "shocked even those people who had considerable respect for the cloth until he knocked it out of them." *The Detroit Free Press* was unsurprised by the "flagrant scandal," explaining that during his visit to their city Capel had "earned the reputation of being a showy, glittering and thoroughly insincere man of the world masquerading in priestly garb."

The Catholic World, published out of New York, weighed in on the other side of the debate and railed against the "filthy, false and malicious fabrications about Catholic priests" which were a disgrace to the profession of journalism. "Let some low, vile, contemptible gutter-snipe hand in a piece of 'copy' assailing the character of a priest, and it is gloated over as if no more precious article of news could possibly be obtained." Purveyors of stories such as these were "the maggots of a disreputable press" striving to crawl over the noble form of "a great and good man," the monthly magazine proclaimed.

An indignant Capel added fuel to the fire, issuing strident appeals for a retraction of the allegations made against him. In a series of telegrams to newspapers nationwide, he demanded: "In the name of American liberty and in the name of the honor due to American women, let the journal that has given publicity to it publish the name of the human monstrosity capable of and responsible for giving its false and malicious Californian charge against me, or stand convicted of gross falsehood and cowardice."

Contrary to Capel's hopes, what followed was a flood of allegations in the press concerning his earlier behaviour in California. Two reports revolved around events which had taken place when he was residing at the Palace Hotel in San Francisco. The first involved a convivial evening he shared with the Marquis D. J. Oliver, an Irish-born pillar of the local Catholic community who had been bestowed with the title "Marquis" by Pope Pius IX for his contribution, monetary and otherwise, to the Church.

"It was said that one night at dusk he and the Marquis Oliver left the Palace Hotel together, and much to the scandal of the Marquis – a good old Irishman who had once been a house painter – the monsignor gave chase to a pretty woman, and was about to walk off with her when the Marquis, forgetting his Roman dignity, fell upon Capel and, with the assistance of a hackman, thrust him into a carriage and drove him home." The night air and a large intake of champagne had been "too much for the monsignor," *The Chicago Tribune*, which broke the story, remarked.

A second revelation concerned the breakup of Capel's partnership with his agent and secretary, George Bradshaw, and again involved the Palace Hotel. Bradshaw revealed how he had tired of Capel's fraternising with women, arguing that instead of focusing on business, the Monsignor's "tomfoolery" was costing them money. The amounts involved were substantial. "I do not remember the figures which Bradshaw told me they had made. They were enormous," a journalist remarked after interviewing him.

"I have had trouble with him everywhere," Bradshaw said. "In one place it was almost necessary to kick the women out of the house in which he was staying....he won't leave the women alone and they won't leave him alone, the utter fools! They give him diamonds and rings and ornaments, and he will give them to some passing girl whose fancy he takes." He should, instead, be focusing on business, Bradshaw declared.

During a work trip to Santa Cruz, Capel had lingered too long for the liking of Bradshaw, who waited impatiently for him at the Palace

Hotel. "Women, it is said, cried," a newspaper reported of the impact he made during that visit, adding that "it was openly whispered abroad that several society ladies were a great deal too much attached to the handsome monsignor." Although ordered to return from Santa Cruz, Capel refused, and Bradshaw cut off the supply of cash. A furious Capel made his way back to San Francisco and headed straight to the hotel, where a vicious row ensued.

"He called me a thief and I called him a frequenter of houses of ill-fame," the agent later recalled, adding that he planned to expose Capel's intrigues and "go to the *Argonaut* with some delectable scandals." A fistfight followed. Bradshaw was magnanimous enough to concede that the Monsignor was a good boxer. "The divine with proper training would have made a good showing with John L. Sullivan," he said, referring to the famous heavyweight champion. Inevitably, Bradshaw lost, and the pair's relationship came to an end.

It wasn't the only time Capel resorted to violence – or at least the threat of it – as a reporter from *The World*, a New York broadsheet, discovered. The newspaper had taken a prominent role in exposing the Monsignor's domestic adventures and sent their reporter to allow him the right of reply. "The Monsignor was absent at the time, so the reporter occupied himself with making a careful observation of all about him," the journalist wrote. He particularly noted how Mrs. Valensin exhibited "much uneasiness" on discovering the purpose of his visit.

A furious Monsignor Capel soon entered the room, and although he hadn't yet read the news report, he had heard about its contents. "I can't believe it," he said. "So far I have always been a friend of *The World*. If this thing continues I shall remember my manhood and act as any Englishman would under the circumstances. Fear is a thing I know not, and, well, I am capable of doing something." At this point, the reporter remarked, "the priest cast a proud glance at his brawny arm." The reporter failed to get an interview.

By Christmas 1886, Monsignor Capel was still firmly embedded at Arno and showing no signs of leaving. At nearby Sacramento, seasonal festivities were in full swing. The Wells Fargo express rolled into town, bringing vast stocks of goods. Weinstock & Lubin and Breuner's, two of the city's great stores, were decorated with mountain berries, mistletoe and evergreens. "The entire city wears a holiday appearance," it was said. Money was plentiful, and trade was brisk.

At Arno, Capel was engaging in his own lavish spending – or, more correctly, helping disperse Mrs. Valensin's fortune. The Monsignor "abhors anything unluxurious," a news report commented, yet the ranch house was rustic and, like most Californian ranch houses, was "not generally well furnished." To remedy matters, "furniture went up by the carload to the house." Capel was also drilling the servants, while educating the Chinese cook in the art of making several Italian dishes which tickled his palate.

He continued to tutor Mrs. Valensin's young son, Pio, who had turned 13 shortly before Christmas. People said he was a fine young boy – generous, high-minded, popular with friends, and an example for other boys to follow. "The child was always around his mother, and she was always fussing with him," a neighbouring farmer remarked. Pio was bright, fluent in Italian, and had an understanding of French. It was noted that under Capel's guidance he was "acquiring quite the conversational charm of the gay master."

Capel also prepared Mrs. Valensin for her divorce case in 1887, arguably with good reason. Her attempt to sever links with Count Valensin two years earlier – shortly before the Monsignor's arrival at Arno – had foundered when her cruelty claim was adjudged not proven. The Supreme Court ordered the case to be retried on a point of law, and the rehearing was scheduled for a time when Capel's residency at the Arno ranch threatened to have an explosive impact on proceedings.

"It has been the talk here that Count Valensin has contemplated for some time making Monsignor Capel a co-respondent in the pending suit for divorce," *The Sun*, a mass-appeal broadsheet published out of New York, reported. "A sensation in San Francisco is expected," the *Brooklyn Times Union*, another New York publication, added. Capel scurried from one law firm to the next, swearing affidavits, preparing for the worst. He need not have bothered as the Count offered no defence, and the divorce was granted in November 1887.

Following the case, Monsignor Capel sank into obscurity. The years passed by and few people heard of the fate of the famous prelate whose name, at one time, was on the lips of every Catholic and Protestant in Europe and America. "As far as the public is concerned he has been practically dead for the last five years," the *St. Louis Post-Dispatch* commented in 1891, although it added that rumours were occasionally surfacing which were anything but complimentary.

The fact was that the Monsignor had never left Arno but, as *The Chicago Tribune* discovered and rather callously put it, was still at the ranch, a self-styled tutor, "living the life of a disappointed man, shorn of his honors and his courtly presence." There, in close companionship with Mrs. Valensin, he lived off the fruits of the rich and prosperous land for the final 25 years of his life.

ARNO

Capel in his 70s

The Restaurant de France, partly run by Frenchman Julien Faure, was one of the finest eating establishments in Sacramento. Located on K Street, in the busy heart of the city, it had been offering first-class dining to its wealthy clientele since pioneer days. Its most recent proprietor, Monsieur Faure, had trained as a chef at Pau, a place close to Capel's heart. Inevitably, the restaurant became popular with the Monsignor during his visits from nearby Arno.

One day, in the early 1890s, Capel was spotted at the restaurant by the San Francisco correspondent of *The Chicago Tribune*. "The doors of the main room were suddenly flung open and I heard a penetrating, commanding voice say, 'Let us sit here,'" the correspondent, who had known Capel from his time in San Francisco, wrote. "My attention was at once arrested. No man but Capel has such a voice. I looked up and it was the monsignor....There were two ladies with him. Both were dressed in black, profusely trimmed with crêpe."

Capel's drink-ravaged appearance shocked his observer: "The little red streaks had increased, and they had crossed and recrossed each other so minutely and so thoroughly in his blooded face that it appeared to me as one great scarlet patch. His eyes had lost their fire. They no longer gleamed from out beneath their shaggy brows like sentinels to a great mind, but their look was dead and colorless."

The Monsignor's overcoat was spotted with greasy stains, his collar dusty and unclean, his hands dirty and stained. He immediately ordered claret, drank heartily, and set about his meal. "The day was warm and the atmosphere moist, and as I saw him mop his face with a red bandana and ram the salad into his mouth and gulp it down I felt that if Disraeli could only have seen his Catesby as he now appeared there would have come to that cynical reader of human nature a sharp pang of sorrow," the journalist remarked.

Capel, who was in his mid-50s, still held sway in the restaurant, capturing the attention of those around him. The waiters left other tables to go to his. The landlord bowed and hurried the orders. The landlady smiled and stood ready to help. And yet, as the astute newsman noted, "the man eating and drinking looked like an unhappy man who had lost all in one huge gamble and who lived a discontented life, despising those who paid homage to him and despising himself for being in those environments."

Visits to Sacramento were about the height of Monsignor Capel's travels during the 25 years following his arrival at the Valensin ranch. The city, although growing, was a long way from London, not only in distance but in culture and style. "It could have disappeared after the fervor of the Gold Rush," wrote Marcos Bretón, journalist and columnist with *The Sacramento Bee*. "It probably should have. Pressed between two rivers, it was oppressively hot, dusty, provincial, dull and lowbrow. Who would have wanted to live here if they could live somewhere else?"

Perhaps understandably in those circumstances, the Monsignor spent most of his time at the Arno ranch. He buried himself in the rambling, 17-room Valensin mansion, tutoring Pio when he was young, writing and reading in his study, and drinking to excess. There was the occasional trip to San Francisco – hardly once a year – and visits to the nearby telephone station to make or receive calls. Otherwise, apart from infrequent local lectures, his life was one of a recluse.

"My work is confined to educating the boy," he remarked. "The rest of my time is devoted to books and writing. The whole of the grain land is rented; the remaining part in pasturage is managed by one of the renters; and a foreman superintends the ground surrounding the residence. There is, therefore, no place for a general manager." Despite the limited scope for his talents, he was occasionally seen strolling around the farm dressed like a cowboy or driving a one-horse buggy.

He had become, as one newspaper remarked, the "pathetic picture of old age in exile." He looked his age, had lost his looks, developed a stout figure, and bore the signs of a life anything but abstemious. He possessed all the telltale indicators of high living, including the flushed face traced with red veins that the correspondent for *The Chicago Tribune* noted at the Restaurant de France in Sacramento.

Capel shared his love of alcohol with his close friend Charles K. McClatchy, the crusading editor of *The Sacramento Bee*, whose father was Irish, from County Antrim. They first met on a train rolling down the Sacramento Valley from the east, when the young McClatchy – then only 26 years old – interviewed the Monsignor as he arrived in California. That meeting kindled a close friendship which endured up to Capel's death.

McClatchy gave the Monsignor extensive coverage in his newspaper, all of it of a complimentary nature. He once described Capel as "the world's greatest theological polemic" with "an intellect surpassingly great, his tongue tipped with the divine fire, his brain, and his heart, and soul in his work." Other coverage was even more fawning. Both men, who shared a deep intellectual curiosity – not to mention their mutual attachment to liquor – often met during Capel's years in Arno.

Another fellow drinker and friend was the controversial newsman John A. Sheehan, who was editor and co-publisher of the *Sunday News*, a weekly broadsheet servicing Sacramento. A writer of rare ability, he became embroiled in allegations of corruption and blackmail little more than a decade before his death at the age of 53. Capel's brother, Arthur, also turned up in Arno, where he stayed as a guest at the Valensin ranch. He, too, had a record for adventures with alcohol, replicating to some extent his brother's predilection.

Perhaps the most intriguing visitor to arrive was Monsignor Germano Straniero, a high-powered, influential Vatican diplomat who, in 1886, traversed America on a fact-finding mission on behalf of Pope Leo XIII. A Private Chamberlain to the Pope, this small, handsome, brown-eyed, 33-year-old was speculated to have met Capel at the ranch "for the purpose of conveying a stern rebuke from Rome."

The speculation may not have been wide of the mark as the Vatican had just finalised the Monsignor's formal severance from his priestly faculties. Dr. O'Callaghan, Rector of the English College in Rome, informed Cardinal Manning of the development. "I write to say that Mgr. Capel has been suspended by the Pope *a divinis*," he wrote in July 1886, meaning Capel could no longer celebrate Mass or administer sacraments anywhere in the world. "The Papal suspension is by a Decree of the H. O. [Holy Office], and I have the information on good authority."

Straniero, who was close to the Pope and au fait with the development, no doubt had a long and lively chat with the Monsignor. Following it, he continued on his American travels before returning to Rome, where he planned to deliver a comprehensive summary of his visit to the Pope. A fine communicator and speaker – he was fluent in six languages – it must have been an interesting conversation.

Back at Arno, Capel was living with another fine conversationalist, Mrs. Valensin, who was said to be one of the best sources of stories in California. She had a vast range of tales to tell – how she had met Abraham Lincoln, had been feted with her wealthy parents at the famous military outpost Fort Laramie, had barely avoided a treason charge after singing *Dixie* in a San Francisco hotel, and had fled with her Confederate-supporting parents to Europe, where she became a dazzling debutante in the European courts of the mid-nineteenth century.

She was well educated, having attended the Convent du Sacré Coeur in Paris, where "so many European noblewomen received their education," she explained. The schooling had obviously paid off. "I read each day from Spanish, French, German or Italian books," she remarked. Her Catholic background and wealth also brought her into contact with Archbishop Riordan, of San Francisco, and Bishop Grace, of Sacramento, who were visitors to the Arno ranch.

By the 1890s and early 1900s, when Capel was firmly ensconced at Arno, Mrs. Valensin was losing her good looks. "I was small and trim, with blue eyes, an attractive face, blonde hair and a vivaciousness that prompted my father in law to call me his 'little witch,'" she reflected on her appearance as a young, eligible lady. With the passage of time, a newspaper claimed, she had become "an unprepossessing woman of the bone and sinew order, with a long, lantern-jawed face and a complexion of yellow leather."

Both Mrs. Valensin and the Monsignor – and their guests – were well looked after by Eliza Matthews, a "colored maid" whose grandparents had come to America as slaves. "Eliza is a granddaughter of a slave woman named Mammy Ann," Mrs. Valensin once explained, adding that she was "not a servant, but a companion." Eliza worked hard, but without pay. "I am a true Southerner," Mrs. Valensin remarked, well accustomed to the use of slaves in her family.

In these cosseted surroundings – being waited on hand and foot – the Monsignor never lost his grandiosity or sense of self-esteem. He falsely alluded to his family as being from the Capell bloodline, holders of the title Earl of Essex. When applying for a California State Library card, he wrote that his father had been "Capt. John Capel," although he had never attained that rank. His mother's father, in Ireland, was a large farmer, he claimed, but that wasn't accurate, either – he only rented 15 acres.

He said he had resigned as the Marquess of Bute's chaplain due to work pressure, ignoring the fact that Bute had fired him. He boasted that he had "been honored with personal relations by His Majesty," King Edward VII of England, despite having met him only once at a royal garden party. When the King died, he wrote to the press about his "loyal allegiance to the deceased monarch" and expressed "heartfelt sympathy with the widowed Queen." He ended his missive with "God save the King."

Even Mrs. Valensin was a victim of his grandiosity. When writing his will, he made her the beneficiary of a trust fund he had inherited in England. Unfortunately for her, it was later discovered that the trust fund – written into the will at Sacramento in April 1891 – didn't exist, at least by the time of his death. The remainder of his estate, worth approximately $1,000, was bequeathed to the children of his brother, Arthur. Mrs. Valensin received nothing.

Capel also had grand ideas about the future of the Arno ranch. "I have decided to build an agricultural college. This institution will be the Monsignor's especial care," he told *The San Francisco Call.* Equally ambitious was his plan to develop sugar beet in the region and his scheme to subdivide the big ranches around Sacramento and inhabit them with new settlers from Europe. "I am an ill-used man," he had frequently remarked. No doubt he felt these new activities might change all that.

He had no difficulty admonishing his superior, Dr. Patrick William Riordan, Archbishop of San Francisco, who he accused of bad-mouthing him during a visit to Arno. "Your Grace's assertion to Governor Stoneman, a Protestant, at the table of this household, that I am fond of wining and dining out, as well as further injurious statements about me....caused painful astonishment!" he wrote. After alleging that the Archbishop had revealed a further sensitive issue to other senior churchmen, he went on to ask for his help in restoring him to priestly office. His audacity knew no bounds.

He was additionally happy to comment on the "unnatural crimes" and "outbreaks of depravity" of his fellow countryman Oscar Wilde, despite his own track record of sexual misbehaviour. He sensed that Wilde's "heavy, sensuous face, the pasty complexion and the mass of loose flesh under the esthete's eyes, were a bad indication of his character." He was revolted, he said, by "the degraded members of the aristocracy who were his associates." Confession, he added, was the best remedy for homosexuality.

The one person he never publicly commented on was his adversary, Count Valensin. Perhaps he had good reason to hold his tongue. Not only was the deserted husband said to be "a morose and disappointed man," but the former duellist harboured a dark hatred for Capel. "Whenever he hears the name of Capel mentioned his cheeks flush angrily and his dark eyes flash with a menacing and dangerous expression," Joseph Pulitzer's *The World* – famous for its sex scandals and other sensational stories – disclosed.

Midway through the first decade of the 1900s, as Capel approached 70, the world had all but forgotten about his existence. There were occasional references to him in the press, mostly relating to his retirement at the Arno ranch. One observer, writing from Los Angeles, noted how he was "still suspended, ecclesiastically, but may sometimes be seen, in the neighbouring church, making the Stations of the Cross." His observation was insightful, as Capel was attempting to return to his priestly activities.

His route back to the priestly fold was facilitated by Bishop Grace of Sacramento, a Wexford-born fellow Irishman who knew Capel well. A kind, unassuming man, he decided to allow Capel deliver sermons and discourses at the Cathedral, especially to children, starting in New Year 1907. The Bishop's decision was no doubt influenced by his friendship with Mrs. Valensin and Charles McClatchy, editor of *The Sacramento Bee*. Capel immediately said "Yes," jumping at the chance of climbing the steps of a pulpit for the first time in decades.

Over the next five years, Capel pumped out discourses on unlikely themes, given his history. He delivered sermons on morality at the Cathedral and elsewhere. "Look at the filthy, suggestive pictures in our newspapers, and the theatres we have which border on the immoral," he declared. He dealt with man's treatment of the opposite sex. "Too often man allows his animal instincts to get the better of him and perhaps exhibits himself before the woman he has sworn to cherish in an intoxicated condition or does other acts equally detestable to her," he preached.

He railed against the evils of liquor and saloons. "Unhappily, experience the world over witnesses to the evil effects of saloons especially to the young, and no stone should be left unturned to avert such dangers," he said. Old sermons from his time at Pau – including "Sins of the Tongue" – were dusted down and redelivered. New themes, "Confession and Satisfaction for Sin," "Conscience and its Culture," and "The Meaning of Mass," were also included in his repertoire. Large audiences came to hear him. As one newspaper remarked, his sermons were "a treat not soon to be forgotten."

The weekend beginning Saturday, 21 October 1911 was another busy one in the diary of Monsignor Capel. He stayed at the residence of Bishop Grace, next to the Cathedral, to be on hand for his regular Sunday morning sermon to children. On Sunday evening, he delivered another sermon before heading to bed. "He was apparently in full health," it was reported, "and those who listened to his discourse at the Cathedral say he was never so brilliant and so alert."

That night, shortly after midnight, a diocesan priest, Fr. Ryan, heard the Monsignor coughing but paid little or no heed. The following morning, at eight o'clock, he became worried on noticing that the prelate was late for Mass. After repeatedly knocking on his door, he entered and found him lying on his bed, his hands close to his chest as if he had suffered a heart attack. Although the body was warm, Monsignor Capel was dead, five days short of his 75th birthday.

Bishop Grace decided that the Monsignor should be given a send-off appropriate to a man of his stature. The body was dressed in purple vestments and placed in a purple coffin with mountings of silver but of simple design. It was then transferred to the Cathedral and placed in front of the pulpit where a few nights earlier the Monsignor had delivered what his friend Charles McClatchy, of *The Sacramento Bee*, described as "his last lecture in the interest of mankind."

Everyone connected with the Church in Sacramento or its hinterland was notified of the imminent funeral, including priests from remote parishes. Many responded, most notably those who were posted to the High Sierras. The majority were of Irish stock. "Gold Rush" priests Fr. O'Kane, of Georgetown, and Fr. Horgan, from Placerville, decided to come. So, too, did another Fr. Horgan, this one from Truckee, a rough-and-tumble mountain town where pistol affrays in barrooms had once been common.

Fr. Brady, of Red Bluff – formerly a busy port for paddle-wheel steamers – packed his bags, as did Fr. Murphy, of Virginia City, where a young Mark Twain had worked as a reporter on the local newspaper. One of the rare non-Irish priests, Fr. Walrath, a Prussian based in Woodland, who early in his career had allowed his Native American converts to end their recitations of the Rosary with an Indian dance, also decided to attend.

The funeral Mass, officiated by Bishop Grace, took place at the Cathedral on Wednesday, 25 October 1911. Shortly afterwards, just after midday, the casket was borne down the steps of the Cathedral to the horse-drawn hearse waiting below. It was a hot Sacramento day, with the sun burning in a clear-blue sky. Hundreds lined the steps, the men in sombre suits of grey and black, the women in long skirts and bonnets.

From there, the cortège silently wound its way to St. Joseph's Cemetery, located on 21st Street, two miles distant. A few chosen priests sang the *Benedictus* at the graveside, asking God to shine his compassion on those who dwell in darkness and to guide the sinner on the path to peace. As the canticle was quietly sung, the body of the Right Rev. Monsignor Capel was lowered to its resting place in the priests' plot, beside the dust of the deceased clergy of Sacramento.

Back in Kensington, autumn had settled in. There were shorter days, morning mists, evening fogs, and the overcast sky was spitting occasional showers. Pathways were covered with leaves and crushed bright-russet chestnuts. The sound of migrating birds filled the air. People indoors, snug before their fires, settled back to catch up with the latest gossip in their newspapers.

Reports of a once famous priest whose star, 40 years earlier, had blazed through the London skyline might have caught their eye. He had done well since leaving England, readers were told. Prior to his death he was employed as the "prelate in charge of the Roman Catholic Church for the district of Northern California" and had been living for ten years "at the residence of Monsignor Grace, the Bishop of Sacramento."

Even in death the Monsignor was still spinning yarns!

EPILOGUE

Monsignor Capel Bust

In September 1940, at the height of the Blitz, the Luftwaffe dropped incendiary bombs on the Church of Our Lady of Victories in Kensington. A nasty red glow lit up the sky. Nothing but the four walls and pillars of the building remained standing. The pulpit of the Pro-Cathedral, where the Monsignor had delivered so many inspirational sermons, was destroyed.

It took a wrecking ball, and not incendiary bombs, to demolish Capel's beloved Cedar Villa. The famous property made way for a block of flats. His other main residence, Scarsdale Lodge, was also demolished for development. The ivy-covered Abingdon House, home to the Catholic University College, met with a similar fate and was replaced by a row of houses.

Within a decade of Capel's move to America, the clerical landscape of the Diocese of Westminster was transformed beyond recognition. Capel's nemesis Cardinal Manning passed away in 1892. Another adversary, the Rev. Walter Croke Robinson, acquired the title of Monsignor having been elevated to Domestic Prelate of the Pope. A noted lecturer and writer, Robinson died in 1914.

Mary Stourton – the object of Capel's ruinous attentions – met with further tragedy later in her life. In July 1887, she married the Irish-born James Graham at the Pro-Cathedral, Kensington, fulfilling a dream she feared might never be realised. Unfortunately, he died when Mary was in her 40s. She then lived in a boarding house in Paddington, London, adjacent to the railway line. She died from cirrhosis of the liver, at the age of 52.

One by one, the Monsignor's Pious Ladies also passed away. Fanny Geldard went to live in a convent, although she never became a nun. Instead, she taught French and music on a live-in basis and worked into old age. She was obliged to do so, as reflected in the £20 she had to her name when she passed away in 1909. Another Pious Lady, Annie Gomess, was also plunged into poverty. When she died in 1906, her effects were valued at less than £120.

The same destiny befell Mrs. Bellew, who had a long and torrid affair with the Monsignor. "I am in great mental distress," she said, following what she described as "the enormity of my sin against Almighty God." She was eventually forced to relinquish her Kensington property and move to Queen's Crescent, Kentish Town, where she died in September 1894. She left behind effects worth less than £300.

Mrs. Rutherford Smith also never fully recovered after her three-year involvement with Capel. Following her divorce, she married again, to a "gentleman" named Charles Holland Hastings, but he subsequently deserted her. Forced to rely on the charity of relatives and friends, in desperation she sued him for alimony of £1 a week. She married for a third time, in 1906, to Henry Hans Scharpenberg, a financier, and lived with him for the last two years of her life. She died aged 55.

Mrs. Valensin, who was Capel's companion in California, suffered no such hardship. She lived a long and prosperous life at her Arno ranch, eventually dying in 1949, at the age of 101. Her former husband, Count Valensin, fared less well in the longevity stakes. Although he became a well-known horse breeder – and once owned Sidney, the fastest trotter in the United States – he died in 1892, aged 40. To everybody's shock, he left Pio, his son, a mere $1 in his will.

There could be no greater contrast to Capel's lifestyle than the path taken by his older sister, Maria, who became a nun. Mother Gabriel, as she was called, was a bright, well-read, charitable woman, and an inspirational teacher. People who knew her said she was deeply in love with the Monsignor and had the highest regard for his intelligence. Undoubtedly, his loss less than a year earlier hastened her death in London, in August 1912.

Another notable Capel family member, Arthur, died in 1904, after excelling in business, retiring when young, and moving to Paris where he and his wife, Berthe, lived an affluent lifestyle. Their debonair son, Arthur "Boy" Capel, made a fortune in shipping, and like his father and uncle, mixed in exalted circles. He had a nine-year affair with Coco Chanel, the fashion designer, and financed her first shops. The affair continued until his death, aged 38, in a car crash.

The Monsignor's Coco Chanel connection didn't end there. To this day, visitors to her opulently-decorated apartment at 31 Rue Cambon, Paris, can see an imposing, beautifully-sculpted bust sitting on her mantelpiece. The bust is the same marble sculpture of Monsignor Capel that once graced Cedar Villa. With his resolute jaw, aquiline nose, pursed lips, confident gaze, and dressed in Monsignor's robes, Capel surveys the lavish furnishings and artworks around him, looking perfectly pleased.

ACKNOWLEDGEMENTS

The philosopher John Stuart Mill described the Victorian era as "the age of newspapers, railways, and the electric telegraph." The period he was referring to roughly coincided with the 50 years from 1860 – 1910, which is considered the golden age of newspaper publishing. Technological innovation allied to growing levels of literacy led to an enormous number of titles being presented for sale. The fact that the Monsignor's career spanned the era was crucial to the writing of this book.

We had a vast range of newspapers to choose from. Among them were *The Times*, published out of London since the 1780s, and its competitor *The Daily Telegraph*, which by 1876 had the largest circulation of any newspaper in the world. Like their counterparts, *The Scotsman*, from Edinburgh, and the Marquess of Bute's *Western Mail*, from Cardiff, these broadsheets found sizeable readerships in their immediate areas and, via steam train, in surrounding hinterlands. A century and a half later, they became priceless resources for us.

The Tablet, which was launched in 1840 and is still going strong, was among the 250 or so British dailies or weeklies we turned to in the course of our research. It was a wonderful source for tracking the Monsignor's activities, especially his career in Kensington. *The Illustrated London News* – the world's first illustrated news magazine, which was published on a weekly basis – was also priceless, as were its rivals, the downmarket *Penny Illustrated Paper* and *The Graphic* whose artwork impressed the Dutch painter Vincent van Gogh while living in London at the height of Monsignor Capel's fame.

Other valuable titles include the *Morning Post*, *Pall Mall Gazette*, *John Bull*, *Evening Standard*, *Daily News*, *South London Chronicle*, *Globe*, *Yorkshire Post*, *Manchester Evening News*, *Manchester Weekly Times*, *Preston Chronicle*, *Birmingham Daily Post*, *Newcastle Journal*,

Bradford Daily Telegraph, Norwich Mercury, Lancaster Gazette, Sheffield & Rotherham Independent, York Herald, Northampton Mercury, Burnley Advertiser, Glasgow Herald, and *Edinburgh Evening News.*

Local newspapers helped identify Capel's victims, most notably Mary Stourton and Mrs. Rutherford Smith. Stourton's family was sufficiently wealthy and well known that the *Isle of Wight Observer,* along with the *Hampshire Advertiser, Hampshire Telegraph* and *Hampshire Chronicle,* allowed us to build a profile of her life. Without the *Taunton Courier, Gloucestershire Chronicle, Bristol Times and Mirror, Southern Times,* and *Exeter and Plymouth Gazette,* we may never have discovered the background of Mrs. Rutherford Smith.

The fame and power of the Marquess of Bute ensured that almost every Welsh newspaper, local and otherwise, covered his dealings with the Monsignor, including the *Welshman, North Wales Chronicle, Aberystwyth Times, Rhyl Record and Advertiser, Cardiff Times, Cardiff and Merthyr Guardian, South Wales Daily News,* and *Carnarvon and Denbigh Herald.* Likewise, the activities of some of the Capel family – most notably the Monsignor's mother – were covered by the *Hastings and St. Leonards News, Hastings Chronicle,* and *Hastings & St. Leonards Observer.*

A brief list of other useful local or regional papers includes the *Dover Telegraph, Islington Gazette, Bedfordshire Mercury, Stroud News, Oxford Chronicle & Berks & Bucks Gazette, Oxfordshire Weekly News, Leamington Advertiser, Rugby Advertiser, Reading Mercury, Shepton Mallet Journal, Hendon & Finchley Times, Chelmsford Chronicle, Folkestone Express,* and *Crewe Guardian.*

Irish newspapers also covered Capel's career, not because of his Irish birth and maternal connections but due to his extraordinary fame and occasional visits. Among the most important were the *Freeman's Journal, Nation, Irish Times, Cork Constitution, Cork Examiner, Dublin Evening Mail, Evening Telegraph, Belfast News Letter, Belfast Telegraph, Kerry Evening Post, Kilkenny Journal, Nenagh Guardian, Fermanagh Herald,* and *Derry Journal.*

Many magazines and journals were helpful, among them *Vanity Fair* whose "Men of the Day" feature, in September 1872, was the first to refer to Capel as the "Apostle to the Genteel," a sobriquet that stuck with him for the rest of his days. The magazine held back little in its sarcasm, referring, for example, to his manners as stretching to "a point of suavity amounting nearly to fawning." *Vanity Fair*'s observations, while often amusing, may even have been accurate.

Other priceless resources included *The Month*, a Jesuit-published review which would later feature great writers like Graham Greene and Evelyn Waugh; *The London Review*, which at its foundation in 1860 declared its intention to cater for "intelligent readers of this much-reading age"; and *The Whitehall Review*, "a journal of politics, literature, art, and country pursuits," published on Thursdays and priced sixpence. *The Bulwark or Reformation Journal*, a Scottish Reformation Society publication designed to expose "Popery," was also of value.

The Monsignor's thought-reading experiment was featured in *The Eclectic Magazine*, Vol. 45, 1887, in an article written by Stuart Cumberland. Monsignor Capel's visit to the girls' convent school near Paris appeared in *Scribner's Monthly*, Vol. 15, Nov. 1877 – April 1878. Valuable descriptions of the Monsignor's time in Pau were contained in *The Galaxy*, Vol. 10, July 1870 – Jan. 1871. Although these three magazines were American-published, the events they covered pertained to his life and times in Europe.

While one would be hard-pressed to find any newspaper in the English-speaking world that did not refer to Monsignor Capel at the height of his career, surprisingly not a single biography or detailed analysis was ever written about this remarkable man. Inch by inch research was required instead. This task led us on a journey from the beaches of Ardmore and Whiting Bay to his stomping grounds in Britain, France, Italy and America, and through many dozens of archives, record offices and libraries along the way.

We extend a special word of thanks to the Westminster Diocesan Archives, Kensington, London, which possesses an extraordinary collection of material relating to Monsignor Capel. Many of the documents, reports, letters and notes we reference in this book – primarily relating to his pre-America years – were sourced in the archives and are listed at the end of this book. Not only were we given access over a number of visits, but we were graciously received and assisted by their archivists, Fr. Nicholas Schofield, Susannah Rayner and Judi McGinley. Our sincere gratitude goes out to them for their hospitality and generosity.

We are additionally indebted to the National Archives, Kew, Surrey, where we sourced records concerning John Capel's naval and coast-guard careers, along with his son's application for entry to the upper school of the Royal Hospital, Greenwich. The British Library in London, and Angie Shelton of the Library Services at St. Mary's University, Twickenham, were also most helpful, as was Gil Newman of Hastings Library, who discovered a rare report concerning the death of John Capel, the Monsignor's father.

In Ireland, we received help from the public library in Lismore, County Waterford, and the National Library, Dublin. Further assistance was provided by Dungarvan photographer Sean Byrne, who helped prepare the cover image of the book, and by author and poet John Daly, who kindly read the first draft of the text and provided encouragement and advice. We are also grateful to Ber Mangan O'Farrell for her contribution to the artwork.

We are additionally obliged to archivist Noelle Dowling, of the Dublin Diocesan Archives, who went to great lengths to source material from their impressive historical collections. Our thanks also go to Linda Monahan, Barbara Ryan and Roy Thewlis, of Typeform, for their expertise. Likewise, we are grateful to Professor Con Timon for his much-valued care and support.

A wide range of books helped us construct the Monsignor's life as a boy. Included among them were *Ardmore Memory and Story*, by Siobhán Lincoln; *Guide to Youghal, Ardmore and the Blackwater*, by Samuel Hayman, 1860; *The History, Topography and Antiquities of the County and City of Waterford*, by Richard Hopkins Ryland, 1824;

Ireland: Its Scenery, Character, etc., by Mr. and Mrs. S. C. Hall, 1846; *The Smugglers*, by Charles G. Harper, 1909; and *Cornelia Connelly: A Study in Fidelity*, by Mother Marie Thérèse.

We also consulted a large number of books with information relevant to the Monsignor's third-level education. They included *Commitment to Diversity: Catholics and Education in a Changing World*, edited by Dr. Mary Eaton, which contains a chapter on St. Mary's College, Hammersmith, by Noreen Nicholson; and the *Centenary Record of St. Mary's College, Hammersmith 1850 – 1925, Strawberry Hill 1925 – 1950*. Of additional importance were *Nineteenth-Century English Religious Traditions*, edited by Denis G. Paz; and *Religion in Victorian Britain*, edited by Gerald Parsons.

Further books revealed details about Capel's visits to Lourdes and his later career as an educationalist. *The Village of Bernadette*, by Colm Keane and Una O'Hagan, covered the former. Among the most important covering the latter were *English Roman Catholics and Higher Education 1830 – 1903*, by Vincent Alan McClelland; and *Fifty Years of Catholic Life and Social Progress*, by Percy Hetherington Fitzgerald, 1901. The Rise and Fall of the Catholic University College, Kensington, 1868 – 1882, by Tom Horwood, published not in book form but in the *Journal of Ecclesiastical History*, Vol. 54, Issue 2, April 2003, was also excellent.

A number of additional books proved crucial: *Converts to Rome*, by W. Gordon Gorman, 1885; *Life of Cardinal Manning*, by Edmund Sheridan Purcell, 1896; *The History of the Noble House of Stourton*, by Lord Mowbray, 1889; *The Climate of Pau*, by Sir Alexander Taylor, 1845; *Unorthodox London*, by Charles Maurice Davies, 1873; *John Patrick, Third Marquess of Bute*, by Sir David Hunter Blair; and *The Grand Designer, Third Marquess of Bute*, by Rosemary Hannah. Beatrice Webb's memories of Capel as a sermonizer are contained in *Sidney and Beatrice Webb*, Vol. 1, edited by Norman Mackenzie.

Further helpful books included *A Handbook for Travellers in France*, 1867; *Survey of London*, Vol. 42, London County Council, 1986; *Victorian London*, by Liza Picard; *Daily Life in Victorian England*, by Sally Mitchell; *Victorian Britain*, by Brenda Williams; *The Victorian City: Everyday Life in Dickens' London*, by Judith Flanders; *The London Restaurant 1840 – 1914*, by Brenda Assael; *The Railways*, by Simon Bradley; and *A Dictionary of Victorian London: An A – Z of the Great Metropolis*, by Lee Jackson.

A Roman Miscellany: The English in Rome 1550 – 2000, edited by Nicholas Schofield, was valuable in identifying the major English figures in Rome during Capel's era. William Pepperell's hard-to-find *The Church Index*, from 1872, was also most helpful even if the author took an acerbic view of everything to do with the Catholic Church. Pepperell had an astute eye and provided a remarkable insight to the physical layout of the Pro-Cathedral and those who worked in it, including Monsignor Capel.

On the British book front, finally deserving mention are *Lothair*, by Benjamin Disraeli; *David Copperfield* and *The Pickwick Papers*, by Charles Dickens; *The Picture of Dorian Gray*, by Oscar Wilde; *Finnegans Wake*, by James Joyce; and a range of books by Margaret Mary Plues, including *Rambles in Search of Flowerless Plants*.

A large number of directories, calendars and yearbooks also provided priceless information. Among them, covering many years, were the *Catholic Directory, Almanac and Clergy List*; *Sadliers' Catholic Directory*; *Battersby's Catholic Directory, Almanac, and Registry of the Whole Catholic World*; *Catholic Encyclopedia*; and *Catholic Who's Who & Year-Book*.

Other works of reference include *Debrett's Peerage*; *The County Families of the United Kingdom*; *Kelly's Handbook to the Titled, Landed & Official Classes*; and a range of trades, street, city, professional, property and Post Office directories. *The Oxford University Calendar* and *The Navy List* were also important, as were numerous census, birth, marriage, divorce and death records.

Regarding America, we were blessed not only with the country's enormous number of newspapers but with their insatiable appetite for stories concerning Monsignor Capel. Unlike Europe, where a gentlemanly reserve overshadowed press coverage, American editors were uninhibited in their reporting and journalistic styles. Graphic accounts of the Monsignor's exploits were brought to light as a result.

From Capel's arrival in Manhattan to his final years at Arno, well-known newspapers such as the *New-York Times, Chicago Tribune, Boston Globe, Philadelphia Inquirer, Washington Post, Los Angeles Times* and *San Francisco Examiner* covered his progress. Some newspapers, such as New York's *World, Sun, Star, Tribune, Herald* and *Brooklyn Daily Eagle*, took an intense interest in his affairs. Other broadsheets, published out of cities he visited, remained curious about his continuing exploits.

We accessed more than 200 daily and weekly publications from all parts of America. Of great value were the *Sacramento Bee, Sacramento Star*, and the Sacramento-published *Record-Union*. Another important reference point was the *St. Louis Post-Dispatch*. Further excellent sources included the *San Francisco Chronicle, San Francisco Call, Santa Cruz Surf, Santa Cruz Sentinel, Omaha Daily Bee*, and *Detroit Free Press*. This latter newspaper featured author and poet William Augustus Croffut's insightful descriptions of David Dudley Field's dinner party, which are contained in the "On the Road" chapter.

We encountered some intriguing dailies and weeklies along the way. The *Butte Daily Miner*, which reported on the manager's unsuccessful attempts to lure Capel to his Butte Grand Opera House, is a case in point. Set in a tiny mining town, the fact that the newspaper existed at all is remarkable. With the shift in population from east to west, allied to improvements in printing technology and the growing use of the telegraph, there were many newspapers similar to this Montana publication springing up throughout the country. A large number of them proved valuable.

A brief list of useful broadsheets includes: *Frank Leslie's Illustrated Newspaper, Cincinnati Enquirer, Atlanta Constitution, Oakland Tribune, Hartford Courant, Sioux City Journal, Buffalo Evening News, Stockton Mail, Macon Telegraph*, and *Salt Lake Democrat*. Further information was gleaned from the *St. Louis Globe-Democrat, Lancaster Daily Intelligencer, Norfolk Virginian, Indianapolis News, Los Angeles Mirror*, and *Elk City Globe*.

The *Shreveport Times, Shreveport Journal, Leavenworth Standard, St. Paul Globe, Streator Free Press, Kansas City Times, Baltimore Sun,* and *Pittsburgh Daily Post* were also of importance. Some unusual titles were encountered, such as the *Carbon Advocate* from Lehighton, Pennsylvania, *Weekly Capital-Commonwealth* from Topeka, Kansas, and the *Daily Memphis Avalanche* from Memphis, Tennessee. To all of these titles, including those not listed, we offer our sincere thanks.

Many books aided us in the American leg of our research, the following being the most notable: *Journalism in the United States from 1690 – 1872,* by Frederic Hudson; *Retrospect of Western Travel,* Vol. 2, by Harriet Martineau, 1838; *Performing Authorship in the Nineteenth-Century Transatlantic Lecture Tour,* by Amanda Adams; *Greenwich Village Catholics,* by Thomas J. Shelley; *Incredible New York,* by Lloyd Morris; *Henry Ward Beecher: His Life and Work,* by J. T. Lloyd; and *The Transatlantic Marriage Bureau,* by Julie Ferry.

The Baptist preacher Dr. Justin D. Fulton produced some interesting, if now outdated, publications including *Rome in America, Washington in the Lap of Rome, How to Win Romanists* and *The Roman Catholic Element in American History.* He would have been unamused by the invaluable *The Gentleman's Companion,* described by *The New-York Times* as "A Vest Pocket Guide to Brothels in 19th-Century New York for Gentlemen on the Go," published in 1870. *The Baptist Encyclopedia,* by William Cathcart, and *The Encyclopedia of New York City,* edited by Kenneth T. Jackson, were also useful.

Turning to California, *History of Sacramento County, California,* by G. Walter Reed; *An Illustrated History of Sacramento County, California,* by Winfield J. Davis; *Sacramento County and its Resources: a Souvenir of the Bee,* published in 1895; *The Good Life: Sacramento's Consumer Culture,* by Steven Avella; and *Past and Present of Alameda County,* by Joseph E. Baker, were all of importance, as was Steven Avella's book *Charles K. McClatchy and the Golden Era of American Journalism.*

We would like to thank Kate Feighery, Director of Archives and Records Management with the Archdiocese of New York, who was most helpful. Kate provided many notes, letters and copies of telegrams from Rome, Dublin and cities throughout America which were important for our research. While all were significant, some were quoted from and are listed in the notes at the end of this book.

We also extend our gratitude to archivist Chris Doan, who opened up the San Francisco Archdiocesan files and, in particular, led us to an important letter written by the Monsignor to Archbishop Riordan. Bonnie Rodriguez, Managing Editor of *The Galt Herald*, provided guidance and advice, while Dan Tarnasky, Historian/Archivist with the Galt Area Historical Society, went to great lengths to secure the rare image of Alice Valensin featured in the book. Along with Marcos Bretón, of *The Sacramento Bee*, for his description of Sacramento during Capel's era, we would like to thank them all.

Finally, we wish to thank all those American state agencies which provided us with documents regarding births, marriages, deaths and divorces, including the Monsignor's application for a California State Library card. One of those documents was a copy of the Monsignor's death certificate, showing that he died aged 74 years, 11 months and 25 days, with his father's name "unknown," his mother's name also "unknown," and whose "trade, profession, or particular kind of work" was, up to the time of his death, clearly marked as "clergyman."

NOTES

The following is a summary of documents sourced from various diocesan archives. Some documents were referred to on multiple occasions, as can be seen from the following lists.

Westminster Diocesan Archives

Prologue
Sergeant Ahern's statement of events at Cedar Villa is contained in Ma 2/3/204. The quote "He cannot be stopped" was accessed from Ma 2/3/255.

The Rise to Fame
An account of the Monsignor's sexual misbehaviour with two American sisters and their servant in Rome is featured in Ma 2/3/50.

Decline and Fall
Details of J. P. O'Hara's visit to Rome are contained in Ma 2/3/83. The Pickwell observations are outlined in Ma 2/3/410, while Sergeant Ahern's complaints are in Ma 2/3/204. Details regarding the state of the University College accounts were sourced from Ma 2/3/214. Other documents include Ma 2/3/50, Ma 2/3/225, Ma 2/3/354, Ma 2/3/371, Ma 2/3/48, Ma 2/3/232, Ma 2/3/497, Ma 2/3/284, Ma 2/3/126 regarding the complaint of the Reverend Mother, and Ma 2/3/546 which contains Capel's response.

The Mary Stourton Scandal
Mary Stourton was an inveterate letter writer who engaged in extensive correspondence with Cardinal Manning, Monsignor Capel and others. Informative letters include Ma 2/3/8, Ma 2/3/97, Ma 2/3/18, Ma 2/3/271, Ma 2/3/542, Ma 2/3/135, Ma 2/3/306, Ma 2/3/90, Ma 2/3/79, Ma 2/3/99, Ma 2/3/123, Ma 2/3/128, and Ma 2/3/161. Notes written by Cardinal Manning (Ma 2/3/85) and Ma 2/3/130 were also of use. The photograph of Mary Stourton sent to Monsignor Capel (Ma 2/3/89) and used in this book is courtesy of the Westminster Diocesan Archives.

The Mrs. Bellew Affair
Mrs. Bellew's statement to Cardinal Manning and Capel's reply (Ma 2/3/24), Dr. Willington's communications with Cardinal Manning (notably Ma 2/3/150 and Ma 2/3/151), notes from the Vicar General (Ma 2/3/49), and a letter from Mrs. Bellew to Capel (Ma 2/3/93) were of central importance. The anonymous letter (Ma 2/3/72) was also useful.

The Housemaid's Tale
Lucy Stevens' testimony before the Commission of Investigation is contained in Ma 2/3/225 and Ma 2/3/51. Other accounts feature in Ma 2/3/155, Ma 2/3/156, Ma 2/3/151, Ma 2/3/59, and Ma 2/3/68. Capel's response can be found in Ma 2/3/164.

Commission of Investigation
An important summary of the Commission of Investigation's work is contained in Ma 2/3/225. The commission member's quotes were sourced from Ma 2/3/40. Other quotes came from Ma 2/3/24, Ma 2/3/51, Ma 2/3/222, Ma 2/3/233, Ma 2/3/151, Ma 2/3/322, and Ma 2/3/180.

Money Matters
Information concerning Bernard Alfred Fairfield is contained in three documents: one an unnumbered letter from the Reverend Mother of the Sisters of Charity orphanage; the others are Ma 2/3/305 and Ma 2/3/428. Details regarding the Petritzka story were sourced from Ma 2/3/82 and Ma 2/3/449. General money debts are itemised in Ma 2/3/119, Ma 2/3/146, Ma 2/3/388, and Ma 2/3/144.

The Ruin of Miss Plues
The narrative of Margaret Mary Plues was greatly assisted by a series of letters and documents including Ma 2/3/270, Ma 2/3/80, Ma 2/3/497, Ma 2/3/275, Ma 2/3/273, Ma 2/3/77, Ma 2/3/81, Ma 2/3/429, and a letter from Alice Wilmot Chetwode (Ma 2/3/310).

The Mayor, the Maid & the Widows
Two letters (Ma 2/3/131 and Ma 2/3/138) concerning the McSwiney case, one letter (Ma 2/3/338) referring to the Carston case, two further letters (Ma 2/3/99 and Ma 2/3/495) relating to the Davidson will, and another (Ma 2/3/469) regarding Mrs. Richardson were referenced in this chapter.

The Battle for Rome
The correspondence of Fr. Robert Butler provided many insights to events at Rome (especially Ma 2/3/84), as did letters from Bishop William Clifford (notably Ma 2/3/247). Further useful correspondence and notes include Ma 2/3/181, Ma 2/3/169, Ma 2/3/250, Ma 2/3/249, Ma 2/3/74, Ma 2/3/265, and Ma 2/3/243. Cardinal Manning's quotes were excerpted from Ma 2/3/258.

Mrs. Rutherford Smith
Letters from John Hoadley Rutherford Smith (especially Ma 2/3/46), his sworn statement (Ma 2/3/335) and a letter from Mrs. Rutherford Smith's sister (Ma 2/3/361) were central to this chapter. Other letters include Ma 2/3/344, Ma 2/3/370, Ma 2/3/76, and the maid's letter (Ma 2/3/362).

Infamy and Disgrace
A document from Annie Gomess (Ma 2/3/76), remarks by Capel (Ma 2/3/373), and gossip letters (Ma 2/3/312, Ma 2/3/251, Ma 2/3/414 and Ma 2/3/413) were

important. Other documents referenced were Ma 2/3/308, Ma 2/3/46, Ma 2/3/378, Ma 2/3/375, Ma 2/3/371, and Ma 2/3/384. Two further documents (Ma 2/3/4 and Ma 2/3/5) featured the controversy surrounding the baptism of Arthur Capel Jnr.

Bankruptcy
Three file documents (Ma 2/3/313, Ma 2/3/488 and Ma 2/3/46) referred to the attempted fraud by Alice Wilmot Chetwode. The comments from Capel were sourced from Ma 2/3/287.

The Reckoning
News from Rome was imparted in many letters, notably Ma 2/3/402, Ma 2/3/403, Ma 2/3/501, Ma 2/3/471, Ma 2/3/479, Ma 2/3/480, Ma 2/3/84, Ma 2/3/483, Ma 2/3/482, and Ma 2/3/490. Mgr. Capel's triumphant remarks are contained in Ma 2/3/121. Fanny Geldard's comments are contained in Ma 2/3/461. Fr. Butler's encounters with Capel are recalled in Ma 2/3/490, Ma 2/3/496 and Ma 2/3/503; his assessment of the Rome hierarchy is featured in Ma 2/3/84 and Ma 2/3/478; his meeting with the Pope in Ma 2/3/477. The Pope's remark "Why doesn't he go and hide in America?" features in Ma 2/3/491; Fr. Robinson's remark "Bold, insolent, and hard to the last" is contained in Ma 2/3/41.

Farewell New York
Archbishop Corrigan's comment "The sooner he leaves America the better" is taken from Ma 2/3/528.

Arno
Dr. O'Callaghan's news about Capel's suspension by the Pope *a divinis* was sourced from Ma 2/3/540.

Epilogue
The two quotes from Mrs. Bellew were taken from Ma 2/3/194 and Ma 2/3/239.

Dublin Diocesan Archives

Money Matters
The Monsignor's letter seeking money from the Archbishop of Dublin, Cardinal Cullen, is numbered AB4/322/1/I/48 and contained in the "Priest Files" at their archives.

Archives of the Archdiocese of San Francisco

Arno
Capel's letter berating Patrick William Riordan, Archbishop of San Francisco, was extracted from the Deceased Priests Personnel Files, Archives of the Archdiocese of San Francisco (AASF).

Archives of the Archdiocese of New York

The Reckoning
Cardinal Simeoni's letter of recommendation for Capel was sourced from G-76, Folder 12 (Archbishop Corrigan Correspondence), 12 July 1883.

America
Archbishop Corrigan's letter to Cardinal Simeoni concerning Capel's arrival in New York is contained in G-33 (Letters of Abp. Corrigan as Coadjutor Bishop of New York, 1880 – 1885), 31 July 1883.

Farewell New York
Capel's letter excusing his behaviour at Delmonico's features in G-57 (Archbishop Michael Augustine Corrigan: Correspondence and Reports – Series G), 1 March 1885. The eyewitness account of his drinking at the banquet was drawn from the same box source, but is undated. Also drawn from the same source were Archbishop Corrigan's interview with Henry C. Olds concerning Capel's post-banquet visit to a brothel (2 February 1885), Olds' request for an interview with the Archbishop, the notes taken by the Archbishop regarding Capel's activities with a widow at the St. James Hotel, and a letter from Rhoda E. White (11 January 1885) describing his behaviour while staying at her daughter's home. The same box, G-57, contains the telegram from Rome empowering the hierarchy in New York to expel Capel, and the devastating note from Corrigan advising him to leave. Bishop McCloskey's offer to help force Capel out of America came from C-2 (To Abp. Corrigan from Bishops and Other Dignitaries).

California
Cardinal Simeoni's instruction for Capel to return to Europe, and Archbishop Corrigan's reference to same in a letter, were retrieved from G-57 (Archbishop Michael Augustine Corrigan: Correspondence and Reports – Series G).

Mrs. Valensin
Archbishop Riordan's decision to suspend Monsignor Capel is described in a letter from Cardinal Gibbons, C-15 (From Bishops and Other Dignitaries to Abp. Corrigan, 1886 – 1891). Riordan's forlorn attempts to "keep the scandal out of the papers" are also mentioned in the same document.